MW01503137

GOD'S GUARANTEE

ROMANS 8:28-30

Other books by Edmund R. McDavid III

Let God Speak: and Let Us Listen
ISBN 0-9630447-1-0

Infant Salvation & The Age of Accountability:
What Does The Bible Teach?
ISBN 0-9630447-4-5

Hope Publishing Company
P.O. Box 131447
Birmingham, AL 35213

GOD'S GUARANTEE

Are you covered by it?

Edmund R. McDavid III

Hope Publishing Company
P.O. Box 131447
Birmingham, Alabama 35213

God's Guarantee:

Copyright © 2002 by E. R. McDavid III

All rights reserved

All Scripture quoted us from the New International Version except for the chapter on Satan, and that is from The New American Standard.

Scripture taken from the Holy Bible: New International Version. Copyright © 1973, 1978, 1984 by International Bible Society.

Scripture taken from the Holy Bible: New American Standard Copyright © 1960, 1962, 1963, 1968, 1972, 1973, 1975, by The Lockman Foundation.

First printing 2002
Fourth printing 2005

Hardback: ISBN 0-9630447-2-9
Paperback: ISBN 0-9630447-3-7

Published by: Hope Publishing Company
                      P.O. Box 131447
                      Birmingham, Alabama 35213

Printed in the United States of America

Cover design by Jennifer Bromberg Joseph

DEDICATION

To Peg, my wife of 55 years. You have been a real helpmeet and a stabilizing influence in my life. I thank God for giving you to me. I love you very much.

ACKNOWLEDGMENTS

Once again a special thanks goes to my wife, Peg. She played as important a role in this book reaching fruition as she did with my first book, <u>Let God Speak</u>. She took my longhand writing and turned it into a computerized book which became "camera ready" when printed. Only those who write could fully appreciate the many changes, additions and deletions she had to endure before arriving at the finished product.

I also want to acknowledge the help of my son Mike McDavid and his wife Mikelyn and my daughter Peggy Joseph and her husband Thomas. They were gracious to read the manuscript and give me their thoughts and suggestions. They also held the book up in prayer, as did my four grandchildren: Taylor Joseph, Edmund Joseph, Lyndsay McDavid and Michael McDavid. Regardless of the time and effort we put forth in writing this book, we know that it is through prayer and by God's grace that it is now in print.

CONTENTS

PREFACE

All Scripture is meaningful, and all Scripture is profitable. Scripture is the Christian's guide to living as a sojourner in a hostile world. It tells us what we are to be and what we are not to be, what we are to do and what we are not to do, how we are to act and how we are not to act. Scripture is the written Word that reveals to us the Living Word, our Lord and Savior Jesus Christ. We must hear, understand, and believe a certain amount of Scripture before we can come to Christ through faith.

> **13 ..."Everyone who calls on the name of the Lord will be saved."**
> **14 How, then, can they call on the one they have not believed in? And how can they believe in the one of whom they have not heard? 17 Consequently, faith comes from hearing the message, and the message is heard through the word of Christ.**
> (Romans 10:13-14a, 17).

After we are saved, we must progressively know, understand, and believe more and more Scripture if we expect to grow in the grace and knowledge of Christ. Scripture exhorts us to grow.

> **18 But grow in the grace and knowledge of our Lord and Savior Jesus Christ.** (2 Peter 3:18).

We are to grow in grace, which is a gift from Christ, and in knowledge, of which the object is Christ. Is not growing in the grace and knowledge of Christ actually the process of sanctification? That process whereby having been set-aside for God we are now being made holy by God. And what is being holy but being like Christ – Christ is holiness. If we are to be like Christ, then we must have knowledge of Him. Knowledge of Christ is more than knowledge about Him; it is first a personal knowledge of Him through an intimate relationship with Him. Only as we have come to know Him can we understand the truth about Him and continue to grow closer to Him – becoming more like Him. To grow in the grace and knowledge of Christ is to grow spiritually – to continue to mature as a Christian. That is why we must continue to study the Bible, to pray, and seek to walk in obedience to God by the power of the Holy Spirit. It matters not to what extent we have grown spiritually, we are not to think that we have arrived and are in no need of further growth. Those who don't go forward find themselves going backward. When a person who has become physically fit by exercising, eating healthy, etc. quits doing those things, his fitness declines. If a swimmer quits stroking, he begins to sink in the water. When riding a bicycle, if you quit peddling, the bicycle will fall over. In the same way, continuous spiritual growth helps to preserve against our falling into apostasy and finding ourselves in the position of the worthless servant in the Parable of the Talents.

> **28 "'Take the talent from him and give it to the one who has the ten talents. 29 For everyone who has will be given more, and he will have an abundance. Whoever does not have, even what he has will be taken from him. 30 And throw that worthless servant outside, into the darkness, where there will be weeping and gnashing of teeth.** (Matthew 25:28-30).

Even under the most favorable of circumstances, our human nature can give rise to nagging doubts about God. And under adverse circumstances it can lead us to rebel and turn away from Him. Therefore the Bible exhorts us to hold fast to the truth and stand firm in the faith. This holding fast and standing firm is to be done no matter how bad our situation is or how awful the issues are that we face in life. This leads us to the purpose for writing this book. For the issues that we have to face appear to be getting worse, and standing firm in the faith is becoming more difficult. We Christians need words that will comfort us and encourage us to stand firm. We have these words in Romans 8:28-30. It is God's Guarantee to us.

Christians have always had to face tough problems of persecution, trials, and temptations. There is a constant war with the world, the flesh, and the devil. Throughout history the problems Christians have faced were worse at times than at others. Starting approximately thirty years ago, we have seen a continual decline in the moral integrity of American society. The influence of this moral decline has affected many individuals in the church, some with devastating consequences. This naturally has affected the corporate church and its ability to be effective in its work.

In recent years we have seen hostility toward the church and individual Christians. Often these are from sources that you would not expect and on such a scale that it has given rise to much concern. Many Christian leaders have expressed that we are living in a post-Christian society – one that is becoming more pagan day by day. Christians coping in a pagan society is not something new, but it is a new experience to many in this country who remember when Christian principles dominated our society.

With that being the case, let us now consider how we will face the issues of life in this pagan society. Will we succumb to the pressure of persecution? Will we yield to the enticement of the world to join it in its sin? (Public sin that is so prevalent and accepted by our morally decaying society that it goes unnoticed; secret sin in the privacy of our homes readily available at the turn of a TV knob or the push of a VCR button; seducing sin on magazine racks of material that was once considered unfit for the public eye and was kept under the counter; even the subtle sin in newspapers of underwear ads showing scantily clad bodies in provocative poses that invite lingering looks and fantasy thoughts; the greedy sin of materialism that can lead to rationalizing the need to lie and cheat, bend the rules, even break the law to get ahead or keep up with the Joneses).

In our society today, we have illegal drug use in all walks of life, divorce for any reason or no reason at all, sex without marriage is now the norm rather than the exception; abortion is rampant, and the homosexual lifestyle is gaining in acceptability. Our society takes pride in its tolerance of anything and everything. It has been said that the earmark of the twentieth century was the replacement of truth with tolerance. However, we are now going beyond tolerance to the point of condoning and encouraging behavior that is morally below the standards of our past, and is called sin by the Word of God. All of these have an effect on the Christian and the church. The church is slowly being eroded by the constant bombardment of the world. The result is that Christians are seeking divorces and abortions for the same reasons the world does – and at an alarming rate. As society grows more pagan, Christians will feel more pressure: both the pressure of resisting the temptations of the world and that of withstanding persecution by the world.

Add to all of this the everyday problems that go with earning a living, rearing children, caring for elderly parents, the threat of earthquakes, hurricanes, floods, automobile wrecks, the fear of being a victim of crime or terrorism and we get some sense of how many issues we face that can prevent us from living an obedient and fruitful Christian life. For most it is not a question of one issue "doing us in" (although it can happen) but it is the constant struggle with one issue after another that wears us down. At some point an issue can become the straw that broke the camel's back. Will we break under the weight of a severe and lengthy illness – one that we are told is terminal? Will we quit running the race if we suffer financial ruin or if no matter how hard we try, we fail time after time? Will we be fair weather professors of Christ, being faithful as long as life is easy, but turning our backs on Him when the going gets tough? These are questions that cause concern for many Christians. However, if we know the provision that God has made for His children when they undergo trials, we can face them with a confident attitude.

God has given His people a guarantee that took effect the moment we became Christians. He has promised that He will take whatever we encounter, whatever we have to endure, whatever we suffer, and make it work to our good.

By this promise, God has guaranteed us victory in any situation. This is stated so beautifully in Romans 8:28-30.

> **28 And we know that in all things God works for the good of those who love him, who have been called according to his purpose. 29 For those God foreknew he also predestined to be conformed to the likeness of his Son, that he might be the firstborn among many brothers. 30 And those he predestined, he also called; those he called, he also justified; those he justified, he also glorified.**
> (Romans 8:28-30).

Meditating on these verses should bring joy to any Christian. They are verses that all of us should hide in our hearts, relying on them for strength in time of trouble. In fact, if verses of Scripture were ranked according to the importance of their bearing on the Christian life (in the sense of how meaningful and profitable they are) these three verses would rank among the top. It is difficult to find three others where more theology and doctrine are packed. Understanding, believing, and applying the truths of Romans 8:28-30 are vital to our attitude toward God and to our walk with God. Most Christians are familiar with these verses, but how many of us understand and believe them? More importantly, how many live life in the light of the truth these verses teach? By God's grace I pray this book will not only help some to understand the truth of these verses, but that it will also motivate them to apply this truth in their daily living, firmly clinging to it in time of trouble.

The issues of life are many and varied, but God's Guarantee covers them all. Let us take an in-depth look at this wonderful guarantee of Romans 8:28-30. We will then consider some of the troubling issues that become stumbling blocks and cause some to fall. Understanding and believing God's Guarantee as we face these issues can prevent that from happening.

Ed McDavid
January 2002

God's Word tells us we are not only to follow Christ, not only to act like Christ, but we are to be like Christ. We are to be conformed to His image, to His likeness – we are to be like Him, i.e. Christ is compassionate; therefore, we are to be compassionate. We are to not only show compassion outwardly but also be compassionate inwardly. We are to truly feel compassion for others.

Romans 8:28-30

We Know

And <u>we know</u> that in all things God works for the good of those who love him, who have been called according to his purpose. (Romans 8:28).

Looking at Romans 8:28, some readers may question the "we know" at the very onset. They have doubts in their hearts as to whether or not <u>they</u> know, and they assume others have similar doubts. Their assumptions would be correct. Many who profess Christ as Lord and Savior have doubts about this verse, and some actually deny it in time of trouble. However, if we do not believe this verse to be true, can we believe John 3:16 or Ephesians 2:8-9? These verses are all in the same Bible. They are all God's Word.

There is much evidence to give one reason to believe that the Bible is God's Word, and that it is true. Christ says that God's Word is true.

17 "Sanctify them by the truth; your word is truth." (John 17:17).

There is much historical and archaeological evidence that points to the accuracy and reliability of the Bible. The lives and deaths of the writers indicate that the Bible was written by men of integrity - truthful and godly men. The Bible claims to be inspired by God, and the writers make that claim for the Bible.

> **20 Above all, you must understand that no prophecy of Scripture came about by the prophet's own interpretation. 21 For prophecy never had its origin in the will of man, but men spoke from God as they were carried along by the Holy Spirit.**
> (2 Peter 1:20-21).

> **3 All Scripture is God-breathed and is useful for teaching, rebuking, correcting and training in righteousness...** (2 Timothy 3:16).

The fact that the Bible was written over a period of approximately 1500 years by more than forty different writers from different cultures and backgrounds and yet maintains continuity of thought and purpose, certainly gives weight to its being inspired. The enormous amount of fulfilled prophesy is compelling evidence that the Bible is God's Word. So many predictions about people, things, and events were made hundreds of years before they were to take place, and yet each came about just as the Bible predicted. However, as Christians, we see it through the eyes of faith, for it is by faith that we believe the Bible. We must look at Romans 8:28 through the eyes of faith, as we do the rest of God's Word.

The "we know" in the Greek is strong. It indicates certainty. The inference is that not only can we know that what follows is true but that we can rest assured it is. It is an unquestionable fact. It is absolute truth. Just as the Apostle John tells us we can know we have eternal life (1 John 5:13), here Paul tells us we can know that God works all things for our good. It is not a matter of our hoping it is so or thinking it is so - it is a matter of our knowing it is so. There is no room here for doubt; this is positively fact. It is a settled issue. However, on his own the Christian cannot believe this verse.

The Holy Spirit must enlighten him to this truth. We are dependent on God's Holy Spirit to teach us all things and to lead us into all truth.

> **26 But the Counselor, the Holy Spirit, whom the Father will send in my name, will teach you all things...** (John 14:26).

> **13 But when he, the Spirit of truth, comes, he will guide you into all truth.** (John 16:13).

Our knowing that Romans 8:28 is true does not mean that we should expect to know all about it. We do not know how God does what He does; however, we do know that He does it. We must hold fast to this knowledge or we might fail to stand firm in time of trouble. If we don't stand firm, we may find that we fall. Paul warns us to be careful.

> **12 So, if you think you are standing firm, be careful that you don't fall!** (1 Corinthians 10:12).

Knowing that God is making all things work for our good is important anytime, but it is especially important that we know this with certainty when we face persecution or trials. Each of us should ask ourselves, "Do I really believe Romans 8:28?" Am I sure in my heart that God will make "all things" work for my good? If I am not sure, will I perhaps buckle under trials, turn my back on God out of hurt or anger, stop going to church or reading my Bible and praying? Will I perhaps find that I have fallen away, that I never did truly love God, that although I had professed to be a Christian, I really was not. Christ spoke of one who falls away in the Parable of the Sower.

> **20 The one who received the seed that fell on rocky places is the man who hears the word and at once receives it with joy. 21 But since he has no root, he lasts only a short time. When trouble or persecution comes because of the word, he quickly falls away.** (Matthew 13:20-21).

When tragedy comes, it often comes to us suddenly and unexpectedly. If and when it comes, we must be spiritually prepared. We shouldn't wait until it is upon us to decide whether or not we are convinced that God will make it work to our good. We need to be standing firm in our faith when tragedy hits and continue to stand firm in its midst. The teaching of the Bible is clear: it is not those who once prayed a prayer, held up their hand, or walked an aisle, but those who stand firm to the end that will be saved.

> **13 All men will hate you because of me, but he who stands firm to the end will be saved**. (Mark 13:13).

Not knowing what God will send or permit to come our way, let each of us ask Him to give us the faith to know that He will make it all work for our good.

In All Things

> **And we know that <u>in all things</u> God works for the good of those who love him, who have been called according to his purpose.** (Romans 8:28).

We have seen that, by God's grace, we can know for sure that in all things God works for the good of those who love Him. We also have said that this is difficult for some Christians to accept. If "all things" includes bad things, then it raises doubts for a number of people. Nevertheless, it does include the bad things. It is all things; nothing is excluded. Cancer, heart trouble, failed business, war, death of a loved one, persecution, etc. are included in "all things."

Let us not forget that this work of God applies only to the Christian. It does not apply to the non-Christian. Therefore, until we were saved it did not apply to us. It is true that those who come to Christ are elected and that from the beginning God has chosen them to be saved.

> *13* But we ought always to thank God for you,
> brothers loved by the Lord, because from the
> beginning God chose you to be saved...
> (2 Thessalonians 2:13).

From the beginning, God planned to save us. However, until our salvation had actually taken place, we remained as we were when we came into the world – objects of God's wrath.

> *1* As for you, you were dead in your transgressions
> and sins, *2* in which you used to live when you
> followed the ways of this world and of the ruler of
> the kingdom of the air, the spirit who is now at work
> in those who are disobedient. *3* All of us also lived
> among them at one time, gratifying the cravings of
> our sinful nature and following its desires and
> thoughts. Like the rest, we were by nature objects of
> wrath. (Ephesians 2:1-3).

However, at the time we were saved God began to make all things work for our good. The Christian and the unbeliever can share the same trial, suffer with the same disease, be involved in the same plane crash; however, these things are made to work for the good of only the Christian.

When we think of "all things" these are not things that just happen on the spur of the moment. These are things that are connected to all other events by the decree of God. They are connected to both past and future eternity. They are events that are in the plan of God to achieve the purpose of God. God's plan is being worked out. All in the universe is working to our good. He is using things, people, and events in His great work of redemption – all for the good of the redeemed and for His glory.

> 15 All this is for your benefit, so that the grace that
> is reaching more and more people may cause
> thanksgiving to overflow to the glory of God.
> (2 Corinthians 4:15).

The Christian is never to take a fatalistic attitude toward the bad and the evil that affect us all. We know that our Heavenly Father has a plan and a purpose for it.

He tells us in Romans 8:28 that in all things He works for our good. In verse 29 He tells us what that good is: it is to be conformed to the likeness of His Son. In verse 30 He tells us that those who are conformed to the likeness of His Son are those who are glorified – those who enjoy the glory of Christ in heaven for eternity. Though a much better likeness of Christ will be ours in heaven, we are to be growing more like Him on a daily basis while we are here on earth. Therefore, to this end and for our good God works in all things.

The Christian is not told that he will not have trials and suffering. Rather, he is told that he will, and that he is to rejoice and persevere in them.

> *3* **Not only so, but we also rejoice in our sufferings, because we know that suffering produces perseverance;** *4* **perseverance, character; and character, hope.** (Romans 5:3-4).

> *2* **Consider it pure joy, my brothers, whenever you face trials of many kinds,** *3* **because you know that the testing of your faith develops perseverance.** (James 1:2-3).

> **12 Blessed is the man who perseveres under trial, because when he has stood the test, he will receive the crown of life that God has promised to those who love him.** (James 1:12).

The believer is to face trials and suffering not only in the knowledge that God will make them work to his good but also in the knowledge that Christ is with him in his suffering. Christ is with him in a very real way to strengthen and comfort him. Each believer is in a mystical union with Christ.

> *17* **But he who unites himself with the Lord is one with him in spirit.** (1 Corinthians 6:17).

Christ speaks of this union.

> *20* **"On that day you will realize that I am in my Father, and you are in me, and I am in you."** (John 14:20).

This union with Christ is evident in His prayer.

20 "My prayer is not for them alone. I pray also for those who will believe in me through their message, *21* that all of them may be one, Father, just as you are in me and I am in you. May they also be in us so that the world may believe that you have sent me. *22* I have given them the glory that you gave me, that they may be one as we are one: *23* I in them and you in me. May they be brought to complete unity to let the world know that you sent me and have loved them even as you have loved me." (John 17:20-23).

It appears that this union is of such a nature that Christ shares both our sufferings and our blessings. When Saul (Paul) was persecuting the Christians, we see how Christ responded. He did not ask Saul why he was persecuting those people. He did not ask Saul why he persecuted His disciples. He asked Saul, "Why do you persecute Me?"

1 Meanwhile, Saul was still breathing out murderous threats against the Lord's disciples. He went to the high priest *2* and asked him for letters to the synagogues in Damascus, so that if he found any there who belonged to the Way, whether men or women, he might take them as prisoners to Jerusalem. *3* As he neared Damascus on his journey, suddenly a light from heaven flashed around him. *4* He fell to the ground and heard a voice say to him, "Saul, Saul, why do you persecute me?"
5 "Who are you, Lord?" Saul asked.
"I am Jesus, whom you are persecuting," he replied.
(Acts 9:1-5).

In the parable of the sheep and the goats, Christ tells us that when we help a fellow Christian we help Him.

34 "Then the King will say to those on his right, 'Come, you who are blessed by my Father; take your inheritance, the kingdom prepared for you since the creation of the world. *35* For I was hungry and you gave me something to eat, I was thirsty and you

gave me something to drink, I was a stranger and you invited me in, 36 I needed clothes and you clothed me, I was sick and you looked after me, I was in prison and you came to visit me.'
37 "Then the righteous will answer him, 'Lord, when did we see you hungry and feed you, or thirsty and give you something to drink? 38 When did we see you a stranger and invite you in, or needing clothes and clothe you? 39 When did we see you sick or in prison and go to visit you?'
40 "The King will reply, 'I tell you the truth, whatever you did for one of the least of these brothers of mine, you did for me.'" (Matthew 25:34-40).

We know the Bible teaches that Christ suffered for us, and we have seen that in some manner He suffers with us. We also know the Bible teaches that all Christians will suffer to one degree or another, but are we aware that our suffering is to be for Christ?

29 For it has been granted to you on behalf of Christ not only to believe on him, but also to suffer for him... (Philippians 1:29).

17 Now if we are children, then we are heirs—heirs of God and co-heirs with Christ, if indeed we share in his sufferings in order that we may also share in his glory. (Romans 8:17).

10 I want to know Christ and the power of his resurrection and the fellowship of sharing in his sufferings... (Philippians 3:10).

12 Dear friends, do not be surprised at the painful trial you are suffering, as though something strange were happening to you. 13 But rejoice that you participate in the sufferings of Christ, so that you may be overjoyed when his glory is revealed. (1 Peter 4:12-13).

19 So then, those who suffer according to God's will should commit themselves to their faithful Creator and continue to do good. (1 Peter 4:19).

The above verses speak about suffering for Christ, but beyond them we have the clear teaching of the Bible that we are to do everything as for Christ. Everything means just that – everything. Our work, play, stewardship, and our suffering are all included. It is all that we experience as a Christian – all of our Christian life is to be lived for Christ and His glory.

17 And whatever you do, whether in word or deed, do it all in the name of the Lord Jesus, giving thanks to God the Father through him. (Colossians 3:17).

31 So whether you eat or drink or whatever you do, do it all for the glory of God. (1 Corinthians 10:31).

Most Christians readily agree that the Bible speaks of Christians suffering persecution.

20 Remember the words I spoke to you: 'No servant is greater than his master.' If they persecuted me, they will persecute you also... (John 15:20).

But what of other types of suffering such as pain, sickness, loss of finances, loss of health, loss of a loved one, etc.? What about the suffering involved when one is greatly tempted to sin and struggles to resist it? Is not the fight with the world, the flesh, and the devil a constant struggle? If it is not, then we must question the degree of our commitment to Christ – perhaps even question if we have made a commitment.

Paul tells us that the Christian groans as he eagerly looks forward to getting out of his body of flesh, going to heaven, and receiving his glorified body.

23 Not only so, but we ourselves, who have the first fruits of the Spirit, groan inwardly as we wait eagerly for our adoption as sons, the redemption of our bodies. (Romans 8:23).

1 Now we know that if the earthly tent we live in is destroyed, we have a building from God, an eternal house in heaven, not built by human hands.

> **2 Meanwhile we groan, longing to be clothed with our heavenly dwelling, 3 because when we are clothed, we will not be found naked. 4 For while we are in this tent, we groan and are burdened, because we do not wish to be unclothed but to be clothed with our heavenly dwelling, so that what is mortal may be swallowed up by life.** (2 Corinthians 5:1-4).

Contrary to what the health, wealth, and prosperity (HW&P) teachers say, suffering for the Christian is not the exception – it is the norm and is to be expected. And contrary to the HW&P teaching, what happens to us is part of God's plan and it is going to happen whether we like it or not and whether we believe it will or not. God has decreed (ordained) all that will take place. He decreed that Christ would come and die on the cross. This was done before the creation of the world.

> **20 He was chosen before the creation of the world, but was revealed in these last times for your sake.** (1 Peter 1:20).

> **22 The Son of Man will go as it has been decreed, but woe to that man who betrays him.** (Luke 22:22).

> **27 Indeed Herod and Pontius Pilate met together with the Gentiles and the people of Israel in this city to conspire against your holy servant Jesus, whom you anointed. 28 They did what your power and will had decided beforehand should happen.** (Acts 4:27-28).

Whatever trials and suffering we have to go through have also been decreed by God. If it has been decreed, it will come about. Prayer will not change what is decreed nor will having more faith change it. If someone says, "I thought prayer changes things", they would be right from the human perspective. Prayer is most important. Christians need to pray more. God commands and expects us to pray; moreover, He answers prayer. However, when we pray for something to happen and it does, it was decreed by God.

Our prayer, which was also decreed, may well have been the means God used to bring it about. An example of this is King Hezekiah.

> *1* In those days Hezekiah became ill and was at the point of death. The prophet Isaiah son of Amoz went to him and said, "This is what the LORD says: Put your house in order, because you are going to die; you will not recover."
> 2 Hezekiah turned his face to the wall and prayed to the LORD, 3 "Remember, O LORD, how I have walked before you faithfully and with wholehearted devotion and have done what is good in your eyes." And Hezekiah wept bitterly.
> 4 Before Isaiah had left the middle court, the word of the LORD came to him: 5 "Go back and tell Hezekiah, the leader of my people, 'This is what the LORD, the God of your father David, says: I have heard your prayer and seen your tears; I will heal you. On the third day from now you will go up to the temple of the LORD. 6 I will add fifteen years to your life. And I will deliver you and this city from the hand of the king of Assyria. I will defend this city for my sake and for the sake of my servant David.'"
> 7 Then Isaiah said, "Prepare a poultice of figs." They did so and applied it to the boil, and he recovered. (2 Kings 20:1-7).

In the above verses God tells Hezekiah that He has heard his prayer and will heal him. But, both the prayer and the healing were decreed before the world was made. However, God used the prayer as the means to bring about the healing.

God has an ultimate purpose for all of His creation – to bring glory to Himself. What better way for the Christian to glorify God than by remaining faithful, walking in obedience, and praising God – even in the mist of suffering. Job is a good example of this.

> 20 At this, Job got up and tore his robe and shaved his head. Then he fell to the ground in worship 21 and said:

"Naked I came from my mother's womb,
and naked I will depart.
The LORD gave and the LORD has taken away;
may the name of the LORD be praised."
(Job 1:20-21).

7 So Satan went out from the presence of the LORD
and afflicted Job with painful sores from the soles of
his feet to the top of his head. 8 Then Job took a
piece of broken pottery and scraped himself with it
as he sat among the ashes.
9 His wife said to him, "Are you still holding on to
your integrity? Curse God and die!"
10 He replied, "You are talking like a foolish woman.
Shall we accept good from God, and not trouble?"
In all this, Job did not sin in what he said.
(Job 2:7-10).

When we read about the faithfulness of Job, our faith is
strengthened. We are encouraged to glorify God by
remaining faithful in times of adversity. In doing so, we
become an example and encouragement to others. The
weight of affliction can put severe stress on one's faith –
even to the point of our becoming angry with God. Job's wife
told him to curse God (Job 2:9). I have heard people speak
of being angry with God as though they were justified under
the circumstances. That is sin. We never read of Christ
being angry with God. Being angry with God is a sin of pride
that says we deserve better and that we have been done
wrong by God. But what do any of us really deserve? The
Bible makes it clear that we all deserve hell. Think about
your own situation. Does God owe you something? If you
are a Christian, it is because He gave you salvation. He will
keep His promises to His children, but He owes us nothing.
Knowing that we deserve to suffer in hell for eternity but
instead are going to spend eternity in the bliss of heaven is a
real incentive to praise God – in both the easy and the hard
times. Our suffering on earth is of brief duration, and is
nothing when compared to eternity in heaven.

18 **I consider that our present sufferings are not worth comparing with the glory that will be revealed in us.** (Romans 8:18).

17 For our light and momentary troubles are achieving for us an eternal glory that far outweighs them all. (2 Corinthians 4:17).

For further comfort, God tells us that Christ experienced trials and temptation, as well as loss and pain. He suffered in every way that we do; therefore, He can sympathize with us and comfort us.

18 Because he himself suffered when he was tempted, he is able to help those who are being tempted. (Hebrews 2:18).

The word "tempted" in the above verse means more than to entice to sin. That is included, but it is not the strict meaning. There are times when the context denotes enticement to sin in the strict sense; however, the Bible generally uses the word tempted in a manner that means tried or tested. It is in this context that it is used here. Many commentaries explain the Biblical usage of the word tempted. In fact, in Luke 22:28 where the NIB, NAS, and a number of other translations use the word "trials", the KJV uses the word "temptations." However, many commentators who use the KJV make it clear that trials is the meaning.

28 "You are those who have stood by me in my trials." (Luke 22:28).

Christ was tried in the many things He suffered: poverty, hunger, thirst, pain, weariness, reproach, shame, desertion by friends and followers, and desertion by God on the cross. When suffering trials of sickness, pain, persecution, poverty, hunger, etc., man is tempted to react with a bad attitude toward God or man. If he does react with a bad attitude, it is sin. When Christ underwent His trials, He did so without sinning. We should strive to do the same.

15 For we do not have a high priest who is unable to sympathize with our weaknesses, but we have one who has been tempted in every way, just as we are— yet was without sin. (Hebrews 4:15).

Christ suffered greatly in diverse ways. We are told that He learned obedience in His suffering.

7 During the days of Jesus' life on earth, he offered up prayers and petitions with loud cries and tears to the one who could save him from death, and he was heard because of his reverent submission. Although he was a son, he learned obedience from what he suffered. (Hebrews 5:7-8).

What is meant by "Christ learned obedience" is not to be confused with man learning to be obedient. Beginning in childhood, man learns by the carrot and stick method. He learns the advantages of obedience and the consequences of disobedience. His rebellious nature must be brought to a point of submissive obedience. On the other hand, Christ though fully man is also fully God. Being God, He is co-equal with God the Father but voluntarily became man. As man, He was voluntarily obedient to God the Father and was never disobedient. He fulfilled all of the Law. The expression, "Christ learned obedience", does not mean He learned to be obedient or that He learned how to be obedient. It means He experienced obedience. When someone who has never flown makes his first trip by plane, he experiences what it is to fly. As man, Christ actually experienced what it was like to be obedient in the face of all the trials and temptations common to man. He who created the universe, He who spoke things into existence, He who gave orders throughout all creation now learned experientially what it was to be obedient – obedient even when suffering under harsh conditions – obedient even unto death.

5 Your attitude should be the same as that of Christ Jesus: 6 Who, being in very nature God, did not consider equality with God something to be

grasped, 7 but made himself nothing, taking the very nature of a servant, being made in human likeness. 8 And being found in appearance as a man, he humbled himself and became obedient to death— even death on a cross! (Philippians 2:5-8).

Christ, as man, learned what it was like for man to remain faithful under the burden of trials and suffering. He knew what it was to be obedient, because He experienced it – He was obedient. The opposite of this would have been to be disobedient, and that is sin. Though He paid the penalty for our sins, He never sinned. He did not experience what it is to sin. Because we sin, we do know what it is to sin. We have experienced and continue to experience sin. Hopefully, we sin less as we mature spiritually. We also experience obedience when we are obedient to the Word and the leading of the Holy Spirit. Hopefully, as we become more mature, we will find ourselves being more obedient when we are tested by the trials of persecution, by the pain of disease, or by the untimely loss of a loved one. There is one thing for sure, we don't want to be among those that fall away when they are tested.

13 Those on the rock are the ones who receive the word with joy when they hear it, but they have no root. They believe for a while, but in the time of testing they fall away. (Luke 8:13).

God's Word makes it clear that we can expect to face trials and suffering of one degree or another. They are included in the "all things" of our verse. However, no matter what type or how severe the trial, our heavenly Father loves us, and He will make it work for our good.

God Works

28 And we know that in all things <u>God works</u> for the good of those who love him, who have been called according to his purpose. (Romans 8:28).

All of God's Word is amazing, but Romans 8:28 is one of the most profound statements we find. It is telling us that in addition to all the things we call good, all the things we call bad will also be made to work for our good. Furthermore, this is not a casual statement; it is a promise from God. It is a guarantee from the Creator of the universe. We all like to have products or services that are guaranteed. It gives us a feeling of security. However, we learn from experience that the guarantee is no better than the one who makes it. A company can go bankrupt or go out of business or just plain default on its guarantee for many reasons. However, because God is sovereign, His guarantee is 100% reliable throughout eternity. It matters not that the Apostle Paul penned the words in this verse approximately two thousand years ago. God's Word is as up-to-date now as it was then, and it will be up-to-date two thousand or ten thousand years from now. It will be up-to-date for all eternity. God's Word never changes, and God never changes.

8 The grass withers and the flowers fall,
but the word of our God stands forever.
(Isaiah 40:8).

6 "I the LORD do not change" ... (Malachi 3:6).

Yes, God's Word stands, and God's work stands. And lest any think that our God isn't working, that He created everything and now sits idol, let us look at Scripture. We see from it that God has a plan and purpose for His creation.

11 In him we were also chosen, having been predestined according to the plan of him who works out everything in conformity with the purpose of his will... (Ephesians 1:11).

9 Remember the former things, those of long ago;
I am God, and there is no other;
I am God, and there is none like me.
10 I make known the end from the beginning,
from ancient times, what is still to come.
I say: My purpose will stand,
and I will do all that I please.
11 From the east I summon a bird of prey;
from a far-off land, a man to fulfill my purpose.
What I have said, that will I bring about;
what I have planned, that will I do.
(Isaiah 46:9-11).

God is always at work to bring about His plan and purpose.

17 Jesus said to them, "My Father is always at his
work to this very day, and I, too, am working."
(John 5:17).

In the above verse, Jesus says that God works and that He
works too. We find that the purpose of the redemptive work
of Jesus was to glorify God. We see that He completed His
work. Should we not strive to complete ours?

4 I have brought you glory on earth by completing
the work you gave me to do. (John 17:4).

There are references to God working all through Scripture.
We will look at only a few.

10 Then the LORD said: "I am making a covenant
with you. Before all your people I will do wonders
never before done in any nation in all the world. The
people you live among will see how awesome is the
work that I, the LORD, will do for you."
(Exodus 34:10).

24 How many are your works, O LORD!
In wisdom you made them all;
the earth is full of your creatures.
25 There is the sea, vast and spacious,
teeming with creatures beyond number—
living things both large and small.
26 There the ships go to and fro,

and the leviathan, which you formed to frolic there.
27 These all look to you
to give them their food at the proper time.
28 When you give it to them,
they gather it up;
when you open your hand,
they are satisfied with good things.
29 When you hide your face,
they are terrified;
when you take away their breath,
they die and return to the dust.
30 When you send your Spirit,
they are created,
and you renew the face of the earth.
31 May the glory of the LORD endure forever;
may the LORD rejoice in his works—
(Psalm 104:24-31).

3 "Neither this man nor his parents sinned," said Jesus, "but this happened so that the work of God might be displayed in his life." (John 9:3).

God works and He expects us, His servants, to work. If the master works should not the servant work? The servant is not greater than the master.

16 I tell you the truth, no servant is greater than his master, nor is a messenger greater than the one who sent him. (John 13:16).

God's Word is clear: the Christian is expected to work. If he doesn't, his claim to have faith is hollow. A profession of faith without deeds to confirm it is a useless faith; moreover, it is a dead faith, unable to save.

14 What good is it, my brothers, if a man claims to have faith but has no deeds? Can such faith save him? 17 In the same way, faith by itself, if it is not accompanied by action, is dead. (James 2:14,17).

Doing good deeds does not save us; however, if we are saved we will do good deeds. The Christian is to work out the salvation that God has already worked in him.

> *12* **Therefore, my dear friends, as you have always obeyed—not only in my presence, but now much more in my absence—continue to work out your salvation with fear and trembling...** (Philippians 2:12).

We find that God has foreordained the work each of us is to do.

> *10* **For we are God's workmanship, created in Christ Jesus to do good works, which God prepared in advance for us to do.** (Ephesians 2:10).

It is only because God works that we do our work. He works in us to enlighten us to the work He would have us do, to move us to do it, and to enable us to do it.

> *13* **for it is God who works in you to will and to act according to his good purpose.** (Philippians 2:13).

Our work is laid out for us. For what are we waiting? There will come a time when no one can work.

> *4* **As long as it is day, we must do the work of him who sent me. Night is coming, when no one can work.** (John 9:4).

Considering Romans 8:28, we see thus far that we know for sure (we are absolutely positive) that in all things (everything that happens, whether it is good or bad) God is at work. God brings it about, causes it to happen, or permits it to happen. In all cases He controls the results it produces. As we read more of the verse, we see that God is not only working but that He works everything for the good of those who love Him. It is here that some who profess Christ have a problem. They have trouble believing that the corruption, the sin, the suffering, the pain, and the evil in this world could be made to work to the good of God's people. They know that the verse says, "in all things", and they believe it to be God's Word. Moreover, they do not believe that God would lie. In fact, most probably know the Bible says God cannot lie.

2 ...which God, who does not lie... (Titus 1:2).

18 ...it is impossible for God to lie... (Hebrews 6:18).

Therefore, if God's Word says it (and God does not lie), then their reason for not believing it must be because they don't believe God can do it. The message of the verse is clear. It is not difficult to understand. However, there are situations, circumstances, and problems that can make the message of Romans 8:28 hard to accept and difficult to believe. Many Christians who doubt the reality of this verse do so because they don't understand the absolute totality of God's sovereignty – not because they doubt God's Word. They are prone to think of God's creation as having gotten off track and running amuck, with evil men and Satan out of control. They don't understand that all of creation is proceeding according to God's plan and purpose, and that everything that happens has been decreed to happen by God. With that in mind, before we go any further with Romans 8:28, let us briefly consider God's sovereignty.

God's Sovereignty

Some people think God made earth and man, and then left man free to do as he pleases. Others agree with this view, but think God steps back into the affairs of man on certain occasions. Some see God as knowing what is going to happen, but unable to prevent it. None of these views are Scriptural. The Bible teaches that God is totally sovereign. He has complete and absolute control over all of His creation.

35 All the peoples of the earth
are regarded as nothing.
He does as he pleases
with the powers of heaven
and the peoples of the earth.
No one can hold back his hand
or say to him: "What have you done?" (Daniel 4:35).

...What I have said, that will I bring about;
what I have planned, that will I do. (Isaiah 46:11).

35 This is what the LORD says,
he who appoints the sun
to shine by day,
who decrees the moon and stars
to shine by night,
who stirs up the sea
so that its waves roar—
the LORD Almighty is his name... (Jeremiah 31:35).

37 For nothing is impossible with God. (Luke 1:37).

If God were not sovereign, then we would be captive to chance – good or bad luck some would say. If God were not sovereign, how would we fair against the unrestrained sinful nature of man, the turbulence of planets out of control, weather out of control, the fury of the devil and his demons, or our own unrestrained sinful nature? Seeing how things are <u>even with</u> the restraints that God puts on evil, would you want to live in a world <u>without</u> God's restraints? I think we would all agree that we prefer having God in control. Anyone who would be brazen enough to tell God to leave him or her alone would be foolish indeed. If God did so for one split second, he or she would be gone. God not only created everything, He holds it all together.

2...but in these last days he has spoken to us by his Son, whom he appointed heir of all things, and through whom he made the universe. 3 The Son is the radiance of God's glory and the exact representation of his being, sustaining all things by his powerful word. (Hebrews 1:2-3).

28 'For in him we live and move and have our being.' (Acts 17:28).

People are prone to say that man makes history. He does make history, but only the history that God has decreed and in His providence brings about. The history that man makes is the unfolding of God's plan for His creation. The plan was made before the world was made. The world and all that happens are all part of the plan. God made time. We live and see things in a time frame. But what we see in time, God determined in eternity past before the world or time were made. We would have no time without the sun, the rotating earth, etc.

It was Shakespeare who spoke of the world as being a stage. He said that all men and women are merely actors who spend a brief period of time on the stage. There is a touch of reality to what Shakespeare said. We do enter the stage of life in response to God's decree. We remain on the stage for the period of time that He had decreed, and we exit the stage at the moment He has decreed. Yet, there is no script that we are forced to follow. Each of us is free to act out our part as we think best, and each of us is fully responsible for his own performance. God is our audience and He will pass judgment on our performances.

> **10 For we must all appear before the judgment seat of Christ, that each one may receive what is due him for the things done while in the body, whether good or bad.** (2 Corinthians 5:10).

Here we have the unexplainable paradox between God decreeing what man will do and man freely choosing what he will do. If man is not free to do as he wills, he is a robot. If God is not in control of His creation, He is not God. However, at all times, man freely chooses to do what God has decreed.

> **9 In his heart a man plans his course,**
> **but the LORD determines his steps.** (Proverbs 16:9).

> **27 Indeed Herod and Pontius Pilate met together with the Gentiles and the people of Israel in this city to conspire against your holy servant Jesus, whom you anointed. 28 They did what your power and will had decided beforehand should happen.**
> (Acts 4:27-28).

Let me warn that we must guard against taking the position that if God decreed it, we are not responsible. It would be dangerous to our spiritual well being to ignore the fact that we are free agents. We are free to choose our course of action; therefore, we are held accountable for it.

> **19 One of you will say to me: "Then why does God still blame us? For who resists his will?" 20 But who are you, O man, to talk back to God? "Shall what is formed say to him who formed it, 'Why did you make me like this?'"** (Romans 9:19-20).

God is not the author of sin, but He has decreed that sin will be in the world. God does not tempt man to sin nor cause him to sin.

> **13 When tempted, no one should say, "God is tempting me." For God cannot be tempted by evil, nor does he tempt anyone...** (James 1:13).

However, when man does sin, God has decreed it. Also when man overcomes a sin, God has decreed that to happen. If we find ourselves tolerating sin in our lives, we cannot excuse it on the basis that God decreed it. We must repent and look to God for the strength to be obedient. While on this earth, none of us will be totally free of sin. However, if we look to the Holy Spirit for strength and strive for a goal of total obedience, we will be amazed at how much sin God has decreed us to overcome.

As we think through the complex issue of God being sovereign and man being free to choose, we begin to realize that (although we can't understand it) the Bible teaches it; therefore, we believe it. We see that the smallest details and events are all included in God's decree. We become aware of the fact that what man calls an accident did not happen by chance. We realize that what appears to be coincidence to man is decreed by God. Although man makes free choices within the framework of God's sovereign decree, he has no more control over events in this world than he does over the stars in the sky. The sun rises and sets no matter what man does. The ocean tides rise and ebb independent of man's will. God has decreed it to be so. God has also decreed the steps men take and the events of history. When men are faced with making a decision (perhaps to go to war or not), the decision made is man's responsibility – man is accountable for the results. Nevertheless, the decision reached has been decreed by God to take place. This is the teaching of the Bible, and it is logical. After all, if man is free to resist God's will then God is not free to do what He chooses. He is prevented by man. God is then unable to work out His plan for His creation. If God is to be sovereign, it must be the other way around. Man must be captive to God's will.

Man has a problem accepting the absolute sovereignty of an infinite God. Man's finite mind cannot understand how a loving God could let bad things happen: suffering, sickness, rape, murder, etc. Man thinks he deserves better. His sinful pride prevents him from seeing how truly corrupt he is and how holy God is. Man may speak of hell but most do not realize that we all deserve to be sent there. Few who are going there think they are. As a consequence of Adam's fall, we all come into this world in a fallen state – justly deserving hell. The evidence of just how sinful man can be when God loosens the restraints was seen when God was provoked by man's sinfulness and sent the flood.

> **5 The LORD saw how great man's wickedness on the earth had become, and that every inclination of the thoughts of his heart was only evil all the time. 6 The LORD was grieved that he had made man on the earth, and his heart was filled with pain. 7 So the LORD said, "I will wipe mankind, whom I have created, from the face of the earth—men and animals, and creatures that move along the ground, and birds of the air—for I am grieved that I have made them." 8 But Noah found favor in the eyes of the LORD.** (Genesis 6:5-8).

Rather than question how a loving God could let bad things happen, man should be awed that a just God was willing to die for man's sin; moreover, that God is patient with man in giving him time to repent.

> 9 ...He is patient with you, not wanting anyone to perish, but everyone to come to repentance. (2 Peter 3:9).

Some people see God as sovereign but not as decreeing the bad things that happen. They say that God knows all that will happen before it happens but does not decree it to happen. That is a contradiction. It is not logical. A sovereign God has the power to create or to destroy - to bring about an event or to keep an event from happening. An omniscient and omnipotent God can foresee what a Hitler will do and not create him. A sovereign God can keep all evil men and things out of His creation. Therefore, if they exist, logic tells us it has to be because God decreed them to exist. Even the non-Christian, when he blames God for his troubles, is acknowledging God's sovereignty.

Man does not want to be a robot; he wants to be free to do as he wills. However, when someone else does a wicked deed, he wants God to restrain that one's freedom of will. Of course, God does restrain sin and evil – both man's and that of Satan. The rebelling of Satan did not catch God by surprise. He had decreed it to happen. Satan would not exist if God had not made him (he was good when he was made). God could speak a word and destroy Satan in a split second. He permits Satan to do certain things, as in the example we have in the book of Job. However, Satan can do nothing more than God permits. On one hand, we know it is God's desire that none should perish – but on the other hand the teaching of Scripture is that God allows many to justly perish because of their sin.

> 3 This is good, and pleases God our Savior, 4 who wants all men to be saved and to come to a knowledge of the truth. (1 Timothy 2:3-4).

> *13* "Enter through the narrow gate. For wide is the gate and broad is the road that leads to destruction, and many enter through it. *14* But small is the gate and narrow the road that leads to life, and only a few find it." (Matthew 7:13-14).

> 19 This is the verdict: Light has come into the world, but men loved darkness instead of light because their deeds were evil. (John 3:19).

We find in God's decree a conflict between God's own wish and man's freedom to choose. Man is permitted to freely choose to reject that which God wishes. Christ shows us a good example of this.

> 34 "O Jerusalem, Jerusalem, you who kill the prophets and stone those sent to you, how often I have longed to gather your children together, as a hen gathers her chicks under her wings, but you were not willing!" (Luke 13:34).

We must not lose sight of the fact that in the above verse, man's unwillingness is not man disrupting God's plan. It is man fulfilling God's plan. It is man doing, by his own will, that which God has decreed him to do.

> 21 Many are the plans in a man's heart,
> but it is the LORD's purpose that prevails.
> (Proverbs 19:21).

> *1* Then Job replied to the LORD:
> 2 "I know that you can do all things;
> no plan of yours can be thwarted." (Job 42:1-2).

I hope this brief discussion of God's sovereignty has been helpful to some.

For The Good

And we know that in all things God works <u>for the</u> <u>good</u> of those who love him, who have been called according to his purpose. (Romans 8:28).

Having briefly considered God's sovereignty, let us return to Romans 8:28. We have discussed how very certain is the "we know", how all encompassing is the "all things", and the fact that "God works." Now we find that the work God does is to make all things work for our good – if we truly love Him. Those who love God are children of God, and it is for them that He makes all things work for good - the good being to conform them to the image of Christ thereby providing assurance of their salvation. Isn't it wonderful to know that whatever happens, (whether good, bad or otherwise) God is going to turn it to our good. He is going to cause it to produce good results and work for our good. What a comfort and feeling of security is ours, if we believe this word from God.

We are not promised that we will have no trouble. In fact we are told that we will have it. However, Christ tells us that we can have peace in spite of trouble.

33 "I have told you these things, so that in me you may have peace. In this world you will have trouble. But take heart! I have overcome the world." (John 16:33).

Contributing to the peace we have is the fact that our God is the sovereign ruler of the universe. As such, He can and does do all that He has promised. He works all things to our good. If we truly believe Romans 8:28, it makes it much easier for us to carry out Philippians 4:6 and 1 Peter 5:7.

6 Do not be anxious about anything, but in everything, by prayer and petition, with thanksgiving, present your requests to God. (Philippians 4:6).

7 Cast all your anxiety on him because he cares for you. (1 Peter 5:7).

We can refrain from being anxious when we believe that our Heavenly Father not only knows what is happening in our lives, but also controls it and is making it work for our good. Many who profess Christ have an incorrect understanding of Romans 8:28. Perhaps they have not studied the verse in context or maybe they were given an incorrect explanation by a preacher or teacher. Generally this incorrect understanding is simply that whatever the problem and no matter how bad the situation, God will make it all work out good for us. However, there is a real difference in things <u>working out good for us</u> and <u>things working for our good</u>.

Things working out good for us is how we see them from our perspective. The flesh tells us that if we are physically fit, financially sound, achieving much, having it our way, and getting what we want, then things are <u>working out good for us.</u> Things <u>working for our good</u> is from God's perspective. God does not promise that a given situation will work out good for us, but He does promise that He will make that situation work for our good. He is the One who determines whether or not things work for our good. If they are helping to conform us to the image of Christ, then they are working for our good. We are blessed that God makes sure that all things do.

Many in the health and wealth gospel teach the idea of things always working out good for us. This teaching claims that God wants all His children to be healthy and wealthy. Therefore, if you are sick, He will heal you. If you are having financial problems, He will see that you get enough money. Whatever your problems, He will provide a solution so that everything turns out good every time. From a human perspective this sounds great, but it could lead to spiritual decline, if not decay. Becoming rich certainly appeals to the flesh, but it could well be something that <u>works out good for us</u> instead of something that <u>works for our good</u>. Wealth can give one a feeling of power and such a sense of security that one is less dependent on God. Christ says it is hard for the rich to be saved.

> **23 Then Jesus said to his disciples, "I tell you the truth, it is hard for a rich man to enter the kingdom of heaven."** (Matthew 19:23).

A lack of affliction could also cause many people to live independently of God. If they are rolling on through life with no problems, troubles, pain, suffering, or heartaches, they can easily be tempted to see no need to look to God for help or guidance. They are doing just fine on their own. With this attitude it is easy to go astray. The Psalmist tells us that when God's children do stray, God is faithful to afflict them in order to bring them back to the path they should follow.

> **67 Before I was afflicted I went astray,
> but now I obey your word.
> 71 It was good for me to be afflicted
> so that I might learn your decrees.
> 75 I know, O LORD, that your laws are righteous,
> and in faithfulness you have afflicted me.**
> (Psalm 119:67,71,75).

As a loving mother gives bitter medicine to a sick child for physical healing, our loving Heavenly Father gives the bitter pill of affliction to his children for spiritual healing. What a comfort it is to know that although affliction can be most unpleasant, our God has promised to make it work for our good.

"The grand design of God in all the afflictions that befall His people is to bring them nearer and closer to himself."
Thomas Brooks

Those Who Love Him

And we know that in all things God works for the good of <u>those who love him</u>, who have been called according to his purpose. (Romans 8:28).

If we would be one for whom God is making all things work for good, we must be one who loves Him. For the promise, the guarantee, the blessing of Romans 8:28 is for those who love Him and no one else. Many, eager to lay hold of the promise, would profess love for God. But how many of those who profess love, really do love God? True love comes from the heart.

13 The Lord says:
"These people come near to me with their mouth
and honor me with their lips,
but their hearts are far from me. "
(Isaiah 29:13).

Is there some way that we can know we love God? Christ says there is. He says it is through our obedience that we show our love.

23 Jesus replied, "If anyone loves me, he will obey my teaching. My Father will love him, and we will come to him and make our home with him. 24 He who does not love me will not obey my teaching. These words you hear are not my own; they belong to the Father who sent me." (John 14:23-24).

Does this mean that we must follow the teachings of Christ to perfection – never committing a sin to show that we love God? No, that is our goal, but we cannot attain perfection. Christ was the only man who lived a sinless and perfect life. However, we should strive, in the power of the Holy Spirit, to live as sinless a life as we can and to be obedient to the teachings of Christ. We must commit to this and ask God for the grace to enable us to do it. We know God would have us to pray, study the Bible, witness to others, visit the sick, etc., but how obedient are we to these commands? What reasons do we offer to God for not doing these things? How can we obey the teaching of Jesus if we do not know what He taught? How can we know what He taught if we do not study the Bible? What excuses do we use to convince ourselves that God understands how busy we are, and therefore He doesn't expect us to do anymore than we are doing? How do we reconcile our reasons and excuses with what the Apostle John tells us in 1 John 2:3-6?

> **3 We know that we have come to know him if we obey his commands. 4 The man who says, "I know him," but does not do what he commands is a liar, and the truth is not in him. 5 But if anyone obeys his word, God's love is truly made complete in him. This is how we know we are in him: 6 Whoever claims to live in him must walk as Jesus did.** (1 John 2:3-6).

I do not want to be misunderstood at this point. I am not suggesting that we should take a legalistic approach to serving God, nor a fanatical one of thinking that no matter what we do it is not enough. I am suggesting that each of us should find time to take a serious look at how obedient we are. We should ask God to show us where we are falling short and to lead and empower us to do that which He would have us do. There are a number of Christians who are faithful in their service to our Lord, but there are many others who fall short (some very short) in being obedient. Looking back to our passage (John 14:23-24), we see that verse 23 tells us that we love if we obey, and verse 24 tells us that we do not love if we disobey. This automatically raises a question that each of us must answer for ourselves: Am I living my life in obedience to God, thereby showing my love for God? If the answer is yes, then we can have confidence that we not only love God but that He also loves us.

> **21 Whoever has my commands and obeys them, he is the one who loves me. He who loves me will be loved by my Father, and I too will love him and show myself to him.** (John 14:21).

As we give thought to the question of love, we see that the love Christ calls for in the above verse is a commitment-not an emotion. People are prone to mistake physical attraction as love. They often think that their emotional reaction to someone meeting their needs is love. The Bible does allow for physical love, brotherly love, and platonic love. These are forms of love that anyone may experience. However, the Bible speaks of a much higher form of love that is experienced only by Christians. We are told to love God with all our heart, mind, and soul and to love our neighbor as our self. There are no conditions attached to this love. It is a command from God that calls for a commitment to God. This command to love can only be obeyed in the power of God. It is a supernatural love. Therefore, when we say we love God, let it be with this type of love. Anything less will not do.

Another indication that we love God is that we love God's children. God's children are believers who are members of the body of Christ. God's Holy Spirit indwells them all. They are in union with Christ, and through Christ they are in union with each other. All believers are kindred in the Lord – regardless of anything: race, color, ethnic background, age, etc. God has chosen them just as He has chosen you. They are His children, and He loves them. Could you not love what is His – what He loves?

> *1* **Everyone who believes that Jesus is the Christ is born of God, and everyone who loves the father loves his child as well.** *2* **This is how we know that we love the children of God: by loving God and carrying out his commands.** (1 John 5:1-2).

> *7* **Dear friends, let us love one another, for love comes from God. Everyone who loves has been born of God and knows God.** (1 John 4:7).

Love is a grace. It is fruit of the Spirit. Love for God, love for fellow believers, and love for unbelievers is precious. When we have a precious jewel it is important to us. We guard it carefully. Do we guard our love that way?

If our hearts love God, then our hearts belong to God, and all that we are and have belong to Him also. Those who don't love God don't know God, for to know Him is to love Him. The better we know Him the more we will love Him. Those in heaven will love God. Will it not require love for Him to get to heaven? I realize that it is through our faith that we are saved by grace; however, true faith is a faith that is enmeshed in love. We would not have faith if God did not love us. We would not love God if He had not first loved us. Christ said the first great commandment is to love God. We speak strongly of faith – and we should, but sometimes we Christian fail to stir up in our hearts the love of God that should be there. Proper love for God results in proper love for man. Without love we are nothing.

1 If I speak in the tongues of men and of angels, but have not love, I am only a resounding gong or a clanging cymbal. 2 If I have the gift of prophecy and can fathom all mysteries and all knowledge, and if I have a faith that can move mountains, but have not love, I am nothing. 3 If I give all I possess to the poor and surrender my body to the flames, but have not love, I gain nothing.
4 Love is patient, love is kind. It does not envy, it does not boast, it is not proud. 5 It is not rude, it is not self-seeking, it is not easily angered, it keeps no record of wrongs. 6 Love does not delight in evil but rejoices with the truth. 7 It always protects, always trusts, always hopes, always perseveres.
8 Love never fails. But where there are prophecies, they will cease; where there are tongues, they will be stilled; where there is knowledge, it will pass away. For we know in part and we prophesy in part, 10 but when perfection comes, the imperfect disappears. 11 When I was a child, I talked like a child, I thought like a child, I reasoned like a child. When I became a man, I put childish ways behind me. 12 Now we see but a poor reflection as in a mirror; then we shall see face to face. Now I know in part; then I shall know fully, even as I am fully known.
13 And now these three remain: faith, hope and love. But the greatest of these is love.
(1 Corinthians 13:1-13).

If we profess to love God, we should exhibit some of the characteristics of those who do. We should resist sinning against God as Joseph did.

> **9 "No one is greater in this house than I am. My master has withheld nothing from me except you, because you are his wife. How then could I do such a wicked thing and sin against God?"**
> (Genesis 39:9).

When we do sin, we should feel sorrow.

> **75 Then Peter remembered the word Jesus had spoken: "Before the rooster crows, you will disown me three times." And he went outside and wept bitterly.** (Matthew 26:75).

When we sin, we should confess our sins.

> **9 If we confess our sins, he is faithful and just and will forgive us our sins and purify us from all unrighteousness.** (1 John 1:9).

We should feel the need to speak of God.

> **18 Then they called them in again and commanded them not to speak or teach at all in the name of Jesus. 19 But Peter and John replied, "Judge for yourselves whether it is right in God's sight to obey you rather than God. 20 For we cannot help speaking about what we have seen and heard."**
> (Acts 4:18-20).

We should always rejoice.

> **4 Rejoice in the Lord always. I will say it again: Rejoice!** (Philippians 4:4).

If we love God, we will not love the world.

> **15 Do not love the world or anything in the world. If anyone loves the world, the love of the Father is not in him.** (1 John 2:15).

We will love God more than anyone.

> **26 "If anyone comes to me and does not hate his father and mother, his wife and children, his brothers and sisters—yes, even his own life—he cannot be my disciple."** (Luke 14:26).

The word "hate" in this verse does not mean we are to literally hate our mother and father, etc. The Bible teaches us to love, and certainly expects us to love our family. The word "hate" is a Biblical way of describing the great difference in our love for anyone (including ourselves) and our love for God. There should be such a degree of difference, that by comparison it would appear to be hate.

Let us remember an important point about loving God: that having professed love for God in the past is not sufficient for today. Furthermore, today's love for God will not suffice for tomorrow. We must love God afresh each day and continue in our love for Him. A heart that can stop loving God is a heart that never really loved Him. In its deceit it pretended it did. It may have sounded sincere when it said it did – but it really never did love God. If we don't guard our hearts, the sin in us and the sin around us can gain ground and cause our love to wane. If this happens, we must repent and seek to regain it. If we do not, we may find that we are apostates who never had real love for God. We should heed Christ's warning to the church in Ephesus.

> **4 Yet I hold this against you: You have forsaken your first love. 5 Remember the height from which you have fallen! Repent and do the things you did at first. If you do not repent, I will come to you and remove your lampstand from its place.**
> (Revelation 2:4-5).

If we are obedient Christians, we will seek to prevent a decline in our love and strive to have an abounding love for God. If our love is not increasing, it probably is decreasing. Paul prayed for the Philippians' love to abound more and more.

9 And this is my prayer: that your love may abound more and more in knowledge and depth of insight... (Philippians 1:9).

We would be wise to ask God to cause our love for Him to grow.

Who Have Been Called

And we know that in all things God works for the good of those who love him, <u>who have been called</u> according to his purpose.
(Romans 8:28).

It is very important for us to understand the full meaning of the world "called" in Romans 8:28. When we think of someone calling, we know that the one called may or may not hear the call. Even if he does hear, he may or may not answer the call. If the call is for him to come, he may refuse. God gives a call to mankind to repent and be saved, but it is a call that can be ignored or resisted. This call is a general call by God to man. It is not the call that refers to those who are the "called" in our verse. The "called" in our verse refers to people who have received a special call. They have received a call that is above and beyond the general call. It is an irresistible call – an effectual call. It must be, and it will be, answered. The call is to salvation. God is the one who calls; His elect are the ones called. They are called by the means of God's Word and God's Spirit. All the elect without exception come when called.

From the beginning, God planned not only to provide salvation for the elect but also to apply it to them and to bring it about. Understanding God's sovereignty in election and our freedom in choosing to trust Christ to save us is not what is at stake here – no one can understand it. The question is: Do we believe it? Do we see that God's Word teaches that there is a general call and an effectual call?

The general call is for anyone and everyone, but the effectual call is directed only to the elect – those that God has chosen to save. The general call is an outward call; the effectual call is an inward call. The outward call is heard with natural ears – the inward call with spiritual ears. The outward call may change a sinner temporarily; the inward call will change him permanently. The outward or general call is through the Word; the inward or effectual call is the through the Word and by the Holy Spirit. You might say that the effectual call is the general call plus the God-given ability to understand and to obey the call. It is the work of the Spirit that gives us the ability to understand and believe the Word. Many today hear the gospel, but they do not understand or believe it. This is the way it has always been. The general call goes out, but only those who are effectually called respond. Christ tells us that it is this way.

> **63 "The Spirit gives life; the flesh counts for nothing. The words I have spoken to you are spirit and they are life. 64 Yet there are some of you who do not believe." For Jesus had known from the beginning which of them did not believe and who would betray him. 65 He went on to say, "This is why I told you that no one can come to me unless the Father has enabled him."** (John 6:63-65).

Paul tells us that it is the Spirit that enables us to know the truth of God.

> **10 ...but God has revealed it to us by his Spirit.** (1 Corinthians 2:10).

> *17* **I keep asking that the God of our Lord Jesus Christ, the glorious Father, may give you the Spirit of wisdom and revelation, so that you may know him better.** (Ephesians 1:17).

The writer of Psalm 119 knew that it is God who opens our understanding of His Word.

> **18 Open my eyes that I may see
> wonderful things in your law.
> 34 Give me understanding, and I will keep your law
> and obey it with all my heart.** (Psalm 119:18,34).

John tells us that Christ gives us understanding.

> **20 We know also that the Son of God has come and
> has given us understanding, so that we may know
> him who is true.** (1 John 5:20).

Luke tells us that Christ opened the minds of His disciples so that they could understand the Scriptures.

> **44 He said to them, "This is what I told you while I
> was still with you: Everything must be fulfilled that is
> written about me in the Law of Moses, the Prophets
> and the Psalms."
> 45 Then he opened their minds so they could
> understand the Scriptures.** (Luke 24:44-45).

We see in the book of Acts that the Lord opened the heart of Lydia so that she would respond to Paul's message.

> **13 On the Sabbath we went outside the city gate to
> the river, where we expected to find a place of
> prayer. We sat down and began to speak to the
> women who had gathered there. 14 One of those
> listening was a woman named Lydia, a dealer in
> purple cloth from the city of Thyatira, who was a
> worshiper of God. The Lord opened her heart to
> respond to Paul's message.** (Acts 16:13-14).

There are many other examples of this in the Bible; however, these should be sufficient to make it clear that our understanding of the Word of God is totally a work of God. It matters not to which of the three persons of the Godhead the work is attributed; it is all the work of God. When God calls with an effectual call, "the called" will come. Those whom God calls will in turn call on God.

> **32 And everyone who calls
> on the name of the LORD will be saved;**

**for on Mount Zion and in Jerusalem
there will be deliverance,
as the LORD has said,
among the survivors
whom the LORD calls.** (Joel 2:32).

Immediately the question of "free will" arises in the minds of many people. They think of the elect as either being forced to come or as being robots. Neither is correct. They need to understand that although those who receive this special call will always come, it is never against their will. To the contrary <u>they will</u> to come. They have a desire to come, and they freely choose to come. Here we have another example of those paradoxes between God's sovereignty and man's free will. We don't understand how it works, but it is taught in God's Word, and we accept it as the truth it is.

When Christ called His apostles, they all followed without question. Consider the odds against this happening even once, much less each time Christ called. Was this their "free will", or was it a call that they could not refuse? Scripture teaches it was both. The same is true when God calls one of His elect to be saved. He cannot and will not resist the call – yet he gladly comes of his own free will. He does not feel forced to come, and no violence is done to his will. He freely chooses to come. This is the doctrine of election, and this is the teaching of God's Word. God has decreed it to be so, and what God has decreed man will do.

God's decrees are never conditioned upon anything. However, they contain many things that are conditional. But even then, God provides the means for the conditions to be met. We speak of God's decrees, but actually there is only one decree. God has eternally known what He would do. We see events as past, present, and future, but our omniscient God sees them all at one time.

There are objections to the doctrine of election due to a number of reasons. These include misconceptions, lack of understanding, and pride. The objections are not unique to 21st-Century man. They are objections that man has always voiced when faced with the doctrine of election. God's absolute sovereignty and man's total dependency in salvation are things that unsaved man rejects and saved man resists. Paul is aware of those objections and addresses them in Romans 9.

> 10 Not only that, but Rebekah's children had one and the same father, our father Isaac. 11 Yet, before the twins were born or had done anything good or bad—in order that God's purpose in election might stand: 12 not by works but by him who calls—she was told, "The older will serve the younger." 13 Just as it is written: "Jacob I loved, but Esau I hated."
> 14 What then shall we say? Is God unjust? Not at all! 15 For he says to Moses,
> "I will have mercy on whom I have mercy,
> and I will have compassion on whom I have compassion."
> 16 It does not, therefore, depend on man's desire or effort, but on God's mercy. 17 For the Scripture says to Pharaoh: "I raised you up for this very purpose, that I might display my power in you and that my name might be proclaimed in all the earth." 18 Therefore God has mercy on whom he wants to have mercy, and he hardens whom he wants to harden.
> 19 One of you will say to me: "Then why does God still blame us? For who resists his will?" 20 But who are you, O man, to talk back to God? "Shall what is formed say to him who formed it, 'Why did you make me like this?'" 21 Does not the potter have the right to make out of the same lump of clay some pottery for noble purposes and some for common use?
> 22 What if God, choosing to show his wrath and make his power known, bore with great patience the objects of his wrath—prepared for destruction? 23 What if he did this to make the riches of his glory known to the objects of his mercy, whom he prepared in advance for glory— 24 even us, whom he also called, not only from the Jews but also from the Gentiles? (Romans 9:10-24).

From these verses we see that God's kingdom is not a democracy. There is no vote taken on what is to be done or not done. The majority does not rule – the sovereign Lord

God rules. He is the potter – man is the clay. Paul anticipated man's questions and man's wrong attitude toward God, upon hearing the teaching of election. His answer was God's Word. Moreover, this is not the only place in His Word that God makes this point using the potter and clay as an illustration, i.e.:

> 8 Yet, O LORD, you are our Father.
> We are the clay, you are the potter;
> we are all the work of your hand.
> (Isaiah 64:8).

> 1 This is the word that came to Jeremiah from the LORD: 2 "Go down to the potter's house, and there I will give you my message." 3 So I went down to the potter's house, and I saw him working at the wheel. 4 But the pot he was shaping from the clay was marred in his hands; so the potter formed it into another pot, shaping it as seemed best to him.
> 5 Then the word of the LORD came to me: 6 "O house of Israel, can I not do with you as this potter does?" declares the LORD. "Like clay in the hand of the potter, so are you in my hand, O house of Israel.
> (Jeremiah 18:1-6).

> 9 "Woe to him who quarrels with his Maker,
> to him who is but a potsherd among the potsherds on the ground.
> Does the clay say to the potter,
> 'What are you making?'
> Does your work say,
> 'He has no hands'?
> 10 Woe to him who says to his father,
> 'What have you begotten?'
> or to his mother,
> 'What have you brought to birth?'
> 11 "This is what the LORD says—
> the Holy One of Israel, and its Maker:
> Concerning things to come,
> do you question me about my children,
> or give me orders about the work of my hands?
> (Isaiah 45:9-11).

Attempting to grasp this meaty doctrine with our finite intelligence alone is futile. The Holy Spirit must open our minds and hearts to these truths. However, if we will study the doctrine of election with an open mind (putting aside our pride and pre-conceptions) and ask God to show us His truth, I am convinced we will be pleased with the understanding we gain. We may find that we become more aware of how sinful man is and how helpless he is to understand or believe God's Word, apart from God's illuminating grace.

> **5 Surely I was sinful at birth,**
> **sinful from the time my mother conceived me.**
> (Psalm 51:5).

> **6 All of us have become like one who is unclean,**
> **and all our righteous acts are like filthy rags;**
> **we all shrivel up like a leaf,**
> **and like the wind our sins sweep us away.**
> (Isaiah 64:6).

> **36 "When they sin against you—for there is no one**
> **who does not sin...** (2 Chronicles 6:36).

> **6 We all, like sheep, have gone astray,**
> **each of us has turned to his own way;**
> **and the LORD has laid on him**
> **the iniquity of us all.** (Isaiah 53:6).

> **7 ...the sinful mind is hostile to God. It does not**
> **submit to God's law, nor can it do so.** (Romans 8:7).

The Word of God paints a clear picture of the total depravity of unregenerate man. He is not as rotten as he could be, but he is rotten throughout. God restrains evil, and if some men find themselves to be not as sinful as most, it is by God's grace. When we see men whom we think of as really evil, we should not think of them as an exception of human nature, but rather as an example of human nature that has been allowed to run its course. Except for the grace of God, any of us could be as they are. Sinful human nature is sinful human nature. A snake is a snake. A tiger is a tiger, and it has the nature of a tiger. A tiger born and raised in captivity may act differently from one born and raised in the wild, but their natures are the same. This is the way it is with man. Environment, situations, and circumstances can affect how men act and react, but their natures are the same – they are sinful. It is not just the fact that we sin but also the fact that we are sinful. It is not just what we do but what we are. As we study election, perhaps we will also realize the plight of man without Christ.

> **8 He will punish those who do not know God and do not obey the gospel of our Lord Jesus. 9 They will be punished with everlasting destruction and shut out from the presence of the Lord and from the majesty of his power...** (2 Thessalonians 1:8-9).

We should now better understand the need of God's electing grace. It is apparent that without it, all mankind would end up in hell. For we have learned that man is sinful and headed to hell, and the only thing that will prevent that from happening is for him to turn to Christ. However, when he hears the Gospel, he doesn't understand it or believe it because he is unable.

> **14 The man without the Spirit does not accept the things that come from the Spirit of God, for they are foolishness to him, and he cannot understand them, because they are spiritually discerned.**
> (1 Corinthians 2:14).

Furthermore, man suppresses the evidence that God gives him of Himself through His creation and by writing His Law on man's heart. Sinful man does not want to give up his sinful pleasures; he wants to live his life as he pleases – not as pleases God. Therefore, as a stubborn and unrepentant sinner, he is without excuse before God. He is not only deserving of God's wrath, but he continues with time to store up more wrath against himself.

15 ...since they show that the requirements of the law are written on their hearts... (Romans 2:15).

18 The wrath of God is being revealed from heaven against all the godlessness and wickedness of men who suppress the truth by their wickedness, 19 since what may be known about God is plain to them, because God has made it plain to them. 20 For since the creation of the world God's invisible qualities—his eternal power and divine nature—have been clearly seen, being understood from what has been made, so that men are without excuse. (Romans 1:18-20).

5 But because of your stubbornness and your unrepentant heart, you are storing up wrath against yourself for the day of God's wrath, when his righteous judgment will be revealed. (Romans 2:5).

We see from Scripture that unregenerate man is not righteous – he is wicked. Moreover, he not only does not understand the things of God, he does not even care to. He suppresses the truth that is evident and makes no attempt to seek the true God.

**10 As it is written:
"There is no one righteous, not even one;
11 there is no one who understands,
no one who seeks God.** (Romans 3:10-11).

Therefore, he will go to hell unless God intervenes – and that is what God does in the case of the elect.

The elect are those who, while spiritually dead, are made spiritually alive by God. God regenerates them. They are given spiritual life. When this is done, and only then, are they capable of understanding, believing, and responding to the Gospel. Some mistakenly think that you trust Christ first and then you are given spiritual life. However, they are wrong. The spiritually dead cannot respond to spiritual stimuli any more than the physically dead can respond to physical stimuli. Lazarus was physically dead; however, God, through Christ, made him physically alive (John 11:38-44). This was a supernatural work of God. God also does a supernatural work when He makes a spiritually dead man spiritually alive. This is what takes place with the elect. They are spiritually dead, but God has decreed to save them; therefore, He gives them spiritual life. Just as one must be born physically to have physical life, one must be born spiritually to have spiritual life.

> **5 Jesus answered, "I tell you the truth, no one can enter the kingdom of God unless he is born of water and the Spirit. 6 Flesh gives birth to flesh, but the Spirit gives birth to spirit. 7 You should not be surprised at my saying, 'You must be born again.' 8 The wind blows wherever it pleases. You hear its sound, but you cannot tell where it comes from or where it is going. So it is with everyone born of the Spirit."** (John 3:5-8).

We see in the above verses that you must be born of the Spirit (have spiritual life) before you can enter the kingdom of God. You do not and cannot enter the kingdom and then get spiritual life. We also see that God's Spirit gives spiritual life to whomever He pleases. Scripture is clear that those to whom He gives spiritual life are the elect. The elect are those God has chosen to be saved. Another word meaning the same as "the elect" or "the chosen" is "the called". Before the world was made, God chose or elected certain people to be saved. Those elect people, though sure to be saved at some point in time, are unsaved until it pleases God to save them. In His time He calls them to salvation. At that time He regenerates them, giving them spiritual life and enabling them to respond positively to His call. Let us remember that no one deserves to be saved, and all that go to hell get justice. They get what they deserve. All of the called (the elect) deserve hell just as much as the others; however, God shows them mercy, and for His own glory He saves them.

Before the elect are called to salvation, they are no different from the non-elect. They are not more moral, nicer, or smarter than the non-elect. There is no special reason or condition as to why they were chosen to be saved and others were not. They are saved because it pleased God to save them. The Bible teaches that God's election of man is unconditional. If it were not, then it must be conditional. If it were conditional, what is or are the conditions? It certainly could not be doing good works or living right, for the Word makes it clear that you cannot earn salvation.

> **28 For we maintain that a man is justified by faith apart from observing the law.** (Romans 3:28).

> **10 All who rely on observing the law are under a curse, for it is written: "Cursed is everyone who does not continue to do everything written in the Book of the Law."** (Galatians 3:10).

> **10 For whoever keeps the whole law and yet stumbles at just one point is guilty of breaking all of it.** (James 2:10).

You cannot buy salvation by giving money to the church or other worthy causes, for that also falls into the category of good works. If it can't be earned, then salvation must be a free gift, and that is exactly what God says it is.

> **8 For it is by grace you have been saved, through faith—and this not from yourselves, it is the gift of God— 9 not by works, so that no one can boast.** (Ephesians 2:8-9).

The above passage makes it clear that salvation is totally a work of God. All who truly know Christ would agree with the above verse. They would agree that salvation is by grace but this comes through faith. However, the verse tells us that our faith (our understanding, our ability, and our desire of trusting Christ) is not of ourselves but is a gift from God. It is a God-given faith through which we believe unto salvation. Another reference to faith being given to us is found in Romans 12:3.

3 For by the grace given me I say to every one of you: Do not think of yourself more highly than you ought, but rather think of yourself with sober judgment, in accordance with the measure of faith God has given you. (Romans 12:3).

There are those of the Arminian persuasion who will say they were saved by grace, but the decision to trust Christ was their own. Even in the face of the above verses, they will claim that their faith is their own and not a gift from God. Their way of thinking is that God provided a way of salvation, but it was their decision to take the provided way. They do not see this as being works, but it is questionable as to why it is not. After all, if they had chosen not to trust Christ, they would not be saved. Therefore, in their case, God did not save them by Himself – they had to help Him; they made a contribution. They actually have something to boast about if trusting Christ is simply up to man. They have a right to feel superior, because most people are either not morally good enough or smart enough to trust Christ.

If the reader is of Arminian belief, I would ask you this question: Are you not better and have you not achieved much more than all the unbelievers? You have to be proud of yourself. You have made a choice that they aren't good enough or smart enough to make. They are headed to hell, and by your wise decision you are headed to heaven. There is a big difference in them and you. You may feel sorry for them and wish that they had the good sense you have, but regardless, you have to be proud of yourself. After all, look at how many people don't trust Christ and how few do. That makes you one of an elite group. You and your group are winners; all the others are losers. However, let us look again. Let us take a closer look and see if you could have made the decision to come to Christ on your own – before God regenerated you. I believe we will see that the Bible says you could not.

We will begin with the premise that man is a lost sinner headed to hell – unless and until he repents and trusts Christ to save him. I assume we are in agreement on that statement. Considering what you were before you came to Christ, let us see how God describes your situation at that time. He says that you lacked understanding and were separated from Him,

> **18 They are darkened in their understanding and separated from the life of God because of the ignorance that is in them due to the hardening of their hearts.** (Ephesians 4:18).

The preaching of Christ crucified was a stumbling block or foolishness to you.

> **23 ...but we preach Christ crucified: a stumbling block to Jews and foolishness to Gentiles....**
> (1 Corinthians 1:23).

Lacking faith in Christ, everything you did was sin in God's eyes.

> **23 ...and everything that does not come from faith is sin.** (Romans 14:23).

You were perishing (on your way to hell) and the message of the cross was foolishness to you.

> **18 For the message of the cross is foolishness to those who are perishing, but to us who are being saved it is the power of God.** (1 Corinthians 1:18).

You would not accept the things of God. You could not understand them.

> **14 The man without the Spirit does not accept the things that come from the Spirit of God, for they are foolishness to him, and he cannot understand them, because they are spiritually discerned.**
> (1 Corinthians 2:14).

You had your own way of believing – your own religion, but it was leading you to hell.

> **12 There is a way that seems right to a man,**
> **but in the end it leads to death.** (Proverbs 14:12).

You did not seek God. You were worthless. You did nothing good.

> *10* **As it is written:**
> **"There is no one righteous, not even one;**
> **11 there is no one who understands,**
> **no one who seeks God.**
> **12 All have turned away,**
> **they have together become worthless;**
> **there is no one who does good,**
> **not even one."** (Romans 3:10-12).

Your righteous acts were like filthy rags to God.

> **6 All of us have become like one who is unclean,**
> **and all our righteous acts are like filthy rags...**
> (Isaiah 64:6).

You not only did not do good, you could not do good.

> **23 Can the Ethiopian change his skin**
> **or the leopard its spots?**
> **Neither can you do good**
> **who are accustomed to doing evil.**
> (Jeremiah 13:23).

You were hostile to God, controlled by your sinful nature, and you could not please God.

> **7 ...the sinful mind is hostile to God. It does not**
> **submit to God's law, nor can it do so. 8 Those**
> **controlled by the sinful nature cannot please God.**
> (Romans 8:7-8).

The above descriptions of the unsaved person are true of everyone before being saved. Therefore, they are true descriptions of you and me before we were saved. There are many more Scriptures that express similar ideas about man without Christ; however, these should suffice. In light of these, is there any way you can claim to have trusted Christ on your own without denying logic and reason - much less the truth of Scripture? I do not see how anyone can. I am not alone in the position I hold. It is the same position that Christ, Paul, and the other Apostles held. It is the position held by Saint Augustine, Martin Luther, John Calvin, and Charles Spurgeon.

Luther made clear that this was his position in his well-known work <u>The Bondage of The Will</u>. The writings of the well-known Catholic Theologian Augustine confirm that this was also his position, and we will see this as we read a couple of passages from Calvin's "Institutes" as he quotes Augustine. In his "Institutes" Calvin says:

"Since the will of man is held fast in the bondage of sin, it cannot move towards good; much less can it cleave to good. A movement towards good is the first step in conversion to God; and in the Scriptures this is always attributed entirely to His grace. Hence the prophet Jeremiah prays, "Turn Thou me, and I shall be turned." (Jeremiah 31:18). And yet man still possesses a will: for when by his fall he subjected himself to the necessity of serving sin, his will was not taken away from him, but became diseased. Hence the mere faculty of will belongs to man; the will to evil belongs to his depraved nature; the will to good belongs to grace. I wonder that any should think it a harsh saying that the will of man, having lost its freedom, is by necessity drawn or led to evil, There is nothing absurd in the statement: but it offends those who cannot distinguish between necessity and compulsion, and yet if they were asked whether God is necessarily good, or whether the devil is necessarily evil, how could they deny it? The goodness of God is so connected with His divinity that He is as necessarily good as He is necessarily God. And the devil by his fall is so alienated from all that is good that he can do nothing but what is evil. But if any impious caviller should object that, if God is compelled to be good, small praise is due to Him for His goodness, the answer is easy: His own infinite goodness, not some forcible constrain,

makes it impossible for Him to do evil. If therefore the fact that God is necessarily good is no hindrance to the freedom of His will in the exercise of His goodness, and if the devil, who can only do evil, exercises his own will in the commission of evil; who will venture to say that, because man is under a necessity to commit sin, he does not sin willingly? Augustine everywhere maintains this, and he does not hesitate to say that 'by the exercise of his freedom man became a sinner; but now a penal state of depravity has turned his freedom into a necessity to commit sin.' In short, therefore, let this distinction be observed: man, corrupted by the fall, sins willingly; sins because the affection of his mind is eagerly disposed towards evil, not because he is subject to violent compulsion; sins by a movement of his own desire, not by eternal constraint. In this I bring forward no new doctrine, but that which Augustine taught long ago with the consent of all godly men...

Since this is a point of cardinal importance, I will prove it by the clearest testimonies of Scripture; and having done so I will show that Augustine bears testimony to the same truth; for I consider it not unimportant to point out that I am in agreement with a man whom all godly people justly regard as an authority...

And now let us listen to Augustine. His words will show that we are not, as our adversaries allege, contradicted by the unanimous voice of the ancient fathers. I will briefly outline Augustine's opinion, using his own words...

In another place Augustine says that grace does not deprive man of his will, but changes it from a bad will to a good one, and afterwards assists it; by which he means that man is not driven as it were, by some external impulse, but is so affected within that he obeys from the heart. He also says in one of his letters: "We know that the grace of God is not given to all men; and that where it is given, it is not given on the ground of the merits of man's works or man's will, but by free favor: and we know that where it is not given, it is withheld by the just judgment of God."

The great Baptist preacher Spurgeon also knew that man left to himself is unable to trust Christ. He knew that it takes the work of the Holy Spirit to regenerate man (give him spiritual life), to enable him to trust Christ, and he knew that is what God does for His elect. One of the better-known sermons on election is by Spurgeon. The following quote is taken from that sermon.

"But," say others, "God elected them on the foresight of their faith." Now, God gives faith, therefore he could not have elected them on account of faith, which he foresaw. There shall be twenty beggars in the street, and I determine to give one of them a shilling; but will any one say that I determined to give that one a shilling; that I elected him to have the shilling, because I foresaw that he would have it? That would be talking nonsense. In the like manner, to say that God elected men because he foresaw they would have faith, which is salvation in the germ, would be too absurd for us to listen to for a moment. Faith is the gift of God. Every virtue comes from him. Therefore it cannot have caused him to elect men, because it is his gift...

..."He will have mercy on whom he will have mercy:" he saves because he will save. And if you ask me why he saves me, I can only say, because he would do it. Was there any thing in me that should recommend me to God? No; I lay aside every thing. I have nothing to recommend me. When God saved me, I was the most abject, lost, and ruined of the race. I lay before him as an infant in my blood. Verily, I had no power to help myself. Oh how wretched did I feel and know myself to be! If you had something to recommend you to God, I never had. I will be content to be saved by grace, unalloyed, pure grace. I can boast of no merits. If you can do so, I can not. I must sing:

"Free grace alone, from the first to the last,
Hath won my affection and held my soul fast."

Spurgeon has been used greatly by God to put forth the doctrine of election not only among Baptist, but also among Christians from many denominations. The fact that one hears little preaching or teaching of election today does not diminish the truth of the doctrine as given to us in God's Word. For many years there has been a watering down of the Word within the church. This trend seems to be accelerating. It has carried over into the seminaries and produced many preachers who are unable to articulate the meaty doctrines of Scripture. This in turn gives us many people sitting in the pew who know nothing beyond the milk of the Word. Often they know very little of that. They may talk about grace, but they know little of the experience of grace. They are unstable, double minded, and easily blown about by every wind of doctrine. They become prime targets for the cults. It is the author's hope that as more Christians learn who the "called" are, (the called are the chosen, the elect) they will begin to see how clearly and how often this meaty doctrine of election is found in Scripture. Hopefully they will then begin to question their leaders as to why it is not being preached and taught in their church.

The doctrine of Election is not a denominational doctrine anymore than is the doctrine of Salvation or the Sovereignty of God. It is Bible doctrine for all Christians. Before it became neglected by the church, it was preached and taught in many denominations. Although now it is seldom ever mentioned, the doctrine of Election is still included in the doctrinal statements of a number of denominations. One of these is the Baptist Confession of Faith of 1689, as it was known in England and Wales. In America, it became known simply as the Baptist Confession. C. H. Spurgeon had this to say about it:

"This little volume is not issued as an authoritative rule, or code of faith, whereby you are to be fettered, but as an assistance to you in controversy, a confirmation in faith, and a means of edification in righteousness. Here the younger

members of our church will have a body of divinity in small compass, and by means of the Scriptural proofs, will be ready to give a reason for the hope that is in them.

Be not ashamed of your faith: remember it is the ancient gospel of martyrs, confessors, reformers and saints. Above all, it is the truth of God, against which the gates of Hell cannot prevail.

Let your lives adorn your faith, let your example adorn your creed. Above all live in Christ Jesus, and walk in Him, giving credence to no teaching but that which is manifestly approved of Him, and owned by the Holy Spirit. Cleave fast to the Word of God which is here mapped out for you."

The Baptist Confession states the following:

2 Although God knoweth whatsoever may or can come to pass upon all supposed conditions, yet hath he not decreed anything because he foresaw it as future, or as that which would come to pass upon such conditions.
Acts 15:18. Rom. 9:11, 13,16,18.

3 By the decree of God, for the manifestation of his glory, some men and angels are predestinated, or foreordained to eternal life through Jesus Christ, to the praise of his glorious grace; others being left to act in their sin to their just condemnation, to the praise of his glorious justice.
1 Tim. 5:21, Mat. 25:34. Eph. 1:5,6. Rom. 9:22,23, Jude 4.

4 These angels and men thus predestinated and foreordained are particularly and unchangeably designed, and their number so certain and definite, that it cannot be either increased or diminished.
2 Tim. 2:19, John 13:18.

5 Those of mankind that are predestinated to life, God, before the foundation of the world was laid, according to his eternal and immutable purpose, and the secret counsel and good pleasure of his will, hath chosen in Christ unto

everlasting glory, out of his mere free grace and love, without any other thing in the creature as a condition or cause moving him thereunto.
Eph. 1:4, 9, 11, Rom. 8:30, 2 Tim. 1:9, 1 Thess. 5:9, Rom. 9:13, 16, Eph. 2:5, 12.

6 As God hath appointed the elect unto glory, so he hath, by the eternal and most free purpose of his will, foreordained all the means thereunto; wherefore they who are elected, being fallen in Adam, are redeemed by Christ, are effectually called unto faith in Christ, by his Spirit working in due season, are justified, adopted, sanctified, and kept by his power through faith unto salvation; neither are any other redeemed by Christ, or effectually called, justified, adopted, sanctified, and saved, but the elect only.
1 Pet. 1:2, 2 Thess. 2:13, 1 Thess. 5:9, 10, Rom. 8:30, 2 Thess. 2:13, 1 Pet. 1:5, John 10:26; 17:9; 6:64.

In the Articles of Religion of the Episcopal Church in the United States of America, the 17th Article states the following pertaining to Election:

"Predestination to life is the everlasting purpose of God, whereby (before the foundations of the world were laid) he hath constantly decreed by his counsel secret to us, to deliver from curse and damnation those whom he hath chosen in Christ out of mankind, and to bring them by Christ to everlasting salvation, as vessels made to honor. Wherefore they which he endued with so excellent a benefit of God be called according to God's purpose by his Spirit working in due season: they through grace obey the calling: they be justified freely: they be made sons of God by adoption: they be made like the image of his only-begotten Son Jesus Christ: they walk religiously in good works, and at length, by God's mercy, they attain to everlasting felicity."

In the Thirty-nine Articles of the Church of England there is a similar statement to that of the Episcopal Church.

The <u>Waldensian Creed</u> that was written around the 12th century says:

"That God saves from corruption and damnation those whom he has chosen from the foundations of the world, not for any disposition, faith, or holiness that he foresaw in them, but of his mere mercy in Christ Jesus his Son, passing by all the rest, according to the irreprehensible reason of his own free-will and justice."

The <u>Westminster Confession of Faith</u> which is widely used by many, especially several Presbyterian Denominations says the following about Effectual Calling:

1. All those whom God hath predestinated unto life, and those only, He is pleased, in His appointed and accepted time, effectually to call, by His Word and Spirit, out of that state of sin and death, in which they are by nature to grace and salvation, by Jesus Christ; enlightening their minds spiritually and savingly to understand the things of God, taking away their heart of stone, and giving unto them a heart of flesh; renewing their wills, and, by His almighty power, determining them to that which is good, and effectually drawing them to Jesus Christ: yet so, as they come most freely, being made willing by His grace.

11. This effectual call is of God's free and special grace alone, not from any thing at all foreseen in man, who is altogether passive therein, until, being quickened and renewed by the Holy Spirit, he is thereby enabled to answer this call, and to embrace the grace offered and conveyed in it.

We have seen that natural man, (man without God's Holy Spirit) in his unregenerate and sinful state, is helplessly and hopelessly lost. He does not even have it in him to accept God's provision of salvation in Christ. We have also seen that a number of doctrinal statements of different denominations teach that God saves His elect out of this hopeless situation. Let us look at some verses that confirm this.

> 5 Jesus answered, "I tell you the truth, no one can enter the kingdom of God unless he is born of water and the Spirit. 6 Flesh gives birth to flesh, but the Spirit gives birth to spirit. 7 You should not be surprised at my saying, 'You must be born again.' 8 The wind blows wherever it pleases. You hear its sound, but you cannot tell where it comes from or where it is going. So it is with everyone born of the Spirit." (John 3:5-8).

> 13 When you were dead in your sins and in the uncircumcision of your sinful nature, God made you alive with Christ. (Colossians 2:13).

> 14 "Then he said: 'The God of our fathers has chosen you to know his will and to see the Righteous One and to hear words from his mouth. (Acts 22:14).

> 1 After Jesus said this, he looked toward heaven and prayed:
> "Father, the time has come. Glorify your Son, that your Son may glorify you. 2 For you granted him authority over all people that he might give eternal life to all those you have given him. (John 17:1-2).

> 21 For just as the Father raises the dead and gives them life, even so the Son gives life to whom he is pleased to give it. (John 5:21).

> 4 But when the kindness and love of God our Savior appeared, 5 he saved us, not because of righteous things we had done, but because of his mercy. He saved us through the washing of rebirth and renewal by the Holy Spirit, 6 whom he poured out on us generously through Jesus Christ our Savior, 7 so that, having been justified by his grace, we might become heirs having the hope of eternal life. (Titus 3:4-7).

26 I will give you a new heart and put a new spirit in you; I will remove from you your heart of stone and give you a heart of flesh. (Ezekiel 36:26).

4 But because of his great love for us, God, who is rich in mercy, 5 made us alive with Christ even when we were dead in transgressions—it is by grace you have been saved. (Ephesians 2:4-5).

17 Every good and perfect gift is from above, coming down from the Father of the heavenly lights, who does not change like shifting shadows. 18 He chose to give us birth through the word of truth, that we might be a kind of firstfruits of all he created. (James 1:17-18).

48 When the Gentiles heard this, they were glad and honored the word of the Lord; and all who were appointed for eternal life believed. (Acts 13:48).

27 "All things have been committed to me by my Father. No one knows the Son except the Father, and no one knows the Father except the Son and those to whom the Son chooses to reveal him. (Matthew 11:27).

3 Praise be to the God and Father of our Lord Jesus Christ, who has blessed us in the heavenly realms with every spiritual blessing in Christ. 4 For he chose us in him before the creation of the world to be holy and blameless in his sight. In love 5 he predestined us to be adopted as his sons through Jesus Christ, in accordance with his pleasure and will— 6 to the praise of his glorious grace, which he has freely given us in the One he loves. (Ephesians 1:3-6).

13 ...for it is God who works in you to will and to act according to his good purpose. (Philippians 2:13)

16 You did not choose me, but I chose you... (John 15:16).

20 And Isaiah boldly says,
"I was found by those who did not seek me;
I revealed myself to those who did not ask for me."
(Romans 10:20).

These verses confirm that God saves His elect out of their hopeless situation. They make it clear that God gives His elect spiritual life. He makes them spiritually alive. He regenerates them – they are born again.

In the beginning of this discussion on the "called" we said that there is a general call and an effectual call. Scripture makes it clear that the "called" (who are the same as the "chosen" or the "elect") are the ones who receive the effectual call. In the Gospel of Matthew, we see that Christ issues a general call – an invitation to come to Him.

28 "Come to me, all you who are weary and burdened, and I will give you rest. 29 Take my yoke upon you and learn from me, for I am gentle and humble in heart, and you will find rest for your souls. 30 For my yoke is easy and my burden is light."
(Matthew 11:28-30).

We also see in Matthew's Gospel that Christ says the invitation to be saved goes out to many; however, only a few are chosen to receive the free gift of salvation. Those few are the elect. They were chosen to receive the effectual call; therefore, being designated the "called."

14 "For many are invited, but few are chosen."
(Matthew 22:14).

Without the grace of God, we would be what we were – by the grace of God, we are what we are. The Apostle Paul was a most unlikely person to become a Christian. He approved the killing of Stephen and guarded the clothes of those who killed him.

> **19 "'Lord,' I replied, 'these men know that I went from one synagogue to another to imprison and beat those who believe in you. 20 And when the blood of your martyr Stephen was shed, I stood there giving my approval and guarding the clothes of those who were killing him.'** (Acts 22:19-20).

However, Paul was effectually called to salvation by God and became what he was by the grace of God.

> **15 But when God, who set me apart from birth and called me...** (Galatians 1:15).

> **10 But by the grace of God I am what I am, and his grace to me was not without effect. No, I worked harder than all of them—yet not I, but the grace of God that was with me.** (1 Corinthians 15:10).

It becomes obvious that we are called out of the darkness and into the light. We respond to the call by God's grace and pass from spiritual death to spiritual life. We move from unknowingly being servants of Satan to knowingly being servants of God. We are called out of Satan's kingdom and into the kingdom of God.

In bringing this discussion to a close, I would like to make a few random remarks:

1. As the doctrine of Election is clearly taught in the Bible, we would do well to spend less time questioning God's right to elect and more time making sure we are the elect.

2. Man is prone to resist the Gospel even when it is presented in the fashion of Arminianism (the belief that man is a sinner but not so morally corrupt that he is unable, in his own strength and by his own volition, to make a positive response to the Gospel). He bows his back up still further when confronted with the Gospel as presented in the tradition of Calvinism (the belief that man is a sinner and so morally corrupt that

he is unable and unwilling to respond in a positive way to the Gospel unless God gives him spiritual life). Man doesn't like to be called a sinner but has an even greater dislike for being told he is totally depraved and totally dependent on God to save him.

3. How we view a particular doctrine will affect our thinking on other doctrines and issues. A belief in total depravity and election will serve to give us patience and understanding of those who reject the Gospel. The Arminian belief would leave us open to look down on those who reject the Gospel as being morally bad or too stupid to understand.

4. We must guard against trying to be a Christian on our own terms, willing to accept Biblical salvation but not other doctrines. We must come to Christ on His terms, live as He says live, and believe what He says believe.

5. God, in election, is not keeping people out of heaven. No, He is making certain that there will be people there.

6. God is not obligated to save any, but He has a right to save some if He so desires. He also has a right to save whomever He chooses.

7. God has called us not only to salvation but also to sanctification. Knowing that it is God who brings about our salvation and sanctification (by "working in us to will and to do"), we must make it our priority to proceed to work out that which God has worked in.

8. Christ prepares a place for us. He also prepares us for that place. As heaven is holy, we must be holy.

9. We are not saved by our works; however, if we are saved, we will do good works because our heart now is bent decisively toward God.

    10 For we are God's workmanship, created in Christ Jesus to do good works, which God prepared in advance for us to do. (Ephesians 2:10).

10. If you say Christ has saved you (that you are one of the "called"), then look for evidence. Has your life changed; moreover, your thoughts, words, and deeds? Do you keep Christ's commands? Are you actively seeking to become more like Him? Is the desire of your heart to live for Him and glorify Him?

Election is a humbling doctrine. Patrick Hues Mell was president of the Southern Baptist Convention for 17 years. The following is a quote from a booklet he wrote on Predestination and Election:

"It tends to produce humility. When we feel that we shape out own destiny – that our own power or wisdom has procured for us our advantages or successes, we are tempted to entertain exalted conceptions of our own importance; but when we believe that God rules above and rules below and works all things after the counsels of His own will – that He not only called us into being, but selected according to His sovereign pleasure, the time and place and circumstances of our existence – circumstances too, that exert a controlling influence upon our destiny – that He chooses out our changes for us and directs our steps – that He accomplishes His own purposes in our lives, working in us, and by us, for the manifestation of His own glory; we feel that, in the presence of God, we are nothing and less than nothing and vanity."

If, as an unbeliever, you are concerned that perhaps you are not elect, it may be a good thing. It could indicate that you have some understanding of God's sovereignty – understanding of the fact that His will is sure to be done. If your concern is such that you are really seeking the God of the Bible, you can take heart. When we find an unbeliever who is sincerely seeking the true God, we have every reason to think God is drawing him.

If you are sincerely seeking the true God, I suggest that you throw yourself on God's mercy by repenting of your sins, looking to Christ for forgiveness, and trusting Christ alone to save you. You may well discover that you are elect, that you are one of "the called." For God's Word tells us that if we seek God with all our heart we will find Him.

> **13 You will seek me and find me when you seek me with all your heart.** (Jeremiah 29:13).

According to His Purpose

> **28 And we know that in all things God works for the good of those who love him, who have been called <u>according to his purpose</u>.** (Romans 8:28).

God has one ultimate purpose for His creation – to bring glory to Himself. He has decreed the ways and means by which He is glorified. Those who love Him are the "called" according to His purpose, and they glorify Him as they are conformed to the likeness of His Son. God is the only being deserving of glory. He is God, and all the rest of us are merely creatures. God is a glorious being whose glory is eternal. There is nothing intrinsic or inherent about us that would commend or qualify us as deserving of glory. We come into this world as sinful creatures, under condemnation, and deserving of God's wrath. It is only when God saves us and works in us, that we can do anything good. This is all to His glory. It is His enabling us to do that which pleases Him. We can take no credit, and we deserve no credit. We can only praise and glorify Him for bringing it about.

Christ tells us that we are totally dependent on Him to do anything that is of spiritual value.

> **5 "I am the vine; you are the branches. If a man remains in me and I in him, he will bear much fruit; apart from me you can do nothing.** (John 15:5).

Paul makes it clear that we can do all that God would have us do, if we look to Him for the strength to do it.

> **13 I can do everything through him who gives me strength.** (Philippians 4:13).

Man rebels at this truth of the Bible, and even many professing Christians are tempted to bow up their backs when confronted with this fact. People like to think of themselves as independent – not dependent. They want to be their own man or own woman. Many in the Christian world are happy to do the work that Christians are called to do. Although they may not be conscious of doing it, they approach the work independent of God. They see themselves as good guys doing good work. They may not admit it, but they feel they deserve any pats on the back they get. In essence, they are trying to do God's work for God, instead of being used to do God's work by God.

The unbelieving world is constantly seeking glory from the world. Christians must guard against joining them in that endeavor. We must also be careful not to infringe upon God's glory, as Eve was tempted to do, because God will not share His glory with anyone.

> **8 "I am the LORD; that is my name!**
> **I will not give my glory to another...**
> (Isaiah 42:8).

Satan tempted Eve to share God's glory by telling her that she would be like God.

> 5 "For God knows that when you eat of it your eyes
> will be opened, and you will be like God, knowing
> good and evil." (Genesis 3:5).

Throughout history, there have been rulers of empires who took great pride in their achievements and powers, as though God had no control over them. King Nebuchadnezzar was one such ruler. He ruled over Babylonia and build splendid temples and palaces in its capital city Babylon. He built the Hanging Gardens of Babylon, which were considered to be one of the Seven Wonders of the Ancient World. He captured Jerusalem in 586 BC but seemed to take more pride in making Babylon a magnificent city than he did in his military conquest. However, he found that God would not tolerate his pride and boasting, for it is God who raises up kings and it is God who brings them down.

> 19 Then Daniel praised the God of heaven 20 and
> said:
> "Praise be to the name of God for ever and ever;
> wisdom and power are his.
> 21 He changes times and seasons;
> he sets up kings and deposes them.
> (Daniel 2:19-21).

Nebuchadnezzar had to learn the hard way that God is able to humble those who walk in pride.

> 28 All this happened to King Nebuchadnezzar. 29
> Twelve months later, as the king was walking on the
> roof of the royal palace of Babylon, 30 he said, "Is
> not this the great Babylon I have built as the royal
> residence, by my mighty power and for the glory of
> my majesty?"
> 31 The words were still on his lips when a voice
> came from heaven, "This is what is decreed for you,
> King Nebuchadnezzar: Your royal authority has been
> taken from you. 32 You will be driven away from
> people and will live with the wild animals; you will
> eat grass like cattle. Seven times will pass by for you
> until you acknowledge that the Most High is
> sovereign over the kingdoms of men and gives them
> to anyone he wishes."

33 Immediately what had been said about Nebuchadnezzar was fulfilled. He was driven away from people and ate grass like cattle. His body was drenched with the dew of heaven until his hair grew like the feathers of an eagle and his nails like the claws of a bird.
34 At the end of that time, I, Nebuchadnezzar, raised my eyes toward heaven, and my sanity was restored. Then I praised the Most High; I honored and glorified him who lives forever.
His dominion is an eternal dominion;
his kingdom endures from generation to generation.
35 All the peoples of the earth
are regarded as nothing.
He does as he pleases
with the powers of heaven
and the peoples of the earth.
No one can hold back his hand
or say to him: "What have you done?"
36 At the same time that my sanity was restored, my honor and splendor were returned to me for the glory of my kingdom. My advisers and nobles sought me out, and I was restored to my throne and became even greater than before. 37 Now I, Nebuchadnezzar, praise and exalt and glorify the King of heaven, because everything he does is right and all his ways are just. And those who walk in pride he is able to humble.
(Daniel 4:28-37).

It is interesting that, of the inscriptions thought to pertain to Nebuchadnezzar, there is this one: "In Babylonia is the palace of my dwelling for the glorification of my dominion." Compare that to verse 30 that we just read:

30...he said, "Is not this the great Babylon I have built as the royal residence, by my mighty power and for the glory of my majesty?"
(Daniel 4:30).

Nebuchadnezzar's objective was to glorify his own name, until God taught him that our real purpose is to glorify His name. Of those who head nations today and those who have reached the top of their chosen profession (whether it is the field of science, entertainment, law, sports, business or education) one has to wonder how many know that it is God who raises up and God who can bring down. Their achievements have been decreed by God. They should acknowledge this and glorify Him.

> **16 Give glory to the LORD your God**
> **before he brings the darkness...**
> (Jeremiah 13:16).

However, it is not just those at the top who need to be concerned about glorifying God. All men, regardless of importance, achievements, race, or nationality, are told to glorify God.

> **7 Ascribe to the LORD, O families of nations,**
> **ascribe to the LORD glory and strength.**
> **8 Ascribe to the LORD the glory due his name;**
> **bring an offering and come into his courts.**
> (Psalm 96:7-8).

Glorifying God was the objective for man from the beginning, and we see in Revelation that it is the objective right up to the end.

> **6 Then I saw another angel flying in midair, and he**
> **had the eternal gospel to proclaim to those who live**
> **on the earth—to every nation, tribe, language and**
> **people. 7 He said in a loud voice, "Fear God and give**
> **him glory, because the hour of his judgment has**
> **come. Worship him who made the heavens, the**
> **earth, the sea and the springs of water."**
> (Revelation 14:6-7).

Man without saving faith is man who is not saved, and unsaved man cannot glorify God nor enjoy the glory of God.

> **6 And without faith it is impossible to please God,**
> **because anyone who comes to him must believe**
> **that he exists and that he rewards those who**
> **earnestly seek him.** (Hebrews 11:6).

> *23* **for all have sinned and fall short of the glory of God...** (Romans 3:23).

Furthermore, from the beginning, unsaved man has made no effort to glorify God.

> **21 For although they knew God, they neither glorified him as God nor gave thanks to him, but their thinking became futile and their foolish hearts were darkened.** (Romans 1:21).

The unsaved may be religious and attend church, but they do not have true faith. Their worship is not from the heart.

> **13 The Lord says:**
> **"These people come near to me with their mouth**
> **and honor me with their lips,**
> **but their hearts are far from me.**
> (Isaiah 29:13).

Right up to the end, the unsaved will make no effort to glorify God. In fact with hardened hearts they will stubbornly refuse to do so.

> **8 The fourth angel poured out his bowl on the sun, and the sun was given power to scorch people with fire. 9 They were seared by the intense heat and they cursed the name of God, who had control over these plagues, but they refused to repent and glorify him.** (Revelation 16:8-9).

Those whom God saves are called to glorify Him in all that they do. Their whole life is to be aimed at glorifying God. Is that the aim of your life?

> **17 And whatever you do, whether in word or deed, do it all in the name of the Lord Jesus, giving thanks to God the Father through him.** (Colossians 3:17).

> **31 So whether you eat or drink or whatever you do, do it all for the glory of God.** (1 Corinthians 10:31).

All of God's creation will glorify Him in one manner or another. The Bible tells us that the heavens declare His glory.

> **The heavens declare the glory of God;**
> **the skies proclaim the work of his hands.**
> **2 Day after day they pour forth speech;**
> **night after night they display knowledge.**
> **3 There is no speech or language**
> **where their voice is not heard.**
> **4 Their voice**
> **goes out into all the earth,**
> **their words to the ends of the world.**
> (Psalm 19:1-4).

Not only do the heavens declare God's glory, but the angels in heaven sing of His glory.

> **11 Then I looked and heard the voice of many angels, numbering thousands upon thousands, and ten thousand times ten thousand. They encircled the throne and the living creatures and the elders. 12 In a loud voice they sang:**
> **"Worthy is the Lamb, who was slain,**
> **to receive power and wealth and wisdom and strength**
> **and honor and glory and praise!"**
> (Revelation 5:11-12).

All workmen have some end in mind – some purpose for their work. God has the highest end for His work. It is to manifest His glory. His work of creation includes the wicked as well as the righteous. God is not the author of sin. However, He has allowed sin and evil to be in the world. He does not compel men to be wicked, but He allows them to be. They are responsible for their sinfulness. The purpose for those who rebel against God and fight against the people of God is the same as the purpose for all the rest of His creation – to bring Him glory. Only God has the power and wisdom to turn the evil of wicked men to His own glory, and this He does.

> **4 The LORD works out everything for his own ends—**
> **even the wicked for a day of disaster.**
> (Proverbs 16:4).

Pharaoh and the Egyptians were examples of God being glorified as He displayed His mighty power against them. His destruction of the Egyptians brought forth praise from the Israelites.

> *13* **Then the LORD said to Moses, "Get up early in the morning, confront Pharaoh and say to him, 'This is what the LORD, the God of the Hebrews, says: Let my people go, so that they may worship me, *14* or this time I will send the full force of my plagues against you and against your officials and your people, so you may know that there is no one like me in all the earth. *15* For by now I could have stretched out my hand and struck you and your people with a plague that would have wiped you off the earth. *16* But I have raised you up for this very purpose, that I might show you my power and that my name might be proclaimed in all the earth.**
> (Exodus 9:13-16).

> *1* **Then Moses and the Israelites sang this song to the LORD:**
> **"I will sing to the LORD,**
> **for he is highly exalted.**
> **The horse and its rider**
> **he has hurled into the sea.**
> **2 The LORD is my strength and my song;**
> **he has become my salvation.**
> **He is my God, and I will praise him,**
> **my father's God, and I will exalt him.**
> (Exodus 15:1-2).

A number of Christians are eager to praise God for His love but are reluctant to praise Him for His justice and wrath. However, they should not be. Everything that God is and everything He does is perfect. God is righteous, and He does nothing but what is right and good. He is a just God who passes out His justice on an unbelieving world.

6 On the wicked he will rain
fiery coals and burning sulfur;
a scorching wind will be their lot.
7 For the LORD is righteous,
he loves justice;
upright men will see his face. (Psalm 11:6-7).

9 A third angel followed them and said in a loud
voice: "If anyone worships the beast and his image
and receives his mark on the forehead or on the
hand, 10 he, too, will drink of the wine of God's fury,
which has been poured full strength into the cup of
his wrath. He will be tormented with burning sulfur
in the presence of the holy angels and of the Lamb.
11 And the smoke of their torment rises for ever and
ever. There is no rest day or night for those who
worship the beast and his image, or for anyone who
receives the mark of his name." (Revelation 14:9-11).

God's punishment of unbelievers is not because He likes to
see them suffer but because He wants justice done. It is not
suffering for the sake of suffering but justice for the sake of
justice. Does not mankind call for justice to be done? Are not
many of man's problems caused by real or imagined
injustices? If a man commits a horrible cold-blooded murder
and the system allows him to go free, are we not appalled?
Do we not feel that an injustice has been done? When sinful
man continues to rebel and sin against Holy God, ignoring
Him and living as though there were no God, denying and
trampling under foot the precious Son of God, should not
justice be done? Is not justice called for? The slain saints of
Revelation 6:9 think so.

9 When he opened the fifth seal, I saw under the
altar the souls of those who had been slain because
of the word of God and the testimony they had
maintained. 10 They called out in a loud voice, "How
long, Sovereign Lord, holy and true, until you judge
the inhabitants of the earth and avenge our blood?"
(Revelation 6:9-10).

God will bring about justice for His people, His chosen ones.

> 7 And will not God bring about justice for his chosen ones, who cry out to him day and night? (Luke 18:7).

> 19 Do not take revenge, my friends, but leave room for God's wrath, for it is written: "It is mine to avenge; I will repay," says the Lord.
> (Romans 12:19).

> *4* Therefore, among God's churches we boast about your perseverance and faith in all the persecutions and trials you are enduring.
> 5 All this is evidence that God's judgment is right, and as a result you will be counted worthy of the kingdom of God, for which you are suffering. 6 God is just: He will pay back trouble to those who trouble you 7 and give relief to you who are troubled, and to us as well. This will happen when the Lord Jesus is revealed from heaven in blazing fire with his powerful angels. 8 He will punish those who do not know God and do not obey the gospel of our Lord Jesus. 9 They will be punished with everlasting destruction and shut out from the presence of the Lord and from the majesty of his power...
> (2 Thessalonians 1:4-9).

However, God is patient. He does not wish anyone to go to hell but would like to see all people repent and be saved.

> 23 Do I take any pleasure in the death of the wicked? declares the Sovereign LORD. Rather, am I not pleased when they turn from their ways and live?
> (Ezekiel 18:23).

> 9 The Lord is not slow in keeping his promise, as some understand slowness. He is patient with you, not wanting anyone to perish, but everyone to come to repentance. (2 Peter 3:9).

While He is patiently waiting for men to repent, His Holy Spirit is working to convict them of their sin.

> *8* When he comes, he will convict the world of guilt in regard to sin and righteousness and judgment: *9* in regard to sin, because men do not believe in me;
> (John 16:8-9).

Although God is patient and shows mercy to man by giving him time to repent rather than cutting him down at the slightest sin, He will not wait indefinitely

> *3* Then the LORD said, "My Spirit will not contend with man forever, for he is mortal; his days will be a hundred and twenty years." (Genesis 6:3).

We have seen that God's purpose for His creation is that He might be glorified. He is glorified in His inanimate creation, in His display of power and justice toward unbelievers, and in His love and mercy for those He saves. God has a plan by which He achieves His purpose. He has decreed the people, things, and events that are the means of His receiving glory. Mary was chosen to glorify Him as the mother of Jesus.

> *46* And Mary said:
> "My soul glorifies the Lord
> 47 and my spirit rejoices in God my Savior,
> (Luke 1:46-47).

The shepherds who went to Bethlehem to see the baby Jesus were chosen that they might praise and glorify God.

> 15 When the angels had left them and gone into heaven, the shepherds said to one another, "Let's go to Bethlehem and see this thing that has happened, which the Lord has told us about."
> 16 So they hurried off and found Mary and Joseph, and the baby, who was lying in the manger. 17 When they had seen him, they spread the word concerning what had been told them about this child, 18 and all who heard it were amazed at what the shepherds said to them. 19 But Mary treasured up all these things and pondered them in her heart. 20 The shepherds returned, glorifying and praising God for all the things they had heard and seen, which were just as they had been told. (Luke 2:15-20).

Peter was chosen to glorify God both in his life and in his death. Christ told him that he would die for His glory.

> **18 I tell you the truth, when you were younger you dressed yourself and went where you wanted; but when you are old you will stretch out your hands, and someone else will dress you and lead you where you do not want to go." 19 Jesus said this to indicate the kind of death by which Peter would glorify God. Then he said to him, "Follow me!"**
> (John 21:18-19).

We know that David sinned greatly, but we know that he also lived a life that brought much glory to God. God had a purpose for David and when David had fulfilled all that God had for him to do, he died.

> **36 "For when David had served God's purpose in his own generation, he fell asleep; he was buried with his fathers and his body decayed.** (Acts 13:36).

Christ came to carry out God's purpose for Him.

> **23 This man was handed over to you by God's set purpose and foreknowledge; and you, with the help of wicked men, put him to death by nailing him to the cross.** (Acts 2:23).

If we are to be conformed to the likeness of Christ, we must have the attitude of Christ. His attitude was to serve God by doing the will of God and thereby bringing glory to God.

> **38 For I have come down from heaven not to do my will but to do the will of him who sent me.**
> (John 6:38).

> **4 I have brought you glory on earth by completing the work you gave me to do.** (John 17:4).

As Christians we need to understand and take seriously the fact that we are here to glorify God. Before we ever came on the scene, God had already planned the work He wants us to do.

8 This is to my Father's glory, that you bear much fruit, showing yourselves to be my disciples.
(John 15:8).

10 For we are God's workmanship, created in Christ Jesus to do good works, which God prepared in advance for us to do.
(Ephesians 2:10).

The question we must ask ourselves is, "Have I looked to God to show me what He would have me do and am I being obedient to do it?" If not, then I am living my life as I please and doing what I choose to do, unconcerned about God's will for my life. That is sin.

17 Anyone, then, who knows the good he ought to do and doesn't do it, sins. (James 4:17).

Professing Christ is no excuse to be complacent; rather it is a call to commitment. Knowing that our purpose is to serve and glorify God, we don't want to be found ignoring or resisting Him. To continue living in willful sin is to indicate that perhaps we don't really belong to God.

26 If we deliberately keep on sinning after we have received the knowledge of the truth, no sacrifice for sins is left, 27 but only a fearful expectation of judgment and of raging fire that will consume the enemies of God. (Hebrews 10:26-27).

Let us seek to do as Paul did, serve God by letting Him work through us in the power of the Spirit.

17 Therefore I glory in Christ Jesus in my service to God. 18 I will not venture to speak of anything except what Christ has accomplished through me in leading the Gentiles to obey God by what I have said and done— 19 by the power of signs and miracles, through the power of the Spirit. (Romans 15:17-19).

If we do, we will find and fulfill our purpose for being: that of glorifying God by being more and more conformed to the likeness of the Son of God. Then with a sincere heart we can say with David:

> **12 I will praise you, O Lord my God, with all my heart;**
> **I will glorify your name forever.** (Psalm 86:12).

Those God Foreknew

> **28 And we know that in all things God works for the good of those who love him, who have been called according to his purpose. 29 For those God foreknew he also predestined to be conformed to the likeness of his Son, that he might be the firstborn among many brothers.** (Romans 8:28-29).

Romans 8:29 begins with "For those God foreknew." Who are the people referred to as "those God foreknew?" Let us look back to Romans 8:28, and we will find that God works for the good of those who love Him. And who are those that love Him but those who have been called. Those who have been called and those who love Him are one and the same. They also are one and the same with those God foreknew. These then are three different descriptions of the same group of people. Those that God foreknew are those that God loves. Before the world was made, He elected them to be saved; in His time He effectually called them to salvation, and as a result, they love God.

Some people, resisting God's absolute sovereignty in election and salvation, attempt to explain that those God foreknew are those whom He saw would accept Christ. However, the verse does not say that. It does not say "those God foreknew would accept Christ." It just says "those God foreknew." When the Scriptures refer to one person knowing another, so often the words "know " or "knew" are translations of the Hebrew or Greek that mean an intimate relationship. Such is the case where the KJV uses "knew" in Genesis 4:1, 17, 25 to indicate an intimate relationship between Adam and Eve, and Cain and his wife.

In John 8:19 we see that Jesus tells the Pharisees they do not know Him. Now the Pharisees are looking at Jesus, they are talking with Him, and this is not their first exposure to Him. They know about Him, but they do not know Him. They do not have an intimate relationship with Him. If they did, they would have an intimate relationship with God the Father.

> **19 Then they asked him, "Where is your father?"**
> **"You do not know me or my Father," Jesus replied.**
> **"If you knew me, you would know my Father also."**
> (John 8:19).

We agree that in Romans 8:29, God foreknew they would accept Christ. However, that is not because He is omniscient and knew they would, but because He is omnipotent and decreed that they would. The God that is all knowing obviously knows all that will happen. However, this same God is all-powerful and has decreed all that will happen. Therefore, what He knows will happen and what He has decreed to happen, are one and the same. Our Sovereign God has not left His creation to run at random. To the contrary, He controls every detail. He is working out His plan and purpose for it.

> **11 In him we were also chosen, having been predestined according to the plan of him who works out everything in conformity with the purpose of his will...** (Ephesians 1:11).

Furthermore, the word foreknew in verse 29 is not followed by the words "who would accept Christ." The phrase, "those God foreknew" can stand by itself. As in verse 28 the phrases "who love Him" and "who have been called", can stand alone as indicating God's elect; so also

The phrase "those God foreknew" indicates elect. You could replace the word foreknew with the words "elected", "chose", or "called" without changing the meaning of the verse.

The meaning of the word foreknew in Romans 8:29 is actually foreordained. Those God foreknew are those He foreordained (decreed) to be those He loved, those He called, those He saved, and those that He conforms to the likeness of His Son Christ.

The words foreknew, foreknowledge, and know often are used in the Bible to indicate a special relationship. In 1 Peter, we see the word foreknowledge means foreordination or decree and refers to the relationship between God and those He has chosen to be saved, His elect.

> **1 Peter, an apostle of Jesus Christ,**
> **To God's elect, strangers in the world, scattered throughout Pontus, Galatia, Cappadocia, Asia and Bithynia, 2 who have been chosen according to the foreknowledge of God the Father, through the sanctifying work of the Spirit, for obedience to Jesus Christ and sprinkling by his blood:**
> **Grace and peace be yours in abundance.**
> (1 Peter 1:1-2).

We find the word foreknew again in Romans 11, and again it refers to a special relationship between God and His people.

> **2 God did not reject his people, whom he foreknew...**
> (Romans 11:2).

Kenneth S. Wuest (Teacher Emeritus of New Testament Greek at the Moody Bible Institute) produced an expanded translation of the Greek New Testament. In Romans 8:29 and Romans 11:2, instead of translating the Greek as "foreknew", he translated it as "foreordained". Also in 1 Peter instead of translating the Greek as "foreknowledge" he translated it foreordination. A study of commentaries and Bible dictionaries will confirm that Wuest's translation carries the basic meaning of the Greek. It is an intimate and loving relationship between God and His elect that He determined to take place before the world was ever made.

We find that Christ speaks of knowing His sheep and His sheep knowing Him. Once again a relationship is what is being stressed.

> **14 "I am the good shepherd; I know my sheep and my sheep know me—...** (John 10:14).

His sheep are the believers, but Christ knows everyone based on the common usage of the word "know". Therefore, we see that the Biblical usage of "know" in this instance denotes love and a special relationship.

In Matthew 7, we see an example where "not knowing someone" indicates a lack of a relationship. Here we have Christ making it clear that everyone who claims to know Him is not necessarily one of His. He certainly knew who these people were, but He did not have a relationship with them. They were not His.

> **21 "Not everyone who says to me, 'Lord, Lord,' will enter the kingdom of heaven, but only he who does the will of my Father who is in heaven. 22 Many will say to me on that day, 'Lord, Lord, did we not prophesy in your name, and in your name drive out demons and perform many miracles?' 23 Then I will tell them plainly, 'I never knew you. Away from me, you evildoers!'** (Matthew 7:21-23).

He Also Predestined

> **28 And we know that in all things God works for the good of those who love him, who have been called according to his purpose. 29 For those God foreknew he also predestined to be conformed to the likeness of his Son, that he might be the firstborn among many brothers.** (Romans 8:28-29).

We see that those God foreknew are those that God loves, and they are the ones that have been predestined to be conformed to the likeness of Christ. This is all part of God's eternal purpose and decree.

If God has predestined something to take place it will happen. Predestined carries a meaning of foreordained, appointed to, to determine in advance, and it always indicates something that is definite, something that is sure to take place. Those that God foreknew are predestined to be conformed to the likeness of Christ. And that being the case, if we are not growing more like Christ, do we have any reason to think that we are predestined to be like Him? Should we not check our hearts and our commitment to Christ?

People have a problem with predestination, but it is just God's sovereignty, His providential work. He determines what will take place and the means by which it will take place. If we will give thought to God's sovereignty and the fact that He has eternally decreed all that happens, we must logically conclude that He has predestined the destiny of all men, both those who go to heaven and those who go to hell. If that thought gives the reader a problem, let us think our way through it.

To say that a man could get into heaven against God's will would be foolish. It would be equally foolish to say that a man could go to hell against God's will. It is true that God does not desire any to perish; it is not His will that they do in the sense that it is not His wish or desire that they do (2 Peter 3:9). By the same token a judge might wish that no one would commit a crime so that he would not have to send a criminal to jail. However, people do commit crimes, and because he must administer justice, the judge does send them to jail. God must administer His divine justice, or God would not be just. If men could get by without punishment, there would be no fear of God. God and His justice would be ridiculed. But, because God is a God of justice as well as a God of love, He does punish men for their sins. Therefore, men have reason to fear Him.

4 "I tell you, my friends, do not be afraid of those who kill the body and after that can do no more. 5 But I will show you whom you should fear: Fear him

who, after the killing of the body, has power to throw you into hell. Yes, I tell you, fear him. (Luke 12:4-5).

30 For we know him who said, "It is mine to avenge; I will repay," and again, "The Lord will judge his people." 31 It is a dreadful thing to fall into the hands of the living God. (Hebrews 10:30-31).

Those whom God has predestined to be conformed to the likeness of Christ are those whose destiny is heaven by His divine grace. The destiny of all others is hell by His divine justice. In both cases all are free to choose the way they will take. Those who go to heaven, God gives a heart to choose His way. Those who go to hell, God leaves to continue in their own way. In the case of those who go to heaven, God is responsible. In the case of those who go to hell, they themselves are responsible, for God did not decree men to sin – He decreed that men would sin. However, they sin of their own accord. Again we are faced with the paradox that God decrees what man will do, but man is free to choose what he will do.

Consider God before He made the world or anybody. He is all-powerful; nothing is impossible with Him. He is all knowing; nothing is hidden or unknown to Him. He determines to make the world and put people on it. He further determines to give the people a free will; they are free to choose what they will think, what they will say, and what they will do. However, in order to carry out His plan for the world and the people, God must control everything including what the people think, say, and do. Otherwise, He could not have things work out the way He has said they would in His Word. If He could not determine what one individual would do, He certainly could not determine what nations would do. He would have no control over events. This appears to give us a real problem until we come to grips with the fact that God is truly God. He is everything that the name God implies, and with God nothing is impossible. He is able to decree that man will sin and still not be the author of sin.

13 When tempted, no one should say, "God is tempting me." For God cannot be tempted by evil, nor does he tempt anyone... (James 1:13).

He is able to decree that men will reject Christ, and yet states that it is His will that none should perish and that all would come to repentance. He is able to remove from people their heart of stone and to give them a heart of flesh, to make the spiritually dead become spiritually alive, to turn man from being in rebellion against Christ to loving and following Christ. And He does it without doing violence to man's will. We do now know how God does this, and we do not need to know; we just need to know that He does - that much He makes clear in His Word.

Those whom God has predestined to receive divine justice are themselves fully responsible for living a disobedient and sinful life, refusing to repent, suppressing the truth of God, and rejecting Christ. God has decreed it, but man is responsible – remember, nothing is impossible with God. God has not made them sin; He has allowed them to sin. They have sinned of their own accords. Think of when you sinned in the past and when you sin now. Did God make you sin? Does God make you sin now? Certainly not, God does not make anyone sin. Man chooses to sin, likes to sin, and enjoys sin. By nature man is sinful and enslaved to sin, and unless God saves him, he continues throughout his life to pursue sin and to commit willful sin. Again I point out that God does not make men sin. However, He has decreed that they will. I would remind the reader that although we don't understand how God can decree (make certain) that man will sin and yet not be responsible for making him sin, we believe He does. We believe this truth because it is taught in God's Word. God is under no obligation to explain it to us, and it would be beyond our finite understanding anyway. God does not expect us to understand how He does what He does, but He expects us to believe He does what He says He does.

Also, God doesn't need us to apologize or make excuses for Him about anything He does. Everything He does is right and good, and if we think or say differently, we are sinning.

When we speak of men being predestined either to heaven or to hell it raises difficulties; it is a hard teaching. Yet we do not want to become discouraged and turn back as some did when Christ presented them with what they felt was a hard teaching.

> **41** At this the Jews began to grumble about him because he said, "I am the bread that came down from heaven." **42** They said, "Is this not Jesus, the son of Joseph, whose father and mother we know? How can he now say, 'I came down from heaven'?"
> **43** "Stop grumbling among yourselves," Jesus answered. **44** "No one can come to me unless the Father who sent me draws him, and I will raise him up at the last day. **45** It is written in the Prophets: 'They will all be taught by God.' Everyone who listens to the Father and learns from him comes to me. (John 6:41-45).

> **53** Jesus said to them, "I tell you the truth, unless you eat the flesh of the Son of Man and drink his blood, you have no life in you. **54** Whoever eats my flesh and drinks my blood has eternal life, and I will raise him up at the last day. **55** For my flesh is real food and my blood is real drink. **56** Whoever eats my flesh and drinks my blood remains in me, and I in him. **57** Just as the living Father sent me and I live because of the Father, so the one who feeds on me will live because of me. **58** This is the bread that came down from heaven. Your forefathers ate manna and died, but he who feeds on this bread will live forever." **59** He said this while teaching in the synagogue in Capernaum.
> **60** On hearing it, many of his disciples said, "This is a hard teaching. Who can accept it?"
> **61** Aware that his disciples were grumbling about this, Jesus said to them, "Does this offend you? **62** What if you see the Son of Man ascend to where he was before! **63** The Spirit gives life; the flesh counts

for nothing. The words I have spoken to you are spirit and they are life. 64 Yet there are some of you who do not believe." For Jesus had known from the beginning which of them did not believe and who would betray him. 65 He went on to say, "This is why I told you that no one can come to me unless the Father has enabled him."
66 From this time many of his disciples turned back and no longer followed him. (John 6:53-66)

When these disciples turned back, Christ asked the Twelve if they wanted to leave Him too.

67 "You do not want to leave too, do you?" Jesus asked the Twelve.
68 Simon Peter answered him, "Lord, to whom shall we go? You have the words of eternal life."
(John 6:67-68).

Our response to hard teaching and meaty doctrines should be the same as Peter's: Where else is there to go? To whom could we go? Christ has the words of eternal life; Christ is eternal life – he who has the Son has the life. When we are faced with difficult doctrine, we must study hard, pray much and ask God to give us understanding.

Over the centuries there have been Christians who have read and studied these same doctrines with which we grapple. They had the benefit of the knowledge and teaching of those who went before them, and now we have the advantage of studying their sermons and writings. We have looked at The Baptist Confession of Faith and The Westminster Confession of Faith, but let us look further at both as we consider the Doctrine of Predestination.

The Baptist Confession of Faith

4. The almighty power, unsearchable wisdom, and the infinite goodness of God, so far manifest themselves in his providence, that his determinate counsel extendeth itself even to the first fall, and all other sinful actions both of angels and men: and that not by a bare permission, which also he most wisely and powerfully boundeth, and otherwise ordereth and governeth, in a manifold dispensation to his most holy ends; yet so, as the sinfulness of their acts proceedeth only from the creatures, and not from God who being most holy and righteous, neither is nor can be the author or approver of sin.

Rom. 11:32-43, 2 Sam. 24:1, 1 Chron. 21:1. 2 Kings 19:28, Ps. 76:10. Gen. 50:20, Isa. 10:6, 7, 12. Ps. 50:21, 1 John 2:16.

6. As for those wicked and ungodly men whom God, as a righteous judge, for former sin doth blind and harden; from them he not only withholdeth his grace, whereby they might have been enlightened in their understanding, and wrought upon in their hearts; but sometimes also withdraweth the gifts which hey had, and exposeth them to such objects as their corruption makes occasion of sin; and withal, gives them over to their own lusts, the temptations of the world, and the power of Satan, whereby it comes to pass that they harden themselves even under those mean which God useth for the softening of others.

Rom. 1:24-26, 28; 11:7, 8. Deut. 29:4. Matt. 13:12. Deut. 2:30. 2 Kings 8:12, 13. Ps. 81:11, 12, 2 Thess. 2:10-12. Exod. 8:15, 32, Isa. 6:9, 10, 1 Pet. 2:7, 8.

<u>The Westminster Confession of Faith</u>

3. By the decree of God, for the manifestation of His glory, some men and angels are predestinated unto everlasting life; and others foreordained to everlasting death.

4.These angels and men, thus predestinated, and foreordained, are particularly and unchangeably designed, and their number so certain and definite, that it cannot be either increased or diminished.

Both the Westminster and Baptist Confession were set forth in the 17th century. Over the years they have been held in high regard by scholars and laymen alike as stating clearly what the Bible teaches. If this was true of them in the past, then it is true of them now. Today's Christians could profit by reading and studying them. A close look at the above quotes will show that, concerning the Doctrine of Predestination, they confirm that the Bible teaches what we have been expressing. Some verses that teach what the above Confessions state are:

21 I charge you, in the sight of God and Christ Jesus and the elect angels... (1 Timothy 5:21).

34 "Then the King will say to those on his right, 'Come, you who are blessed by my Father; take your inheritance, the kingdom prepared for you since the creation of the world. (Matthew 25:34).

5...he predestined us to be adopted as his sons through Jesus Christ, in accordance with his pleasure and will— 6 to the praise of his glorious grace, which he has freely given us in the One he loves. (Ephesians 1:5-6).

22 What if God, choosing to show his wrath and make his power known, bore with great patience the objects of his wrath—prepared for destruction? 23 What if he did this to make the riches of his glory known to the objects of his mercy, whom he prepared in advance for glory... (Romans 9:22-23).

4 For certain men whose condemnation was written about long ago have secretly slipped in among you. They are godless men, who change the grace of our God into a license for immorality and deny Jesus Christ our only Sovereign and Lord. (Jude 4).

4 The LORD works out everything for his own ends—even the wicked for a day of disaster. (Proverbs 16:4).

8 ...and, "A stone that causes men to stumble and a rock that makes them fall."

**They stumble because they disobey the message—
which is also what they were destined for.**
(1 Peter 2:8).

If the reader would like to take a more extensive look at the Doctrine of Predestination I suggest the following: Systematic Theology by Charles Hodge, Manual of Theology by J. L. Dagg, Systematic Theology by R. L. Dabney, The Reformed Doctrine of Predestination by Loraine Boettner, Abstract of Systematic Theology by James P. Boyce, Systematic Theology by L. Berkhof, and Systematic Theology by Wayne Grudem.

In closing our discussion on predestination let me remind you that God does not arbitrarily send people to hell without a cause or reason. They are condemned to hell because they are sinners who die in their sins; they die with their sins unforgiven and therefore must suffer the penalty for them. The elect do not go to heaven because they are not sinners but because they die with their sins forgiven. Christ has paid the penalty for their sins, and His righteousness has been imputed to them. Now God has predestined, foreordained, decreed all of this, but He is not the author of sin, and He doesn't temp anyone to sin. The sin of both unbelievers and believers, although decreed by God, is the responsibility and fault of the one who sins. Therefore, God is perfectly just in condemning sin and sinners. None deserve to be saved, but God, in love and out of His mercy, elects some of sinful mankind to be saved. However, they are no different from those that God does not elect but leaves in their sin. God's reason for electing those that He has chosen is not based on anything found in them but belongs to His secret counsel and is done because it pleases Him to do it.

29 The secret things belong to the LORD our God, but the things revealed belong to us... (Deuteronomy 29:29).

All sinners deserve hell. Those sinners that God passes by, leaving them to themselves, allowing them to continue pursuing their sinful desires – He condemns to hell. This is justice – divine justice. They get exactly what they deserve. The elect, who deserve the same fate, are not condemned to hell but are saved for heaven. They don't get what they deserve. This is mercy – divine mercy. In doing this, God has not treated those who go to hell unfairly – they have received justice. God's passing them by and not saving them is not the cause of their sin; they were already sinners. He has left them where they want to be, where they have chosen on their own to be – in their unbelief and sin. God is just – He only condemns men because of sin, and God is merciful – He doesn't condemn all men who do sin.

In the providential ordering of the beings He created, God allowed all mankind to suffer a fallen state, and He chooses to save some out of that fallen condition. On the other hand, He only allowed some angels to fall from their first state but chose to leave all that fell in their fallen condition. The elect angels He decreed to hold fast their first state, that of holiness.

God is working out His plan and fulfilling His purpose; both of which were decreed from all eternity. As He does, we can know that all He does is right and good. His Word tells us that He is good to all that He has made.

> **9 The LORD is good to all;**
> **he has compassion on all he has made.**
> (Psalm 145:9).

He is good even to His enemies providing food, rain, and sunshine, etc. for them.

> *45* **He causes his sun to rise on the evil and the good, and sends rain on the righteous and the unrighteous.** (Matthew 5:45).

God does what He does not because of anything outside of Himself, but because it pleases Him to do it.

> *26* **Yes, Father, for this was your good pleasure.**
> (Matthew 11:26).

What pleases God should please God's people. Therefore, we are to be pleased with all that God does.

If after all we have discussed so far, the reader is still having trouble understanding and believing that this is what the Bible teaches about predestination, I suggest that you reread this section. Ask God to show you if this is what His Bible teaches.

For the reader who would call into question God's right to do with His creation as He pleases, I would refer you to the question Paul asked:

> **20 But who are you, O man, to talk back to God?**
> (Romans 9:20).

To Be Conformed

> **28 And we know that in all things God works for the good of those who love him, who have been called according to his purpose. 29 For those God foreknew he also predestined <u>to be conformed</u> to the likeness of his Son, that he might be the firstborn among many brothers.** (Romans 8:28-29).

To be conformed to the likeness of Christ is to be made like Him, to be fashioned like Him, to be made the image of Him. As Christ is holy (John 6:69, Mark 1:24), we must be made holy. Being made like Christ is a spiritual transformation, not physical. It has nothing to do with whether we are male or female or of which race, color, or ethnic background we happen to be. While we are on earth, our physical bodies age and die. We who live in these bodies continue to live, but as Peter said we put them aside as you would a tent.

> **13 I think it is right to refresh your memory as long as I live in the tent of this body, 14 because I know that I will soon put it aside, as our Lord Jesus Christ has made clear to me.** (2 Peter 1:13-14).

However, the time is coming when our bodies will be glorified. At that time our bodies will be like Christ's glorious body.

> **20 But our citizenship is in heaven. And we eagerly await a Savior from there, the Lord Jesus Christ, 21 who, by the power that enables him to bring everything under his control, will transform our lowly bodies so that they will be like his glorious body.** (Philippians 3:20-21).

Those who would be conformed to the likeness of Christ must first have experienced the salvation of Christ. When we were saved, we took on the likeness of Christ. Regardless of how weak and dim the likeness was, it was His likeness in us, and it would grow stronger and brighter with time as we matured spiritually.

> **18 And we, who with unveiled faces all reflect the Lord's glory, are being transformed into his likeness with ever-increasing glory, which comes from the Lord, who is the Spirit.** (Corinthians 3:18).

Growing more and more like Christ is what is expected of all who profess to be Christians. If this is not happening to us, can we have confidence that we are saved? God intends our character and behavior as a Christian to be different from what it was as an unbeliever. Those who have been predestined to be, most certainly will be conformed to the likeness of Christ. However, in this life their conformity will not be total; it will not be complete; they will not be made spiritually perfect. In this world we are in the process of being conformed; in the world to come we will be conformed. What was begun here will be completed there.

The process whereby the Christian becomes more like Christ is the process of sanctification. There is a sense in which we have been sanctified, and yet we are in the process of being sanctified.

> **14 ...because by one sacrifice he has made perfect forever those who are being made holy.**
> (Hebrews 10:14).

Sanctification is the work of the Holy Spirit. Just as the Holy Spirit works in us to bring about our salvation, He works in us to bring about our sanctification. Although it is the work of the Holy Spirit in us, we are not to sit idly by. The Holy Spirit's work in us should be evidenced in the work done by us as we seek to serve our Lord.

> **19 Therefore go and make disciples of all nations, baptizing them in the name of the Father and of the Son and of the Holy Spirit, 20 and teaching them to obey everything I have commanded you. And surely I am with you always, to the very end of the age."** (Matthew 28:19-20).

Under the control of the Holy Spirit, we must seek to be righteous and to do that which is righteous. If we do, we will find that the Holy Spirit is conforming us more and more to the likeness of Christ.

The Likeness of His Son

> **28 And we know that in all things God works for the good of those who love him, who have been called according to his purpose. 29 For those God foreknew he also predestined to be conformed to the likeness of his Son, that he might be the firstborn among many brothers.** (Romans 8:28-29).

From Scripture, we learn that to be conformed to the likeness of Christ is to take on His moral character, share in His suffering in this life, and share in His glory in the life to come. God has predestined the Christian to become like His Son. As Christ does, we are to do, and even more importantly, as Christ is, we are to be. We must be morally righteous, living pure and holy lives if we expect to validate our claim to be like Him and to hold to the hope of one day being with Him.

> **6 Whoever claims to live in him must walk as Jesus did.** (1 John 2:6).

3 Everyone who has this hope in him purifies himself, just as he is pure. (1 John 3:3).

7 For God did not call us to be impure, but to live a holy life. (1 Thessalonians 4:7).

15 But just as he who called you is holy, so be holy in all you do... (1 Peter 1:15).

Our eternal life, our spiritual life is in Christ.

11 And this is the testimony: God has given us eternal life, and this life is in his Son. 12 He who has the Son has life; he who does not have the Son of God does not have life. (1 John 5:11-12).

Spiritual growth, therefore, is growing more like Christ. There is no spiritual growth that is independent of Christ, nor is there spiritual growth that produces character unlike Christ. That is why we say that to grow spiritually is to grow more like Christ – anything less misses the mark. We are not to seek to become a nicer and more moral person according to our standard and certainly not according to the world's standard. We must seek to become more like the One who is the standard, our Lord and Savior Jesus Christ.

Becoming like Christ involves personal holiness. However, to become like Christ we must know what Christ is like. How do we discover what Christ is like? He is the living Word, and we learn about Him through the revealed Word – the Bible. The Bible tells us who He is, what He does, and what He is like.

39 You diligently study the Scriptures because you think that by them you possess eternal life. These are the Scriptures that testify about me... (John 5:39).

44 He said to them, "This is what I told you while I was still with you: Everything must be fulfilled that is written about me in the Law of Moses, the Prophets and the Psalms." (Luke 24:44).

23 They arranged to meet Paul on a certain day, and came in even larger numbers to the place where he was staying. From morning till evening he explained and declared to them the kingdom of God and tried to convince them about Jesus from the Law of Moses and from the Prophets. (Acts 28:23).

It is clear, if we would know what Christ is like, we must study the Bible. Reading the Bible is good, but it is not sufficient. We must study it. We should approach our study prayerfully, asking God to open our understanding to His truth. In the Bible we not only have pictured for us the Christ to whom we are to conform but also the instructions on how to do this. We are told how to obey by the One we are to obey. Let us not deceive ourselves. If we are not being obedient, then we are not being conformed – there is no conformity where there is no obedience. Consequently, the more consistent we are in our obedience to Christ, the greater will be our conformity to Him. Obedience is essential. We realize that we are saved by grace, but some emphasize salvation by grace so strongly that they go overboard and neglect obedience. Obedience is commanded and expected from those who are saved. Being saved is not the end of the Christian life; it is the beginning. There is a sanctified life to be lived out, righteous deeds to be done, and spiritual battles to be won. Having begun with Christ, we must finish with Christ. Professing to know Him, we must persevere in Him, and persevering in Him calls for obedience to His Word. We must study His Word, learn His Word, and obey His word.

16 Let the word of Christ dwell in you richly as you teach and admonish one another... (Colossians 3:16).

If the Word of Christ dwells in us, it has found a home in us; it lives in our hearts and minds. We are to view the world, events, other people, and ourselves in the light of the Word. Our thoughts, our actions, our lives are to be lived in accordance with, and in obedience to, the Word. This can only be done, and therefore will only be done, under the control and in the power of God's Holy Spirit. This is where many who profess Christ fall short. They try to live the Christian life in their own strength, and it cannot be done. The God who made us Christians is the God who enables us to live as Christians; we are dependent on Him. Christ makes this clear in the Scripture He quotes when tempted by Satan.

> **3 The tempter came to him and said, "If you are the Son of God, tell these stones to become bread." 4 Jesus answered, "It is written: 'Man does not live on bread alone, but on every word that comes from the mouth of God.'"** (Matthew 4:3-4).

In the above passage, Christ quotes Deuteronomy 8:3 where the Israelites are reminded of how God sustained them in the wilderness for forty years by feeding them manna. They were shown their total dependence on God. They were dependent on God for their food, clothing, and health, and He provided it all in a miraculous way.

> **2 Remember how the LORD your God led you all the way in the desert these forty years, to humble you and to test you in order to know what was in your heart, whether or not you would keep his commands. 3 He humbled you, causing you to hunger and then feeding you with manna, which neither you nor your fathers had known, to teach you that man does not live on bread alone but on every word that comes from the mouth of the LORD. 4 Your clothes did not wear out and your feet did not swell during these forty years.** (Deuteronomy 8:2-4).

Those who would live for God must learn to depend totally on God. Christ the man performed His miracles, conducted His ministry, and offered Himself on the cross, all in the power of God. We know that Christ walked this earth as fully God and fully man, but as fully man He was led and empowered by the Holy Spirit.

> **22 "Men of Israel, listen to this: Jesus of Nazareth was a man accredited by God to you by miracles,**

wonders and signs, which God did among you through him, as you yourselves know. (Acts 2:22).

38 ...how God anointed Jesus of Nazareth with the Holy Spirit and power, and how he went around doing good and healing all who were under the power of the devil, because God was with him. (Acts 10:38).

14 How much more, then, will the blood of Christ, who through the eternal Spirit offered himself unblemished to God, cleanse our consciences from acts that lead to death, so that we may serve the living God! (Hebrews 9:14).

God also did miracles through His Apostles, and Paul was one of them.

11 God did extraordinary miracles through Paul... (Acts 19:11).

From these and other examples throughout Scripture we can take heart – whatever God wants one of His to do, He will enable that one to do it. If He wants us conformed to the likeness of Christ, He will work in us to will and to do that which He wants.

13...for it is God who works in you to will and to act according to his good purpose. (Philippians 2:13).

However, I would remind the reader that we are not to play a passive part in being conformed to Christ's likeness. We are to be active. We must seek to be controlled by the Holy Spirit.

18 Do not get drunk on wine, which leads to debauchery. Instead, be filled with the Spirit. (Ephesians 5:18).

If we would be controlled by the Holy Spirit, we must constantly be aware of the command to be and our need to be. Christians, when they are controlled by the spirit, are only doing that which is expected of those who would do the will of God and walk in obedience to God. Christ did the will of God, and Christ was obedient to God. If we are to be made like Him, we must strive to do the same.

> **38 For I have come down from heaven not to do my will but to do the will of him who sent me.**
> (John 6:38)

> **31...but the world must learn that I love the Father and that I do exactly what my Father has commanded me.** (John 14:31).

As we attempt to bring this discussion of Christ likeness to a close, let each of us ask ourselves the following questions:
Is becoming like Christ the top priority in my life? If not, why not? If I am not making a real effort to become like Christ, do I have any reason to call myself a Christian? Do I have a reason to consider myself a follower of Christ? Christ says that to follow Him I must put Him above everyone including my family and myself. I must deny my desires and my will. I must do His will.

> **37 "Anyone who loves his father or mother more than me is not worthy of me; anyone who loves his son or daughter more than me is not worthy of me...** (Matthew 10:37).

> **23 Then he said to them all: "If anyone would come after me, he must deny himself and take up his cross daily and follow me.**
> (Luke 9:23).

Those who have been privileged to be Christians have the responsibility to act as becomes Christians. We are called in order to become. Having become Christians, we are now to become like Christ. Our goal is not one of how much we can do for Christ but how much like Christ we can become. The more we become like Him, the more He will have us doing for Him, We will be more and more conforming to His likeness, or we will face the consequences for failing to do so.

Throughout history there have been many false followers of Christ. They followed for many reasons other than the truth. We want to be among those who follow in truth, and who are determined to make their calling and election sure by being conformed to the likeness of Christ.

> **10 Therefore, my brothers, be all the more eager to make your calling and election sure. For if you do these things, you will never fall, 11 and you will receive a rich welcome into the eternal kingdom of our Lord and Savior Jesus Christ.** (2 Peter 1:10-11).

It will pay us to check ourselves from time to time to see if progress is being made in our becoming more like Christ. One helpful way to measure progress is to look at the fruit of the Spirit.

> **22 But the fruit of the Spirit is love, joy, peace, patience, kindness, goodness, faithfulness, 23 gentleness and self-control. Against such things there is no law.** (Galatians 5:22-23).

Christ was the embodiment of the fruit of the Spirit. We are to have and to display this fruit. The more like Christ we become, the clearer and more fully the fruit of the Spirit will be seen in our lives. Another measurement could be in our attitude when we suffer. Christ suffered willingly for us; are we willing to suffer for Him?

> **20 But how is it to your credit if you receive a beating for doing wrong and endure it? But if you suffer for doing good and you endure it, this is commendable before God. 21 To this you were called, because Christ suffered for you, leaving you an example, that you should follow in his steps.** (1 Peter 2:20-21).
>
> **17 Now if we are children, then we are heirs—heirs of God and co-heirs with Christ, if indeed we share**

> **in his sufferings in order that we may also share in his glory.** (Romans 8:17).

We must keep in mind that in the beginning man was made in the image of God.

> **26 Then God said, "Let us make man in our image, in our likeness..."** (Genesis 1:26).

> **27 So God created man in his own image, in the image of God he created him; male and female he created them.** (Genesis 1:27).

The above verses speak of man being made in the image of God before the fall. After the fall man's image of God is greatly marred. However, after the fall God still speaks of man being made in His image.

> **6...for in the image of God has God made man.** (Genesis 9:6).

The unsaved man is prevented by his sinful nature from growing in the image of Christ. The saved man is hindered by his sinful nature. However, God's Holy Spirit works to overcome saved man's sinful nature and through the process of sanctification conforms him more and more to the image of Christ. Though the Holy Spirit is working to bring this about, man is expected to work for this also. The Christian finds this to be not only a difficult task but also an ongoing task – one that continues until physical death. However, as we grow more like Christ we bring God glory. Therefore, let us all work to become more like Christ.

Let me offer this thought for encouragement. We know that Christ is the image of God, and if we have seen the Son we have seen the Father.

> **15 He is the image of the invisible God, the firstborn over all creation.** (Colossians 1:15)

> **8 Philip said, "Lord, show us the Father and that will be enough for us." 9 Jesus answered: "Don't you**

> know me, Philip, even after I have been among you
> such a long time? Anyone who has seen me has
> seen the Father. How can you say, 'Show us the
> Father'? (John 14:8-9).

As Christ is the express image of God, it is apparent that as we are conformed to the image of the Son of God, we are conformed to the image of God. And although this will not take place perfectly now, it will in the future. There is coming a time when we shall see God as He is, and we shall be made perfect in Spiritual likeness.

> 2 Dear friends, now we are children of God, and what
> we will be has not yet been made known. But we
> know that when he appears, we shall be like him, for
> we shall see him as he is. (1 John 3:2).

What a wonderful thought, what a wonderful truth, what a wonderful reality. Praise be to God!

That He Might Be The Firstborn

> 28 And we know that in all things God works for the
> good of those who love him, who have been called
> according to his purpose. 29 For those God
> foreknew he also predestined to be conformed to the
> likeness of his Son, that he might be the firstborn
> among many brothers. (Romans 8:28-29).

We find in the Bible that the firstborn son held a position of privilege and authority. He received a double share from his father (Deuteronomy 21:17), and in the absence of the father he had authority over his brothers and sisters (Genesis 24:55-60). We see that Esau, who was a firstborn son, sold his birthright for a pot of stew.

> 29 Once when Jacob was cooking some stew, Esau
> came in from the open country, famished. 30 He said
> to Jacob, "Quick, let me have some of that red stew!
> I'm famished!" (That is why he was also called
> Edom.)

> 31 Jacob replied, "First sell me your birthright."
> 32 "Look, I am about to die," Esau said. "What good is the birthright to me?"
> 33 But Jacob said, "Swear to me first." So he swore an oath to him, selling his birthright to Jacob.
> 34 Then Jacob gave Esau some bread and some lentil stew. He ate and drank, and then got up and left. So Esau despised his birthright.
> (Genesis 25:29-34).

Because the position of firstborn was one of such importance, the term firstborn is sometimes used figuratively to signify something that surpasses anything else of the same kind. One example is Job 18:13, which indicates the most terrible and miserable of deaths.

> 13 It eats away parts of his skin;
> death's firstborn devours his limbs. (Job 18:13).

Another example is Isaiah 14:30 where "firstborn of the poor" in the KJV means "poorest of the poor" which is the way the NIV translates it.

> 30 The poorest of the poor will find pasture,
> and the needy will lie down in safety.
> But your root I will destroy by famine;
> it will slay your survivors. (Isaiah 14:30).

Of course, the surpassing quality of the term firstborn is also applied to those who are beloved as we find in Exodus 4:22 and Jeremiah 31:9.

> 22 Then say to Pharaoh, 'This is what the LORD says: Israel is my firstborn son... (Exodus 4:22).

> 9 They will come with weeping;
> they will pray as I bring them back.
> I will lead them beside streams of water
> on a level path where they will not stumble,
> because I am Israel's father,
> and Ephraim is my firstborn son. (Jeremiah 31:9).

Believers are called the church of the firstborn, indicating the privilege the elect enjoy as opposed to the non-elect.

> **23 to the church of the firstborn, whose names are written in heaven. You have come to God, the judge of all men, to the spirits of righteous men made perfect...** (Hebrews 12:23).

We see in Scripture that the idea associated with the term firstborn is not one of being first in time but rather being first in rank. The idea is that of excellency, superiority, dominion, etc. Scripture tells us that Christ is not only the firstborn among many brothers but He is the firstborn over all creation. He has pre-eminence over all things.

> *15* **He is the image of the invisible God, the firstborn over all creation.** *16* **For by him all things were created: things in heaven and on earth, visible and invisible, whether thrones or powers or rulers or authorities; all things were created by him and for him.** *17* **He is before all things, and in him all things hold together.** *18* **And he is the head of the body, the church; he is the beginning and the firstborn from among the dead, so that in everything he might have the supremacy.** (Colossians 1:15-18).

> **9 Therefore God exalted him to the highest place**
> **and gave him the name that is above every name,**
> **10 that at the name of Jesus every knee should bow,**
> **in heaven and on earth and under the earth...**
> (Philippians 2:9-10).

Among Many Brothers

> *28* And we know that in all things God works for the good of those who love him, who have been called according to his purpose. *29* For those God foreknew he also predestined to be conformed to the likeness of his Son, that he might be the firstborn <u>among many brothers</u>. (Romans 8:28-29).

Our verse speaks of Christ being the firstborn among many brothers. The reference to brothers in this verse is the equivalent to believers. All believers are children of God and therefore related to the Son of God – He is our brother. Christ is the eternal Son, the Son by nature, we are adopted children, children by grace.

> *5* he predestined us to be adopted as his sons through Jesus Christ, in accordance with his pleasure and will... (Ephesians 1:5).

> 16 The Spirit himself testifies with our spirit that we are God's children. 17 Now if we are children, then we are heirs—heirs of God and co-heirs with Christ... (Romans 8:16-17).

Christ refers to believers as His family members.

> 40 "The King will reply, 'I tell you the truth, whatever you did for one of the least of these brothers of mine, you did for me.' (Matthew 25:40).

> 17 Jesus said, "Do not hold on to me, for I have not yet returned to the Father. Go instead to my brothers and tell them, 'I am returning to my Father and your Father, to my God and your God.'" (John 20:17).

> *46* While Jesus was still talking to the crowd, his mother and brothers stood outside, wanting to speak to him. *47* Someone told him, "Your mother and brothers are standing outside, wanting to speak to you."
> 48 He replied to him, "Who is my mother, and who are my brothers?" 49 Pointing to his disciples, he

> said, "Here are my mother and my brothers. 50 For whoever does the will of my Father in heaven is my brother and sister and mother." (Matthew 12:46-50).

Those who are brothers and sisters of Christ are, through Christ, brothers and sisters to each other. This is true of not only those Christians on earth but of those who have preceded us to heaven and those who will follow us there. We are all one family – the family of God.

> *14* For this reason I kneel before the Father, *15* from whom his whole family in heaven and on earth derives its name.
> (Ephesians 3:14-15).

We should note that Romans 8:29 refers to many brothers. This is in keeping with the teaching of the Bible: there will be a great multitude of people saved.

> *9* After this I looked and there before me was a great multitude that no one could count, from every nation, tribe, people and language, standing before the throne and in front of the Lamb. They were wearing white robes and were holding palm branches in their hands. (Revelation 7:9).

However, we don't want to be confused by that large number as there will also be a great multitude of unbelievers in hell. Throughout history, at any one time, there has always been only a small percentage of the world's population who were true Christians. This, too, is in keeping with the teaching of the Bible.

> *13* "Enter through the narrow gate. For wide is the gate and broad is the road that leads to destruction, and many enter through it. *14* But small is the gate and narrow the road that leads to life, and only a few find it. (Matthew 7:13-14).

The great multitude of believers is an accumulation over time, but nevertheless it is still a great multitude. Imagine the number of brothers and sisters we have at present in heaven. Some Christians on earth may be in a family, a location, or a situation where they feel they are all alone, that they are the only believer left. The prophet Elijah felt like that, but God let him know that He was sovereign over men's hearts, and He had reserved people for Himself.

> **13 When Elijah heard it, he pulled his cloak over his face and went out and stood at the mouth of the cave.**
> **Then a voice said to him, "What are you doing here, Elijah?"**
> **14 He replied, "I have been very zealous for the LORD God Almighty. The Israelites have rejected your covenant, broken down your altars, and put your prophets to death with the sword. I am the only one left, and now they are trying to kill me too."**
> **15 The LORD said to him, "Go back the way you came, and go to the Desert of Damascus. When you get there, anoint Hazael king over Aram. 16 Also, anoint Jehu son of Nimshi king over Israel, and anoint Elisha son of Shaphat from Abel Meholah to succeed you as prophet. 17 Jehu will put to death any who escape the sword of Hazael, and Elisha will put to death any who escape the sword of Jehu. 18 Yet I reserve seven thousand in Israel—all whose knees have not bowed down to Baal and all whose mouths have not kissed him."** (1 Kings 19:13-18).

As believers we are never alone. Through Christ we are members of a huge family of believers with whom we share eternal life. Moreover, we have living within us the One who is Eternal Life, Jesus Christ our Lord and Savior who is also our brother.

Isn't it wonderful that we have the privilege of having the Creator of the universe, our Savior and Lord, the King of Kings and the Lord of Lords, as our brother. The Bible says He is, and furthermore, it says He is not ashamed of us.

> **11 Both the one who makes men holy and those who are made holy are of the same family. So Jesus is not ashamed to call them brothers.** (Hebrews 2:11).

He Also Justified

28 And we know that in all things God works for the good of those who love him, who have been called according to his purpose. 29 For those God foreknew he also predestined to be conformed to the likeness of his Son, that he might be the firstborn among many brothers. 30 And those he predestined, he also called; those he called, <u>he also justified</u>; those he justified, he also glorified.
(Romans 8:28-30).

In Romans 8:30, we find the words "predestined" and "called" repeated. Predestined is found in verse 29 and called in verse 28, and as we have already discussed these we will move on to "justified".

Justification is an act of God that does not change the condition of man but changes the position of man before God. It changes his state, his standing before God. Regeneration is an act of God that changes man's condition; the spiritually dead are made spiritually alive. Sanctification is a process whereby God makes man more and more like Christ. Justification is a judicial act. It is based on the righteousness and work of Christ. With respect to the sinner, all the requirements of the Law have been met and satisfied by Christ. The sins of the sinner have been imputed to Christ, and the penalty for those sins paid for in the death of Christ. The righteousness of the resurrected and ascended Christ has been imputed to the sinner. No longer is the sinner guilty before God, nor is he just forgiven by God; he is now declared righteous before God – fit to be a child of God.

When we use terms like justified, it can raise questions in some reader's minds as to their own position, their standing in God's eyes. Are they children of God (everyone is not), are they saved, are they going to heaven when they die? There might be a few who would be indifferent to these questions, but most would react from a position of either insecurity, false security, or real security. Most who feel insecure have good reason to be; they are not saved.

However, some feel insecure who truly belong to our Lord. They just don't seem to understand the teaching of Scripture concerning the assurance of salvation. However, God wants us to know for sure that we are saved. Although there is much in the Bible that teaches the certainty of salvation, it is not stated any simpler than in 1 John.

> **11 And this is the testimony: God has given us eternal life, and this life is in his Son. 12 He who has the Son has life; he who does not have the Son of God does not have life.**
> *13* **I write these things to you who believe in the name of the Son of God so that you may know that you have eternal life.** (1 John 5:11-13).

I believe that those who have the strongest assurance of being saved are those who believe that salvation is all of God. They believe that the sovereign God who chose them to be saved, and who saved them, will continue to keep them saved.

> *6* **...being confident of this, that he who began a good work in you will carry it on to completion until the day of Christ Jesus.**
> (Philippians 1:6).
>
> *8* **He will keep you strong to the end, so that you will be blameless on the day of our Lord Jesus Christ.**
> (1 Corinthians 1:8).

I don't see how those who think salvation is all of grace but still feel that their coming to Christ was their own doing and not God's work could be as assured. After all, if it was totally up to them to come to Christ, might they not choose to turn their back on Him in the future? If they did not need to be regenerated in order to come to Christ, it would appear they would see no need to be regenerated in order to remain in Christ. Therefore, they must be depending on themselves to continue to believe. Knowing how fickle and changeable man can be, that would be cause for concern. And to say that you can come to Christ without God's help but need His help to remain saved, just does not add up. Of course, there are a number of people who profess Christ but believe you can be saved and lost over and over. They just don't understand the teaching of Scripture.

The people that have a false sense of security about going to heaven would be diversified in their opinions of how one gets there. The Universalist thinks that everyone goes to heaven. It matters not what you are, what you do, or what you believe. This is a common and popular belief, and we find it often in news accounts where people are interviewed and they speak of knowing that so and so is in heaven. In some instances that is true, and there is a basis for someone saying so. However, much of the time it is just the wishful thinking of someone who believes in Universalism.

A very large number of people in the false security group would be religious, but rather than depending on the saving work of Christ, they are depending on the work they do. They are working (trying to be good and to do good) their way to heaven. They don't understand that there is an all-important difference in working to be a Christian and working because you are a Christian. The difference is life and death – heaven and hell. God's Word makes it very clear that no one will be justified by trying to be obedient to God's Law.

28 For we maintain that a man is justified by faith apart from observing the law. (Romans 3:28).

10 For whoever keeps the whole law and yet stumbles at just one point is guilty of breaking all of it. (James 2:10).

16 ...know that a man is not justified by observing the law, but by faith in Jesus Christ. So we, too, have put our faith in Christ Jesus that we may be justified by faith in Christ and not by observing the law, because by observing the law no one will be justified. (Galatians 2:16).

The Law doesn't provide salvation; it awakens sinners to the need of it. Before we can see Christ as our Savior, we have to see our self as a sinner. God's Law pointing out what needs to be done is an instructor to us. It is a mirror showing us how sinful we are. The sinner being confronted with the Law is made aware of his failure and his lost condition. In this manner the Law paves the way to the Gospel.

Becoming a Christian is much more than a matter of man changing the direction of his life; it is dependent on God giving man spiritual life. It is having this spiritual life that enables a man to obey God's command to believe in Christ.

> **29 Jesus answered, "The work of God is this: to believe in the one he has sent."** (John 6:29).

> **23 And this is his command: to believe in the name of his Son, Jesus Christ...** (1 John 3:23).

If, as some claim, man can obey this command without God first working in him, then cannot man obey other commands without God working in him? Why would he need the Holy Spirit or any other help from God? All God would have to do is tell man what He wants done with full confidence that man is able to do it. Repenting and trusting Christ alone for his salvation is the most important thing man can do in this life. If he can do that without the prior work of God in him, then he has accomplished something far greater than if he had gained the whole world. However, God's Word is clear on this subject: man does not, man will not, and man cannot believe in Christ unless God has first worked in him to enable him.

> **65 He went on to say, "This is why I told you that no one can come to me unless the Father has enabled him."** (John 6:65).

Pertaining to God's salvation, I am less concerned with those who say they were saved by grace, but accepted Christ through their own free will without God first regenerating them, I am more concerned about those who think they must not only believe, but also live right and do right to be saved. The first is in error about how they came to Christ, but the second is in error to even think they have come to Christ. There is no salvation found in the Bible based on a belief in Christ plus anything else. If you think getting to heaven is dependent on what you do, your good works, then Christ's death was useless. If you depend on His death plus your works, then His death was only helpful. It is faith in Christ only, in Christ alone. Now, not to be misunderstood about works, I believe strongly in works. We Christians too often are guilty of neglecting to do good works, and that is sin. We are saved by grace. However, the salvation God gives by grace is a working salvation. Once we have been saved by grace, the result will be that we will do good works.

> **17 In the same way, faith by itself, if it is not accompanied by action, is dead.**
> **18 But someone will say, "You have faith; I have deeds."**
> **Show me your faith without deeds, and I will show you my faith by what I do.** (James 2:17-18).

We need to be sure that our resistance to a works salvation and a legalistic sanctification doesn't keep us from active service for God. The fear of doing work in the flesh can cause us to neglect doing work in the Spirit. Our external work for God is evidence of His internal work in us.

If you have been trying to work your way to heaven and after reading this you feel you might have been going down the wrong road, please don't just shrug it off. If you have never in repentance turned to God, confessed that you are a lost sinner, and asked to have your sins forgiven, then please stop at this point and consider where you are headed. If you are not trusting Christ alone to save you, God's Word says you are headed to hell. Have you rejected Christ?

Do you perhaps not believe in hell? Can you imagine the anguish of someone who rejects Christ, experiences the death of their body, and suddenly finds themselves in hell?

What they had thought at one time about hell being just a scary fairy tale proves false. The fairy tale turns to reality, and they find hell more real than anything they experienced while on earth. They find it is what God said it is: a place of torment and punishment. They are there for eternity. The sad thing is that there will be people who have read books similar to the one you are reading now and have been called to repent and trust Christ, but they refused to do so; they rejected Him. I now call on you to repent and be saved. Throw yourself on the mercy of Christ; surrender your life to Him. Confess you are a sinner and ask Him to save you. Don't be among the many who, having heard the Gospel, turn their backs on God's gift of salvation and find themselves in hell. No matter what you have achieved on this earth, if it winds up this way, you loose.

Don't let the fact that you have been looking in the wrong direction for some years keep you from turning to the right direction. People hate to admit they have been wrong, and often the longer they have been wrong the harder it is to admit it and change. As people enter into that category called "senior citizens", they can become even more reluctant to cast aside the years of work they have put forth for their salvation. To say it was all wasted time, wasted effort, and not only not pleasing to God but an offense to Him, is more than they will accept. However, that is what God says it is. He says our deeds done in an attempt to earn salvation are like filthy rags.

> **6 All of us have become like one who is unclean,**
> **and all our righteous acts are like filthy rags;**
> **we all shrivel up like a leaf,**
> **and like the wind our sins sweep us away.**
> (Isaiah 64:6).

Think of the consequences of being stubborn and refusing to admit that you are wrong. This is truly a time when it is better late than never. Act now! Turn to Christ now, and you will be forever grateful to God that you did.

He Also Glorified

28 And we know that in all things God works for the good of those who love him, who have been called according to his purpose. *29* For those God foreknew he also predestined to be conformed to the likeness of his Son, that he might be the firstborn among many brothers. *30* And those he predestined, he also called; those he called, he also justified; those he justified, <u>he also glorified.</u>
(Romans 8:28-30)

Being included in the plan and purpose of God, salvation stems from the love of God and ends in the glorification of the children of God.

13 But we ought always to thank God for you, brothers loved by the Lord, because from the beginning God chose you to be saved through the sanctifying work of the Spirit and through belief in the truth. *14* He called you to this through our gospel, that you might share in the glory of our Lord Jesus Christ. (2 Thessalonians 2:13-14).

10 Therefore I endure everything for the sake of the elect, that they too may obtain the salvation that is in Christ Jesus, with eternal glory. (2 Timothy 2:10).

Our glorification is the final step in our salvation. We are saved from sin and hell and saved for righteousness and heaven. Glorified indicates that state where believers are made perfect in holiness and enjoy both the presence of God and boundless blessings of God. Our being glorified is a certainty. It is God's work. Those God has elected to be saved will be saved; they will remain saved, and they will be glorified. God has decreed it; therefore, it will be done. It is so certain that God sees it as already done.

Scripture makes it clear that our hearts are deceitful, and regardless of what we profess with our lips before we are saved, we do not love God. However, once we are saved then we do love Him. It is only at that time that what is contained in Romans 8:28-30 becomes a reality in our lives. It is when we are justified and before we are glorified that all things are being made to work for our good with the result that we are being made into the likeness of Christ. The time between our justification and our glorification then is the time between our spiritual birth and our physical death. For some it is a long period of time and for others a short period. Whether it is long or short, our top priority during this period is to grow more like Christ. We may have to undergo many trials and much suffering which can try our patience and tempt us to turn away from God. But what comfort and strength we have to draw on when we understand and believe Romans 8:28-30. What a blessing it is to have this Word of God hidden in our heart (Psalm 119:11). Then we are in a position to rely on this truth, and in the power of the Holy Spirit to persevere and endure, and when affliction comes, to continue to persevere and endure to the end – knowing that our glorification awaits us if we do.

Just as no one can get into heaven who does not belong to Christ, there will be no one in heaven who is not conformed to Christ. Persevering in the likeness of Christ is the desired end, and it should be the goal of every Christian. Although our likeness to Him will not be completed until we get to heaven, we should be striving to be like Him before we get there. If we do, we may enjoy the additional blessing of hearing "well done, good and faithful servant!"

Assurance of Romans 8:28-30

These three verses present the believer with truths that are music to his ears. They offer comfort, encouragement, and strength in this life and a guarantee of being glorified by God, and enjoying the glory of God, in the life to come.

Paul states the doctrine taught in these verses with an authority and conviction that conveys certainty and assurance. However, in case others are not as convinced as

Paul and envision trials that may cause them to fall away, Paul appeals to logic and reason as food for their faith to feed on. Once Paul's argument has been filtered through the eyes of faith, hopefully, many readers will also be convinced of its truth and reality. Paul's argument is found in Romans 8:31-39.

> 31 What, then, shall we say in response to this? If God is for us, who can be against us? 32 He who did not spare his own Son, but gave him up for us all—how will he not also, along with him, graciously give us all things? 33 Who will bring any charge against those whom God has chosen? It is God who justifies. 34 Who is he that condemns? Christ Jesus, who died—more than that, who was raised to life—is at the right hand of God and is also interceding for us. 35 Who shall separate us from the love of Christ? Shall trouble or hardship or persecution or famine or nakedness or danger or sword? 36 As it is written:
> "For your sake we face death all day long;
> we are considered as sheep to be slaughtered."
> 37 No, in all these things we are more than conquerors through him who loved us. 38 For I am convinced that neither death nor life, neither angels nor demons, neither the present nor the future, nor any powers, 39 neither height nor depth, nor anything else in all creation, will be able to separate us from the love of God that is in Christ Jesus our Lord. (Romans 8:31-39).

As we consider the above passage, keep in mind that what Paul is writing applies only to true Christians – not false professors of Christ. If you have known or seen someone who professed Christ and then turned his back on Him, that is not an indication that he was saved and then lost, but rather it indicates he never was saved.

> 19 They went out from us, but they did not really belong to us. For if they had belonged to us, they would have remained with us; but their going showed that none of them belonged to us.
> (1 John 2:19).

If anyone had reason to withdraw from the Christian faith, it was Paul. His life was one of untold work, hardships and trials as he spread the Gospel. Furthermore, though Paul was writing under the inspiration of God, a number of the afflictions listed (Romans 8:35-38) he had personally experienced from the hand of God. God had told Paul he would suffer for His name.

> **15 But the Lord said to Ananias, "Go! This man is my chosen instrument to carry my name before the Gentiles and their kings and before the people of Israel. 16 I will show him how much he must suffer for my name."** (Acts 9:15-16).

If we look at several passages of Scripture, we get an idea of what Paul went through and yet continued to persevere and endure, as he stood firm in the faith.

> **9 For it seems to me that God has put us apostles on display at the end of the procession, like men condemned to die in the arena. We have been made a spectacle to the whole universe, to angels as well as to men. 10 We are fools for Christ, but you are so wise in Christ! We are weak, but you are strong! You are honored, we are dishonored! 11 To this very hour we go hungry and thirsty, we are in rags, we are brutally treated, we are homeless. 12 We work hard with our own hands. When we are cursed, we bless; when we are persecuted, we endure it; 13 when we are slandered, we answer kindly. Up to this moment we have become the scum of the earth, the refuse of the world.** (1 Corinthians 4:9-13).

> **23 ...I have worked much harder, been in prison more frequently, been flogged more severely, and been exposed to death again and again. 24 Five times I received from the Jews the forty lashes minus one. 25 Three times I was beaten with rods, once I was stoned, three times I was shipwrecked, I spent a night and a day in the open sea, 26 I have been constantly on the move. I have been in danger from rivers, in danger from bandits, in danger from**

my own countrymen, in danger from Gentiles; in danger in the city, in danger in the country, in danger at sea; and in danger from false brothers. 27 I have labored and toiled and have often gone without sleep; I have known hunger and thirst and have often gone without food; I have been cold and naked. 28 Besides everything else, I face daily the pressure of my concern for all the churches. 29 Who is weak, and I do not feel weak? Who is led into sin, and I do not inwardly burn?
(2 Corinthians 11:23-29).

16 At my first defense, no one came to my support, but everyone deserted me. May it not be held against them. 17 But the Lord stood at my side and gave me strength, so that through me the message might be fully proclaimed and all the Gentiles might hear it. And I was delivered from the lion's mouth. 18 The Lord will rescue me from every evil attack and will bring me safely to his heavenly kingdom. To him be glory for ever and ever. Amen.
(2 Timothy 4:16-18).

Although He does remove some afflictions, God has not promised to remove all of them. However, He has promised that He will bring us safely through all of them. It is not that He will take our affliction away, but that He will keep us from falling away. In affliction and even in the face of death, God gives us the grace to stand firm in the faith in order that He can bring us safely to His heaven. This appears to be the point Paul is making in the passage above in verse eighteen. For in the first half of the verse he says the Lord will rescue him from evil, and in the last half that He will bring him safely to heaven. Paul was writing from Rome where he was chained and imprisoned. He knew he was about to be executed (tradition says he was beheaded). He makes that clear earlier in this same letter to Timothy.

6 For I am already being poured out like a drink offering, and the time has come for my departure. 7 I have fought the good fight, I have finished the race, I have kept the faith. 8 Now there is in store for me the

**crown of righteousness, which the Lord, the
righteous Judge, will award to me on that day—and
not only to me, but also to all who have longed for
his appearing.** (2 Timothy 4:6-8).

Paul was more than a conqueror, and he tells us in verse
thirty-seven of Romans 8 that all Christians are. He was not
concerned that his body was about to die; he was ready to
depart and be with Christ. Whether in threatening or
pleasant circumstances, the Christian's primary concern
should not be the safety of his body but the safety of his
soul.

What then is meant by Paul's statement "in all these
things we are more than conquerors"? It means that our
afflictions are not only overcome and rendered powerless to
harm us but that they are so overcome that they are
conscripted to help us. What appears to be something that
could weaken or destroy our faith is overcome and utilized to
strengthen and preserve it. Although, in and of themselves,
afflictions are bad, by God's grace and God's power they are
harnessed and made to work for our good. This is God's
guarantee to us in Romans 8:28-30. Praise God!

2 **Consider it pure joy, my brothers, whenever you face trials of many kinds, 3 because you know that the testing of your faith develops perseverance.** (James 1:2-3).

Issues We Face

Now, let us look at some of the issues we may have to face, keeping in mind that the issues of bad situations, bad people, bad events, etc. are not crosses to bear but are tests of our faith.

12 Blessed is the man who perseveres under trial, because when he has stood the test, he will receive the crown of life that God has promised to those who love him. (James 1:12).

Some of these issues will affect us in a direct and personal way, others in an indirect and less personal way. They can be temptations to sin or opportunities for spiritual growth, depending on how we react to them. May we always face these issues fully confident that God will make them work for our good.

Sin

I assume that everyone is familiar with the term "sin"; however, I feel sure that there are many different opinions of just what sin is. Sin is something for which man is held accountable to God and to God only. Man may do man wrong, but ultimately all sin is against God. King David who committed adultery with Uriah's wife Bathsheba, and then had Uriah killed, made this point very clear in the 51st Psalm.

> **4 Against you, you only, have I sinned**
> **and done what is evil in your sight...**
> (Psalm 51:4).

As it is God to Whom we are held accountable for our sin, it is to His Word that we must go to learn what sin is. Based on the teaching of Scripture, we find that sin is the transgression of God's Law and the lack of conformity to His Law.

> **4 Everyone who sins breaks the law; in fact, sin is**
> **lawlessness.** (1 John 3:4).

> *17* **Anyone, then, who knows the good he ought to**
> **do and doesn't do it, sins.** (James 4:17).

The sins of those in positions of authority or leadership in society are often more destructive than average because of their influence on the lives of others. In a similar way this is true of parents with their children because they are the authority and leadership in their lives. Before we get into the discussion on sin, I want to be sure that I make my position clear. I am a sinner. Moreover, I do not want anyone reading this book to think that I consider myself better than you. I was saved in 1966, and before that time I may have sinned more or less than you. This is being written in the year 2001, and in the thirty-five years that I have been saved I may have sinned more or less than you. However, I am a sinner saved by grace. I have repented of my sins and asked Christ to forgive them. Have you? I look to the indwelling Holy Spirit to give me the wisdom to recognize sin and the strength to resist it. Do you? I find that as I practice doing this that I am sinning less and less with the passing of time. Do you find it is the same with you? When I do sin, I know that I can turn to God, confess my sin, and He is faithful to forgive me.

> **9 If we confess our sins, he is faithful and just and will forgive us our sins and purify us from all unrighteousness.** (1 John 1:9).

Hopefully, you and I are in step at this point. If so, we will probably not have any major differences as we discuss the subject of sin and sinners. If we are not in agreement at this point, then we could very well have even greater differences as we get deeper into the issue. You might be involved in something you think is not sinful, and I say it is. If this is the case, just remember that I am not standing in judgment of you. I will be quoting what God says. God's Word is our judge.

Sin is like quicksand. The longer you remain in it the deeper you sink, and it slowly pulls you under. The deeper you sink, the further you move away from God. This is because God hates sin.

> **9 You have loved righteousness and hated wickedness...** (Hebrews 1:9).

> **13 Your eyes are too pure to look on evil; you cannot tolerate wrong...** (Habakkuk 1:13).

Because our God hates sin, we should hate sin.

> **13 To fear the LORD is to hate evil...** (Proverbs 8:13).

> **10 Let those who love the LORD hate evil...** (Psalm 97:10).

We should view sin as an enemy to be conquered and shown no mercy. Unfortunately, this is not the case in much of the church today. The world is tolerating evil more and more, and it is having an effect on the church. In many churches you seldom ever hear references to sin, much less preaching against sin. This is particularly prevalent in some of the mainline denominations. As these denominations pull away from teaching the truth about sin and salvation, they discourage missions and evangelism. They no longer have a message for the lost world, and without a message there is no need for a messenger. Many preachers today do not proclaim the Gospel because they don't know the Christ of the Gospel. Those sitting under their preaching are perishing in their sin without even being told that they have sin.

Missionaries who hold to liberal theology also have nothing to offer – no Gospel and no Savior. At best, they offer food and medicine clothed in a form of godliness, but denying the power of it. At worst, they leave the unsaved in their lost condition but with a feeling that they are okay. It is a clear example of the blind leading the blind.

> **14 Leave them; they are blind guides. If a blind man leads a blind man, both will fall into a pit."**
> (Matthew 15:14).

We should look at sin as more dangerous than a poisonous snake. One can do only temporal damage, the other spiritual damage. One can bring physical death and the other can bring spiritual death. With the snake we have a choice – we may kill it or walk away. With sin, there is no choice – either we defeat it, or it will defeat us. We either kill sin, or it will kill us. We must never underestimate the destructive force of sin. Christians speak of their three enemies: the world, the flesh, and the devil. But what do these enemies do in an attempt to cause spiritual harm? They tempt, lure, and entice us to sin. Sin is their constant companion and their weapon against us. This is spiritual war and our future destiny hangs in the balance. As Christians, we know that Christ has defeated Satan, overcome the world, and paid the penalty for our sins. He has won the war for us. Yet, we are to fight this war each and every day. This war that has already been won for us is to be fought by us

until we go to heaven. Are you fighting the war? Are you
fighting the sin in your life? If not, why not? Surely you do not
think you do not sin. The Bible is very clear, we all sin.

> **9 Who can say, "I have kept my heart pure;**
> **I am clean and without sin"?** (Proverbs 20:9).

> **20 There is not a righteous man on earth**
> **who does what is right and never sins.**
> (Ecclesiastes 7:20).

> **46 "When they sin against you—for there is no one**
> **who does not sin...** (1 Kings 8:46).

Our sinfulness can prevent us from even acknowledging that
we do sin.

> **8 If we claim to be without sin, we deceive ourselves**
> **and the truth is not in us.** (1 John 1:8).

If we are honest with ourselves, even the most faithful
Christians can see sin in their lives. However, just seeing sin
is not enough. Today there are too many people who see
their sin but choose to travel that dangerous road of being
complacent about it. Their sin may not be the sin that society
abhors such as rape, robbery, murder, etc., but it is still sin
that God abhors such as putting people and things before
Him, covetousness, pride, etc. If you have been unaware
that there is a spiritual war, and after being told that there is,
you refuse to fight the war, then it would appear that you are
not one that God has called to serve in His army. It would
appear that you are still an unbeliever. Perhaps you had an
emotional reaction in a meeting and held up a hand, walked
an aisle, or prayed a prayer, but there was no sincere
commitment to Christ. If so, as an unbeliever you are serving
Satan.

> **42 Jesus said to them, "If God were your Father, you**
> **would love me, for I came from God and now am**

> here. I have not come on my own; but he sent me. *43* **Why is my language not clear to you? Because you are unable to hear what I say. *44* You belong to your father, the devil, and you want to carry out your father's desire.** (John 8:42-44).

Few, if any, unbelievers are truly aware that they are servants of Satan. However, this is the case with all men before they come to Christ. Furthermore, all men are slaves to sin unless Christ sets them free.

> **20 When you were slaves to sin, you were free from the control of righteousness. 21 What benefit did you reap at that time from the things you are now ashamed of? Those things result in death! 22 But now that you have been set free from sin and have become slaves to God, the benefit you reap leads to holiness, and the result is eternal life. 23 For the wages of sin is death, but the gift of God is eternal life in Christ Jesus our Lord.** (Romans 6:20-23).

If all people sin, both believers and unbelievers, there must be something we have in common – something that causes us to sin. The Bible makes it clear that it is our sinful nature. We were born with this sinful nature.

> **3 Even from birth the wicked go astray;**
> **from the womb they are wayward and speak lies.**
> (Psalm 58:3).

> **5 Surely I was sinful at birth,**
> **sinful from the time my mother conceived me.**
> (Psalm 51:5).

Some people think that we are sinners because we choose to sin. It is true we do choose to sin, but that is not the whole story. Why do we choose to sin? It is because of our sinful nature. The fact that man has a sinful nature is as obvious as the fact that fish swim. The sins we commit do not make us sinful – they only show that we are. A Sinful nature left to its own devices will produce only sinful thoughts and deeds.

> *17* Likewise every good tree bears good fruit, but a
> bad tree bears bad fruit. *18* A good tree cannot bear
> bad fruit, and a bad tree cannot bear good fruit.
> (Matthew 7:17-18).

Our sinful nature is the result of Adam's sin. We stand condemned by his sin. We have in our hearts the root of his sin, and our sinful deeds are fruit of his sin. Adam represented the human race as our federal head. When he fell, we fell with him. We remain fallen unless God raises us up to new life in Christ.

> *12* Therefore, just as sin entered the world through
> one man, and death through sin, and in this way
> death came to all men, because all sinned...
> (Romans 5:12).

The elect angels are sinless. They live in a state of obedience to God. Unregenerate man is sinful, and he lives in a state of disobedience to God. Regenerate man is more complex than either of them. He has righteousness imputed to him, a new heart given to him, and God indwelling him. However, he still has his old sinful nature. He is at times obedient and at other times disobedient. Even in his obedience, his sinful nature keeps him from rising to the spiritual heights he would seek. Likewise, in his disobedience, God mercifully keeps him from falling to the depths of spiritual death.

We sin much more often than most Christians realize. We transgress God's law when we do that which we are told not to do. We fail to conform to God's law when we do not do that which we are told to do. In both situations we sin.

> 3 But among you there must not be even a hint of
> sexual immorality, or of any kind of impurity, or of
> greed, because these are improper for God's holy
> people. 4 Nor should there be obscenity, foolish talk
> or coarse joking, which are out of place, but rather
> thanksgiving. 5 For of this you can be sure: No
> immoral, impure or greedy person—such a man is
> an idolater—has any inheritance in the kingdom of
> Christ and of God. (Ephesians 5:3-5).

8 But now you must rid yourselves of all such things as these: anger, rage, malice, slander, and filthy language from your lips. 9 Do not lie to each other, since you have taken off your old self with its practices 10 and have put on the new self, which is being renewed in knowledge in the image of its Creator. (Colossians 3:8-10).

12 Therefore, as God's chosen people, holy and dearly loved, clothe yourselves with compassion, kindness, humility, gentleness and patience. 13 Bear with each other and forgive whatever grievances you may have against one another. Forgive as the Lord forgave you. 14 And over all these virtues put on love, which binds them all together in perfect unity. (Colossians 3:12-14).

18 **Wives, submit to your husbands, as is fitting in the Lord.**
19 Husbands, love your wives and do not be harsh with them.
20 Children, obey your parents in everything, for this pleases the Lord. 21 Fathers, do not embitter your children, or they will become discouraged. (Colossians 3:18-21).

It is also important that we not be confused by temptation. We can be tempted to do something that is sinful, and we can be tempted to not do something that is good. In either case, being tempted is not a sin – yielding to the temptation is when we sin. God will enable us to resist temptation.

13 No temptation has seized you except what is common to man. And God is faithful; he will not let you be tempted beyond what you can bear. But when you are tempted, he will also provide a way out so that you can stand up under it. (1 Corinthians 10:13).

The Christian is to study God's Word, to learn the "do's" and "don'ts" of God's moral law – all the while looking to the Holy Spirit to provide the understanding, wisdom, and power to live in obedience. Though we cannot attain a state of sinless perfection in this life, it is the goal for which we should strive. Are you doing this? If not, why not?

If we are to overcome sin in our lives, we must go to God's Word. His Word is not a man-made formula to follow; rather it is made alive and energized by God the Holy Spirit. Christians have the Holy Spirit living within them (Romans 8:9). If we will study God's Word, trusting the Holy Spirit to teach us its truth, to give us understanding of its promises, and to empower us to obey its commands, we will find that it is sufficient for life and behavior.

> **16 All Scripture is God-breathed and is useful for teaching, rebuking, correcting and training in righteousness, 17 so that the man of God may be thoroughly equipped for every good work.**
> (2 Timothy 3:16-17).

Particular Sins

We have looked at sin in general. I would now like us to look at some particular sins. One interesting thing about many of these sins is that "so-called" experts have told people that they are not the sinner's fault. They are the result of faulty genes. If it were not for this gene problem, the sinner would not do this thing or behave this way. This is music to the sinner's ears for it enables him to see himself as a victim instead of a villain. Much of society will buy into this idea because often they have a family member or friend who fits this picture of a "faulty gene" victim. Even though this theory has the backing of some in the field of medical science, it is still just a theory. There is no real proof or facts to hold up the theory. However, once the theory is proposed, the media and others pick up on it. Somewhere along the way, pointing out that it is only a theory seems to get dropped, and it becomes accepted as fact. Over a period of time, its acceptance becomes so entrenched among the general population that those who do not accept it are cast as uneducated, primitive in their thinking, and out of step with the world. When they say that the wrong behavior is due to man's sinful nature rather than a gene problem, they are told they are being judgmental and unfair. Let us look at some of the sinful behavior that God calls sin and that man calls a "gene problem".

Alcoholism

Alcoholism is one of the sins that is routinely attributed to a genetic problem. This is done even though alcoholism is not a physical characteristic like skin color or the color of hair and eyes. Moreover, it is often spoken of as the "disease of alcoholism". We think of a disease as being like pneumonia, which is something that happens to you. A disease is not some type of behavior that you do yourself, i.e. drinking too much. A diabetic has a condition or disease with which he must contend. It is not a matter of a choice of behavior as drinking is for the alcoholic. The alcoholic may choose to drink or not to drink. However, no one in his right mind would choose to be a diabetic or to have pneumonia. For a cure of their alcoholism, people often go to Alcoholics Anonymous (AA) or some other similar organization where they have a twelve-step program. When successful, the result they achieve is not freedom from being an alcoholic but the ability to control themselves and not drink. Most of these organizations say there is no cure. The alcoholic is told to admit that they are an alcoholic and therefore can never drink again because one drink and you are off on a binge. However, it really comes down to self-control and how one behaves. The alcoholic chooses to drink or not to drink.

If the alcoholic does not drink, he has overcome the sin of getting drunk. He has not found a remedy for his "genetic problem". Further evidence that it is a matter of willpower and self-control is that in England the alcoholic is often taught how to drink in moderation without getting drunk. I have read that many people in America learn to do the same and that many people get over being an alcoholic on their own – without ever going through a program.

If it is not a genetic problem, then why do people become alcoholics? Why do the "so called" experts push the theory that it is genetic? Let us answer the second question first. One answer is money. They may or may not believe in the genetic theory. They may or may not be sincere in their desire to help people overcome alcoholism. But one thing is certain; there is a tremendous amount of money spent each year on organizations and institutions to help people conquer their alcoholism. The "recovery" industry has convinced the public that they are experts in treating alcoholism. In fact the pseudoscientists have been so convincing that even many Christians have bought their theory, and a number of churches have started their own twelve-step programs. They apparently do not believe that Scripture is sufficient. Perhaps they do not know what it says, do not understand what it says, or do not believe what it says. Certainly they are not practicing what it says. Their claim that the alcoholic, on his own, cannot stop drinking and getting drunk flies in the face of Scripture. God does not speak to man on the basis of whether he can or cannot do something. He speaks to him on the basis of whether he will or will not do something. Moreover, God holds him accountable for doing or not doing it.

When faced with the question of why people become alcoholics, no one has a clear and definite answer. As we have discussed, the experts blame it on a gene problem, but without scientific proof for this we must look elsewhere. Man's sinful nature leaves him prone to sin in many different ways. However, everyone has a sinful nature and since most people are not alcoholics, the sinful nature is not the only reason for being one. Perhaps personality plays its role. One may be very outgoing and like to party to the extent that drinking becomes a habit and a way of life. Or one may be so shy that drinking provides the courage to go and do what one would not do sober. One may enjoy the taste of alcohol more than most people do and therefore drink more than most. One may seek to escape from problems and decisions in heavy or continual drinking. For some people, drinking may help blot out their feelings of guilt. It can serve as an excuse for not trying, or for failing when one does try. Some alcoholics may convince themselves that their condition relieves them of any and all responsibility for their families. Someone else can earn the money, raise the kids, and tend to house repairs, etc. because their alcoholism will not let them do it.

Some people become an alcoholic at a young age, some in mid-life, and some in old age. This certainly shoots holes in the gene theory. Old people who live alone or someone who has lost a loved one sometimes become alcoholics as they react to their situations. Also the loss of a meaningful job, good reputation, or a large fortune may be the catalyst to move someone toward becoming an alcoholic.

God does not tell man he cannot drink. He does not tell man that it is a sin to drink. In fact, God tells man that he made wine to make man happy.

> **14 He makes grass grow for the cattle,**
> **and plants for man to cultivate—**
> **bringing forth food from the earth:**
> **15 wine that gladdens the heart of man,**
> **oil to make his face shine,**
> **and bread that sustains his heart.**
> (Psalm 104:14-15).

However, the enjoyment of drinking can be abused as can other gifts from God. God clearly warns of this.

> **1 Wine is a mocker and beer a brawler;**
> **whoever is led astray by them is not wise.**
> (Proverbs 20:1).

> **29 Who has woe? Who has sorrow?**
> **Who has strife? Who has complaints?**
> **Who has needless bruises? Who has bloodshot**
> **eyes?**

30 Those who linger over wine,
who go to sample bowls of mixed wine.
31 Do not gaze at wine when it is red,
when it sparkles in the cup,
when it goes down smoothly!
32 In the end it bites like a snake
and poisons like a viper.
33 Your eyes will see strange sights
and your mind imagine confusing things.
34 You will be like one sleeping on the high seas,
lying on top of the rigging.
35 "They hit me," you will say, "but I'm not hurt!
They beat me, but I don't feel it!
When will I wake up
so I can find another drink?"
(Proverbs 23:29-35).

In addition to warning us of the pitfalls of abusing drink, God goes still further and commands us not to abuse it.

18 Do not get drunk on wine, which leads to debauchery. Instead, be filled with the Spirit. (Ephesians 5:18).

Many people have experienced directly or indirectly the consequences that come from drinking to excess. Too often they react by blaming the drink rather than the drinker. Also, as stated before, people are prone to attribute alcoholism to a gene problem rather than a sin problem. Regardless of the reasons or excuses man finds for drinking to excess, we see above in Ephesians 5:18 that God commands him not to. Disobey God's command and you sin.

Adultery

Sin is a subject most people prefer to avoid, but they will tolerate it if you talk about robbery, rape, and murder. The reason is because these are sins most people do not commit. And few, if any, people would argue that these are not sinful acts. This would not be the case with the sin of adultery. In today's society adultery is commonplace, and many would argue that it is not sinful. I remember reading about a man and woman who were having an adulterous affair. They professed to be Christians and said that they felt God wanted them to get divorced and marry each other. Their lack of understanding of the Bible is very evident, and the question of whether or not they are truly Christians is certainly raised. Nonetheless, they are an example of how adultery is rationalized and condoned in our society today. However, society is not the final judge – God is. He not only commands us not to commit adultery but will stand in judgment of those who do.

> **14 "You shall not commit adultery.** (Exodus 20:14).

> **4 Marriage should be honored by all, and the marriage bed kept pure, for God will judge the adulterer and all the sexually immoral.**
> (Hebrews 13:4).

The issue of adultery is enormous. Because sex outside of marriage is so available in our free-swinging society, adultery becomes a real temptation for some Christian husbands and wives. For those who are not tempted, there is always the possibility of it happening to their children, grandchildren, or other family members. Adultery causes family upheavals, problems at work, and problems at church. Although the Old Testament Civil Law does not apply to us today, it is well worth remembering that God took such a dim view of adultery that He called for death by stoning for those who committed it.

> **10 "'If a man commits adultery with another man's wife—with the wife of his neighbor—both the adulterer and the adulteress must be put to death.'"**
> (Leviticus 20:10).

Christ tells us that to look at a woman lustfully is to commit adultery in your heart.

> **27 "You have heard that it was said, 'Do not commit adultery.' 28 But I tell you that anyone who looks at a**

**woman lustfully has already committed adultery with
her in his heart."** (Matthew 5:27-28).

Fornication

Like adultery, fornication is another act that God calls sin.
However, many in today's society would argue that it is not.
The term "fornication" is generally applied to sex by an
unmarried person. If a married person has sex with someone
other than his or her spouse, adultery has been committed. If
two unmarried people have sex, they both commit
fornication. There was a time when most everyone
considered fornication to be wrong – it was considered
immoral. Although men who committed it suffered little in the
way of consequences, women fornicators were stigmatized.
Compare that with today's reaction to fornication, and we
see how low society has set the moral gauge. However,
society does not set the standard for man's behavior – God
does. God says that fornication is sin, and He judges those
who commit it.

**8 We should not commit sexual immorality, as some
of them did—and in one day twenty-three thousand
of them died.** (1 Corinthians 10:8).
(In this verse and several others, the KJV uses the term "fornication?
Where the NIV has sexual immorality).

People are not only known to be committing fornication,
but they actually make an open display of it by living
together. Some people pursue this relationship as a means
to have a baby without the obligation and responsibilities that
go with marriage. Of course, most pregnancies resulting
from this lifestyle are accidents that end with an abortion or
an unwanted child. Too often, the mother is a teenager still
in high school and the father an irresponsible drop out. In
most of these cases, the cost to society goes beyond that of
welfare, health care, etc. There is the increase of single
parent families, child abuse, and teen violence. Many of

these children not only do not have a daddy at home, but they do not even know who their daddy is. This in turn deprives them of the extended family of grandparents, aunts, uncles, cousins, etc.

The temptation to become involved in fornication is an issue that affects the unmarried Christian in a very direct way. There are those single Christians who are virgins, those who were involved in fornication before becoming Christians, and those who have been married in the past. For some of these, the temptation to commit fornication is very strong. Those who yield may find themselves guilt ridden and have less assurance of salvation. Their weakened faith leads to a weakened witness. The families of those Christians who succumb to the temptation are often greatly affected by what results. One way or another, the issue of fornication affects us all as it contributes to the downward spiral of society.

Homosexuality   Lesbianism   Bisexuality

For this discussion the term "homosexual" will also apply to the lesbian (a female homosexual) and the bisexual (a male or female who practices homosexual and heterosexual sex). Even though most homosexuals are not married, there are some that are married to heterosexuals and some of these commit adultery. Homosexuals who are unmarried that commit a sex act are guilty of fornication. Although the homosexual act may fall in either the category of adultery or fornication, God has put still another classification on it – He calls it "unnatural" and "perverted".

> 26 Because of this, God gave them over to shameful lusts. Even their women exchanged natural relations for unnatural ones. 27 In the same way the men also abandoned natural relations with women and were inflamed with lust for one another. Men committed indecent acts with other men, and received in themselves the due penalty for their perversion.
> (Romans 1:26-27).

I understand that there was a time when the American Psychological Association considered homosexuality a mental disorder, but the homosexual activists and lobbyists got it to take homosexuality off its "deviant" list. The activists are now trying to get the Association to discourage treatment that is directed at changing the sexual orientation of homosexuals.

A number of groups do treat homosexuality and often with much success. These are not formal groups, and many of them are ministries. However, the groups that use a secular approach to treatment are also successful. Of course, some types of treatment are more effective than others, but none are successful with everyone. However, this is the case with any compulsive or addictive behavior and holds true for alcoholics and people who smoke in the same manner as it does for homosexuals.

Just as God sees the homosexual act as unnatural and perverted, the greater part of society also sees it that way. In America it has always been that way. Although society is becoming more and more tolerant of heterosexual adultery and fornication, it is not accepting homosexuality with the same rate of tolerance. I believe this is due to it being unnatural and perverted and also because the homosexuals insist on pushing their lifestyle. When we look around, we do not find a number of well-organized groups pushing adultery or fornication. People are committing adultery and fornication on an increasing scale, but they are not organizing as a political group to lobby and promote their lifestyle. They are not working to have it taught to young children in school, so that it will become more acceptable and possibly lure some into experimenting with it. Many people think that the sin of the homosexual is the bad sin. It is a bad sin, but then all sin is bad. It is not that homosexual sins are bad and other sins are not, but the fact that the homosexuals want to have government endorse and assist them in fostering theirs. They have already infiltrated the school systems with children being encouraged to read Gloria Goes to Gay Pride, and I understand that even some first graders have

<u>Daddy's Roommate</u> as recommended reading. At one school lesbians passed out information to children six to eleven years old encouraging the lesbian lifestyle. Some colleges and universities have homosexual, lesbian, and bisexual clubs on campus.

Since the courts removed God and the Ten Commandments from schools, we no longer have moral absolutes to teach our children. "What is right for you may not be right for me" is what children are being taught. However, it is not just what children are being taught, it is also what we are failing to teach them both at school and at home. Christians, homosexuals, and other groups all want to set the moral standards for society. In our society everyone is entitled to his opinion, and someone's morals are going to be in effect. However, if it is anyone's morals other than the Christians, they can change with the wind. What was once considered wrong can now be considered what is right. Good can become bad and bad can become good. Today's vice may be tomorrow's virtue. However, the Christian's morals are taken from the Bible, and Biblical morals are from God. Therefore, they do not change because God does not change. Moreover, because God institutes them, they are absolute. All others are not.

Due to the promotional campaigns of the homosexuals and the hype of the liberal media, many Christians are confused about the whole homosexual issue. One point of confusion arises because the homosexuals put out the message that if you are against homosexuality you are homophobic, i.e. you fear homosexuality. This is absurd. You can disapprove of something without being afraid of it. You can disapprove of adultery and fornication, but this does not mean you fear them. Probably the biggest point of confusion is the often repeated assertion that people are just born homosexual – that they cannot do anything about it. It is a gene that causes them to be homosexual. There is no scientific proof of this statement although some within the homosexual community would claim they have made studies that prove it. However, it is only a hollow claim as the proof does not exist.

Let us look at how some people may become homosexuals. In doing so, let us first define what a homosexual is. Webster's Ninth New Collegiate Dictionary says the homosexual is "characterized by a tendency to direct sexual desire toward another of the same sex." Of course, there could be situations where people would indulge in a homosexual practice without having a sexual desire toward the same sex. This is true of some male and female prison inmates. Unable to have heterosexual sex, they turn for relief to homosexual acts. The number of years they have been in prison, the close contact with other prisoners and the influence of those prisoners all play a role in their choosing to commit homosexual acts. There are also some people who are in the homosexual lifestyle as prostitutes. They are not in it for pleasure but for money. However, regardless of the reason, the longer they indulge in the lifestyle the more comfortable they become with it. It can become more habit forming until they find themselves choosing it as a way of life. I read that the brain actually changes over time as a behavior is repeated over and over. This change appears to have influence in making it difficult to break a habit. It seems to reinforce the habit.

Another way one can learn to be a homosexual is from someone who is one. We have all seen situations where a young boy or girl thinks an older boy or girl is terrific. They will do most anything to please the older child and be allowed to spend time with them. If the older boy or girl is homosexual, the younger one may go along to please the older.

Adolescent children often experiment with sex. When two boys or two girls who are close friends get together, they may experiment and stumble on something that is pleasurable or makes them feel good. Wanting to experience that "pleasurable sensation" again, they make a point of getting together for that purpose. This can become a habit. Most children will leave the practice of homosexual sex when they become old enough to date, drive a car, and pursue sexual pleasure with the opposite sex. However, some children may continue this practice as they get older and pursue it with others. They may become conditioned to the "pleasurable sensation" being associated with the homosexual act and seek it out of a habit or addiction. The homosexual lifestyle is one to which people can become addicted, just as they can become addicted to pornography. There would be a number of other factors that could come into play and affect one's choice to lead the homosexual lifestyle. Environment, parents' influence (or lack of it), friends (or lack of them), and an insecure feeling when with the opposite sex are a few possibilities. It seems that homosexuals have to spend little time or money in finding a partner for a one-night stand. This in itself may help to draw some to the lifestyle. I feel sure there are many more factors that we have not even touched on that can influence one to pursue the homosexual lifestyle. I understand that some people go back and forth between practicing homosexuality and heterosexuality several times in their life-time.

One thing we do want to remember is that homosexuality is something that people learn, grow into, and choose to do. It is not a matter of a gene. From the beginning some pagan societies practiced homosexuality, and thus people learned it not only as a lifestyle but also as an accepted lifestyle. Sodom is a good example of this. The percentage of people who were homosexuals in Sodom would be very high. And this would be the case not because of so many people having a homosexual gene, but because it was an accepted lifestyle that people learned and practiced. The push is on today by homosexual groups to revive this acceptance in society. If genes were responsible, would a bisexual person have a homosexual and a heterosexual gene? Is there a child molester gene? If a child molester happens to be a homosexual, then again we would have to have two wrong genes. Are genes responsible for someone being a rapist? How about a sexual fetish? Is there a gene that causes someone to become addicted to pornography? If so, and they are a heterosexual pedophile who rapes little girls, then we have three bad genes. We have a gene for pornography, pedophilia, and rape. If they just happen to be an alcoholic, then we have four bad genes. It does not take much to see how ridiculous the gene theory becomes.

In the last few years I have heard of people who think that perhaps there is a gene that causes people to get divorced, to become sex addicts, become gambling addicts, become compulsive shoppers, compulsive liars, and spouse abusers. Imagine the things that could be added to that list. If anyone does anything to excess, you could say it was due to a faulty gene. On that basis you could have a golf gene, eating gene, pool shooting gene, TV watching gene, internet gene, chronic speeder gene, card playing gene, and even a monopoly playing gene. Actually, in America, we are moving toward blaming a gene, our parents, society, and anything else we are capable of dreaming up, as the reason we do anything wrong or anything to excess. We are relieving ourselves of any responsibility for our sins, failures, and shortcomings.

Let us think a minute. If a gene causes all the above actions, it would then seem to indicate that a gene causes all action of any kind. You could have a gene that causes you to help little old ladies across the street. Perhaps you might have a gene that causes you to give money to charity or do volunteer work at the local hospital. The more real thought you give the gene idea, the more ridiculous it gets. We do have genes that determine physical properties such as color of hair, skin, eyes, etc. Genes play a role in what a person looks like. However, we are not commanded to change the way we look, but we are commanded to change the way we behave.

When it comes to sexual sin, the heterosexual and the homosexual have the same problem. They both have a sinful human nature that likes to sin, enjoys sin, and actually wills and chooses to sin. Also, they both seek ways to not be held accountable for their sin. They rationalize, excuse, deny, and try to find someone or something on which they can blame their sin. This is what Adam and Eve did. Adam blamed Eve and God. Eve blamed the serpent, Satan

(Genesis 3:11-13). Who is to blame when you see a college girl being interviewed on TV and she says she is going to try the bisexual lifestyle? Her reason is that it sounds interesting, and she knows some people who are trying it so she want to experiment with it. Apparently at her school it is sort of a fad or "the in thing to do". This is not a gene bringing this about. It is a choice just as someone might choose to learn to play chess. Now some might see her as a young care-free college girl who is not really doing anything wrong. However, God sees her as committing both heterosexual fornication and lesbianism. In God's eyes both are sin, and we can see that it is not a gene or genes that caused her action but her choosing to do something she expects to enjoy. Over a period of time, depending on how the men and women this young lady has sex with treat her etc., she may choose to lead a heterosexual lifestyle or become a lesbian. Let's say she chooses the heterosexual way of life. The fact that she experimented with lesbianism does not make her a lesbian or a bisexual. She is someone who committed lesbian acts, who experimented with the bisexual lifestyle, but she is not a lesbian or a bisexual. She is not now practicing the lesbian or bisexual way of life. Someone who gets drunk a few times is not called a drunkard. A teenager who steals something once cannot be thought of as a thief when he is forty years old. Adolescent girls or boys who experiment with sex and commit homosexual acts but grow up to live heterosexual lives are not homosexual. One act, or repeated acts for a brief period, (i.e. our bisexual college girl) do not make you a lesbian, homosexual, drunkard, thief, etc. A young person that commits fornication one or two times, but is not living that lifestyle would not be classified as a fornicator. It is true that they have committed fornication, but fornication is not a way of life for them. However, even those who are drunkards, homosexuals, thieves, etc. as a way of life for a number of years are no longer to be thought of as that way, if Christ has freed them of that. God makes this clear through the writings of the Apostle Paul.

> **9 Do you not know that the wicked will not inherit the kingdom of God? Do not be deceived: Neither the sexually immoral nor idolaters nor adulterers nor male prostitutes nor homosexual offenders 10 nor thieves nor the greedy nor drunkards nor slanderers nor swindlers will inherit the kingdom of God. 11 And that is what some of you were. But you were washed, you were sanctified, you were justified in the name of the Lord Jesus Christ and by the Spirit of our God.** (1 Corinthians 6:9-11).

We see that Christ sets these people free from the power of sin in their lives. They are freed from certain sins in particular. The sin of homosexuality is only one sin among the group of sins mentioned in the above verses. Although it is not the only sin and may not be the worst sin, it is still sin according to God.

Someone may have lived for years as a lesbian, thief, or drunkard and then find salvation in Christ. Christ can and does break the bondage of sin in our lives. When we come to Him, He changes us – He makes us new creatures. If we do not believe this can happen to someone else, it may be because it has not happened to us. If we profess to trust Christ but over a period of time we do not see a change in ourselves, it will be hard to believe someone else can change. Perhaps we need to do as Paul said and examine ourselves to see if we are in the faith.

As we come to a close on this issue, I think it is important that we make one point very clear. God so loved the world that He sent His Son to die that the sins of those who repent and put their trust in Christ might be forgiven. The Christian, having God's love in his heart, is to love the homosexual, the lesbian, and the bisexual. The person is to be loved, but the behavior is to be condemned because God condemns it. Disagreeing with the defenders and promoters of homosexuality does not make the Christian a bigot. He must oppose the homosexual lifestyle because God does. He does not hate the homosexual but hates the sinful behavior. The Christian is to hate all sin, including his own; moreover, he does not determine what is sin – God does. Any Christian, worth his salt, realizes how much he or she has been forgiven and should not look down on or hate someone else. The old adage still holds true: Hate the sin but love the sinner.

At this point I want to remind the reader that at the beginning of this section on sin, I tried to make it clear that I sin and I do not think of myself as being better than others. I sin less with the passing of time, but I still sin. According to God's Word, everyone sins.

> **23...for all have sinned and fall short of the glory of God...**
> (Romans 3:23).

The fact that someone sins does not disqualify them from pointing out what God says is sin. Sometimes when you point out that what someone is doing is sinful, they immediately come back with "let him who is without sin cast the first stone? (John 8:7), or "judge not that you be not judged" (Matthew 7:1). When Christians point to something that the Bible says is sinful, they are not claiming to be without sin themselves. For example, a Christian may have committed fornication either before or after becoming a Christian. He recognized that when he did, he sinned. That fact does not disqualify or prevent him from saying that fornication is a sin and anyone who does it is sinning. This would apply to any other type of sin as well.

People who resort to the above John 8:7 and Matthew 7:1 as an excuse for, and as a defense of their sinful acts, do not understand what the Bible teaches about sin. The Bible makes it clear: There is no excuse for sin and no defense of sin. Furthermore, there will be eternal punishment for sin unless one repents and trusts Christ as Savior and Lord for the forgiveness of sin.

For those who misunderstand what the verses in question teach, or who use them out-of-context, let us now look at them.

1 But Jesus went to the Mount of Olives. 2 At dawn he appeared again in the temple courts, where all the people gathered around him, and he sat down to teach them. 3 The teachers of the law and the Pharisees brought in a woman caught in adultery. They made her stand before the group 4 and said to Jesus, "Teacher, this woman was caught in the act of adultery. 5 In the Law Moses commanded us to stone such women. Now what do you say?" 6 They were using this question as a trap, in order to have a basis for accusing him.

But Jesus bent down and started to write on the ground with his finger. 7 When they kept on questioning him, he straightened up and said to them, "If any one of you is without sin, let him be the first to throw a stone at her." 8 Again he stooped down and wrote on the ground.

9 At this, those who heard began to go away one at a time, the older ones first, until only Jesus was left, with the woman still standing there. 10 Jesus straightened up and asked her, "Woman, where are they? Has no one condemned you?"

11 "No one, sir," she said.

"Then neither do I condemn you," Jesus declared. "Go now and leave your life of sin." (John 8:1-11).

One of the first things we see is that the men bringing the adulteress to Jesus were doing it to discredit Him, His teaching, and His reputation among the people. Verse six tells us that they were trying to trap Jesus. Matthew 22:15 shows us a similar attempt to trap Him. These Scribes and Pharisees were unhappy that the day before their own temple guards had failed to arrest Jesus (John 7:45). The men probably did not care to see the woman executed because adultery was commonplace in that day. Back then, just as it is at present, a crime was not always punished to the full extent of the law. This woman's reputation had been ruined, her adultery had now been made public, and her husband would probably divorce her. The real purpose in bringing the woman to Jesus was to use her in a clever manner to discredit Him.

Among the people, Jesus had a reputation of being a friend to sinners, publicans, tax collectors, and harlots. If He said to stone the woman, the Pharisees would attack His reputation and denounce Him as a friend to sinners. They could also report Him to the Roman authorities for violating Roman law because the Jews were not allowed to carry out death penalties.

If Jesus said to let her go, the Pharisees could say that He taught contrary to Moses Law and as such was declaring God's Law not to be holy. It was a clever strategy, and we can imagine the Pharisees thought they had Jesus. After all, these men did not need to bring the woman to Jesus. They were the teachers of the Law (Scribes) and the religious leaders (Pharisees). They knew the Law well. They had their system of justice with procedures for bringing charges against someone and carrying out the law.

Let us consider how Christ responded to this scheme of the Scribes and Pharisees. First, He never said that the woman did not sin. In fact He told her to stop sinning. He also never said that her sin was a minor thing. After all, Christ taught against adultery and sin in general.

> **27 "You have heard that it was said, 'Do not commit adultery.' 28 But I tell you that anyone who looks at a woman lustfully has already committed adultery with her in his heart. 29 If your right eye causes you to sin, gouge it out and throw it away. It is better for you to lose one part of your body than for your whole body to be thrown into hell. 30 And if your right hand causes you to sin, cut it off and throw it away. It is better for you to lose one part of your body than for your whole body to go into hell.**
> (Matthew 5:27-30).

Jesus was not going to let these men force Him to take the position of judge at this time.

> **17 For God did not send his Son into the world to condemn the world, but to save the world through him.** (John 3:17).

Christ put the problem in their laps. He referred them to one of the points of the Law with which they would be acquainted. When someone is put to death, the witnesses throw the first stone.

> **5 ...take the man or woman who has done this evil deed to your city gate and stone that person to death. 6 On the testimony of two or three witnesses a man shall be put to death, but no one shall be put to death on the testimony of only one witness. 7 The hands of the witnesses must be the first in putting him to death, and then the hands of all the people. You must purge the evil from among you.**
> (Deuteronomy 17:5-7).

The accusers left, and once they were gone, there were no witnesses to the woman's adultery. The accusers' consciences must have gotten to them. They, of course, knew they were sinners. Possibly they had also committed adultery. From a legal perspective, once the witnesses to the woman's adultery were gone, there was no case to try. Without witnesses, there were no charges being brought. Therefore, there was no guilt or innocence to be determined, no punishment to be imposed.

The other verse that is used so often is Matthew 7:1.

> **1 "Do not judge, or you too will be judged.**
> (Matthew 7:1).

For those who refer to this verse in a manner that implies that what they do is not sinful because no one is supposed to judge them, we need to make clear that the verse does not teach that at all. Christians are to make a judgment as to what is right to do and what is wrong to do. It then follows that when they see people doing what is right or wrong, they cannot help but judge that the person is doing right or wrong – in their opinion. Christ had His opinion, which was always correct and without error.

> **20 For I tell you that unless your righteousness surpasses that of the Pharisees and the teachers of**

the law, you will certainly not enter the kingdom of heaven. (Matthew 5:20).

25 "Woe to you, teachers of the law and Pharisees, you hypocrites! You clean the outside of the cup and dish, but inside they are full of greed and self-indulgence. 26 Blind Pharisee! First clean the inside of the cup and dish, and then the outside also will be clean.
27 "Woe to you, teachers of the law and Pharisees, you hypocrites! You are like whitewashed tombs, which look beautiful on the outside but on the inside are full of dead men's bones and everything unclean. 28 In the same way, on the outside you appear to people as righteous but on the inside you are full of hypocrisy and wickedness."
(Matthew 23:25-28).

Christ had perfect discernment. We do not. Christ knew what was in a person's heart. We do not. However, we are to look to the Holy Spirit to give us discernment and enable us to make good judgments.

14 The man without the Spirit does not accept the things that come from the Spirit of God, for they are foolishness to him, and he cannot understand them, because they are spiritually discerned. 15 The spiritual man makes judgments about all things, but he himself is not subject to any man's judgment... (1 Corinthians 2:14-15).

21 My son, preserve sound judgment and discernment,
do not let them out of your sight... (Proverbs 3:21).

15 "'Do not pervert justice; do not show partiality to the poor or favoritism to the great, but judge your neighbor fairly." (Leviticus 19:15).

1 **Dear friends, do not believe every spirit, but test the spirits to see whether they are from God, because many false prophets have gone out into the world.** (1 John 4:1).

> 15 "If your brother sins against you, go and show him his fault, just between the two of you. If he listens to you, you have won your brother over. 16 But if he will not listen, take one or two others along, so that 'every matter may be established by the testimony of two or three witnesses.' 17 If he refuses to listen to them, tell it to the church; and if he refuses to listen even to the church, treat him as you would a pagan or a tax collector."
> (Matthew 18:15-17).

Having seen from Scripture that Christians are to discern and make judgments, then let us look at the verse that tells us not to judge to see what is meant. If we see it in its full setting, we may can understand it better. Therefore, we will look at the passage, of which it is a part.

> 1 "Do not judge, or you too will be judged. 2 For in the same way you judge others, you will be judged, and with the measure you use, it will be measured to you.
> 3 "Why do you look at the speck of sawdust in your brother's eye and pay no attention to the plank in your own eye? 4 How can you say to your brother, 'Let me take the speck out of your eye,' when all the time there is a plank in your own eye? 5 You hypocrite, first take the plank out of your own eye, and then you will see clearly to remove the speck from your brother's eye." (Matthew 7:1-5).

What Christ is condemning in this passage is a person with a critical and fault-finding attitude. Someone who makes rash and hasty judgments and who is always looking for flaws in another person without considering the sin in his own life. He has a tendency to pass judgment from a self-righteous position. Love and mercy seldom enter into his judgments, and he may even exaggerate the wrong that is done. This passage is for all of us, but it particularly hits home with the teachers of the law and the Pharisees because they were hypocritical in putting on a righteous front and condemning others when they themselves were so guilty of sin. When we look for the speck in someone's eye, we truly need to check to be sure we do not have a plank in our own eye.

Discerning, forming an opinion, and making a judgment about a person, an act, or a thing is not prohibited here. One whose heart is right with God, who has knowledge and understanding of the Word of God, and who is controlled by the Spirit of God need not fear making a judgment. He need not be put on the defensive when someone says, "cast not the first stone" or "judge not". Moreover, if he is to obey many of the commands of Scripture, he must make a judgment. Matthew 7:6 being just one example.

> 6 "Do not give dogs what is sacred; do not throw your pearls to pigs. If you do, they may trample them under their feet, and then turn and tear you to pieces. (Matthew 7:6).

Another area where some explanation is needed concerns the studies of homosexuality by some denominations. The fact that the public reads about a study that takes two or three years to reach a decision can be so misleading. It can give people the idea that the question of whether or not God approves of the homosexual lifestyle is very complex. Therefore, if the answer is that God disapproves, then perhaps the answer is wrong. After all, it is a very complicated question. Many people just do not realize how strong God teaches against this sin. The following are a few verses that should make it clear.

> 1 The two angels arrived at Sodom in the evening, and Lot was sitting in the gateway of the city. When he saw them, he got up to meet them and bowed down with his face to the ground. 2 "My lords," he said, "please turn aside to your servant's house. You can wash your feet and spend the night and then go on your way early in the morning."
> "No," they answered, "we will spend the night in the square."
> 3 But he insisted so strongly that they did go with him and entered his house. He prepared a meal for them, baking bread without yeast, and they ate. 4 Before they had gone to bed, all the men from every part of the city of Sodom—both young and old—

surrounded the house. 5 They called to Lot, "Where
are the men who came to you tonight? Bring them
out to us so that we can have sex with them."

6 Lot went outside to meet them and shut the door
behind him 7 and said, "No, my friends. Don't do this
wicked thing. 8 Look, I have two daughters who
have never slept with a man. Let me bring them out
to you, and you can do what you like with them. But
don't do anything to these men, for they have come
under the protection of my roof."

9 "Get out of our way," they replied. And they said,
"This fellow came here as an alien, and now he
wants to play the judge! We'll treat you worse than
them." They kept bringing pressure on Lot and
moved forward to break down the door.

10 But the men inside reached out and pulled Lot
back into the house and shut the door. 11 Then they
struck the men who were at the door of the house,
young and old, with blindness so that they could not
find the door.

12 The two men said to Lot, "Do you have anyone
else here—sons-in-law, sons or daughters, or
anyone else in the city who belongs to you? Get
them out of here, 13 because we are going to
destroy this place. The outcry to the LORD against
its people is so great that he has sent us to destroy
it." (Genesis 19:1-13).

22 "'Do not lie with a man as one lies with a woman;
that is detestable.'" (Leviticus 18:22).

13 "'If a man lies with a man as one lies with a
woman, both of them have done what is detestable.
They must be put to death; their blood will be on
their own heads.'" (Leviticus 20:13).

4 For if God did not spare angels when they sinned,
but sent them to hell, putting them into gloomy
dungeons to be held for judgment; 5 if he did not
spare the ancient world when he brought the flood
on its ungodly people, but protected Noah, a
preacher of righteousness, and seven others; 6 if he
condemned the cities of Sodom and Gomorrah by
burning them to ashes, and made them an example
of what is going to happen to the ungodly; 7 and if

he rescued Lot, a righteous man, who was distressed by the filthy lives of lawless men 8 (for that righteous man, living among them day after day, was tormented in his righteous soul by the lawless deeds he saw and heard)... (2 Peter 2:4-8).

18 The wrath of God is being revealed from heaven against all the godlessness and wickedness of men who suppress the truth by their wickedness, *19* since what may be known about God is plain to them, because God has made it plain to them. *20* For since the creation of the world God's invisible qualities—his eternal power and divine nature—have been clearly seen, being understood from what has been made, so that men are without excuse.
21 For although they knew God, they neither glorified him as God nor gave thanks to him, but their thinking became futile and their foolish hearts were darkened. 22 Although they claimed to be wise, they became fools 23 and exchanged the glory of the immortal God for images made to look like mortal man and birds and animals and reptiles.
24 Therefore God gave them over in the sinful desires of their hearts to sexual impurity for the degrading of their bodies with one another. 25 They exchanged the truth of God for a lie, and worshiped and served created things rather than the Creator—who is forever praised. Amen.
26 Because of this, God gave them over to shameful lusts. Even their women exchanged natural relations for unnatural ones. 27 In the same way the men also abandoned natural relations with women and were inflamed with lust for one another. Men committed indecent acts with other men, and received in themselves the due penalty for their perversion.
28 Furthermore, since they did not think it worthwhile to retain the knowledge of God, he gave them over to a depraved mind, to do what ought not to be done. 29 They have become filled with every kind of wickedness, evil, greed and depravity. They are full of envy, murder, strife, deceit and malice. They are gossips, 30 slanderers, God-haters, insolent, arrogant and boastful; they invent ways of doing evil; they disobey their parents; 31 they are

senseless, faithless, heartless, ruthless. 32 Although they know God's righteous decree that those who do such things deserve death, they not only continue to do these very things but also approve of those who practice them. (Romans 1:18-32).

Instead of two or three years to study the homosexual issue, two or three minutes is all one needs to see what God says. We must remember that it is only what God says that counts. What people think does not matter.

Another problem is that we have people who call themselves theologians writing articles or books promoting the homosexual lifestyle. Again, we have a situation where much of the public does not know what Scripture says on the subject. Therefore, they may buy into what the "so called" theologians say. In some cases, I believe the theologians are anti-Christian and look for ways to twist the Scriptures. Peter tells us about people like this.

15 Bear in mind that our Lord's patience means salvation, just as our dear brother Paul also wrote you with the wisdom that God gave him. 16 He writes the same way in all his letters, speaking in them of these matters. His letters contain some things that are hard to understand, which ignorant and unstable people distort, as they do the other Scriptures, to their own destruction.
(2 Peter 3:15-16).

I would remind the reader that disagreeing with the defenders and promoters of homosexuality does not make the Christian a bigot. He does not hate the homosexual, he is to love him. However, he must oppose the homosexual lifestyle because God does.

Bestiality

Bestiality is something about which many people probably have never heard. As it relates to sexual sin, it is a sexual relationship between a human and an animal. We have to think that the vast majority of people would be repulsed at the thought of sex with an animal. However, God has commanded man not to do this. In giving the command, He implies that some people are tempted to do it. One might be inclined to think of bestiality as something that may have existed long ago, but not now. It may have existed to a greater degree long ago, as humans were around animals so much more back then. However, I have read and heard of cases of this in our present day. There have been situations where acts of bestiality were performed as "paid for" entertainment.

God condemns it as sin and like all sin, He will punish it. Under the civil law (which we are no longer under) God called for the punishment of death.

> **19 "Anyone who has sexual relations with an animal must be put to death."** (Exodus 22:19).

> **23 "'Do not have sexual relations with an animal and defile yourself with it. A woman must not present herself to an animal to have sexual relations with it; that is a perversion.'"** (Leviticus 18:23).

> **15 "'If a man has sexual relations with an animal, he must be put to death, and you must kill the animal.**
> **16 "'If a woman approaches an animal to have sexual relations with it, kill both the woman and the animal. They must be put to death; their blood will be on their own heads.'"** (Leviticus 20:15-16).

God tells us bestiality is perverted. One has to wonder if some people would say it is caused by a faulty gene. Would the American Psychological Association put it on a "deviant" list? As the morals in our nation continue to crumble, could bestiality become a factor, become tolerated, and in time become accepted. Admittedly, bestiality is not an issue that most Christians have to face now. However, could it be one with which our children or grandchildren will have to contend? I have heard that acts of bestiality are on the Internet. What lies ahead?

As we looked at adultery, fornication, homosexuality, and bestiality we saw how strongly God condemns sexual sin. It is a very addictive sin that seeks its own gratification outside of the boundary that God has set for man's enjoyment of sex. And what is the boundary that God has set for man's enjoyment of sex? It is marriage between a man and a woman.

> **22 Then the LORD God made a woman from the rib he had taken out of the man, and he brought her to the man.**
> **23 The man said,**
> **"This is now bone of my bones**
> **and flesh of my flesh;**
> **she shall be called 'woman,'**
> **for she was taken out of man."**
> **24 For this reason a man will leave his father and mother and be united to his wife, and they will become one flesh.** (Genesis 2:22-24).

Because sexual sin is so dangerous and destructive to one who professes Christ as Savior Christians should hastily flee from it. We are not to spend time thinking about it, rationalizing over it, or toying with it. God tells us to flee from it.

> **18 Flee from sexual immorality. All other sins a man commits are outside his body, but he who sins sexually sins against his own body. 19 Do you not know that your body is a temple of the Holy Spirit, who is in you, whom you have received from God? You are not your own; 20 you were bought at a price. Therefore honor God with your body.**
> (1 Corinthians 6:18-20).

Creation verses Evolution

One issue that Christians face is growing by leaps and bounds in its influence on Christianity. It is the issue of evolution. Its undesirable influence has been strong over the last fifty years. Before that, a considerable percentage of the population, non-Christian as well as Christians, believed in the Biblical account of a six-day creation. It appears that percentage has declined and continues to decline. Evolution is not only being taught in our schools but in very subtle ways it shows up in TV commercials, magazine ads, newspaper stories, etc. It is not that someone is purposely pushing evolution (though some are), but rather that he believes in it, and that belief is reflected in his work. However, the more saturated society becomes with the Theory of Evolution, the more it seeps into the church. And that is what is happening today. As Christians we should know the importance of believing the Creation Account. As we face the issue of evolution, we must remember that it, too, is one of the "all things" referred to in Romans 8:28.

God in God's Book gives the account of creation to us. Man in man's book gives the account of evolution to us. The former is truth from God; the latter is theory from man. Creation and evolution are in total conflict with each other. Even so, of those non-Christians who accept the Theory of Evolution, most would say they believe there is a God. Even a number of those who profess to know Christ try to rationalize mixing a belief in evolution with Christian beliefs. However, a person who claims to be a Christian but believes in evolution is either admitting that he doesn't believe what the Bible teaches, or he doesn't know what it teaches about creation. In turn he would have to deny or plead ignorance of much Bible Doctrine, as the Creation Account is a bedrock of theology upon which so much doctrine stands. Trying to mix a belief in God's Word with evolution is like trying to have your cake and eat it too – it just will not work. It can't be done. As oil and water don't mix, neither do Christian beliefs and evolution.

This is not the place to go into an in-depth study of creation verses evolution, so we will limit ourselves to the consideration of only a few points.

1. Creation calls for a creator; evolution is purely a matter of chance.

2. From planets in synchronized orbit to the wonderful human eye, to chains of DNA, creation calls for a designer. Evolution calls for a series of accidents and mutations, against odds so enormous, that many knowledgeable people say it could not have occurred.

3. Creation says God existed before His work of creation. Evolution, in its truest form, denies God and says that a lump of matter existed before the universe was formed. Which is easier to believe – that God exists eternally or that matter exists eternally? If God is eternal and matter is not, then God existed before matter. If matter is eternal and God is not, then matter existed before God. If they are both eternal, then it would appear that they are on an equal footing, neither having been created by the other, because they both have always been. I suspect that there are few people who can bring themselves to believe that there is no God. Most in this country will believe in God, but their belief, like the Israelites to which Paul referred is not according to knowledge.

> **2 For I can testify about them that they are zealous for God, but their zeal is not based on knowledge.** (Romans 10:2).

4. Many people are prone to believe that God created everything, but that He did it through the process of evolution. They believe that God exists, but they have been taught evolution from childhood. Whether it is the "Big Bang" or some other theory, they go along with that portion of the scientific and academic world that believes in evolution. It is easy to see how the unbeliever can take this position for there is so much about the Bible that he does not know or believe. But, it is difficult to see how one who professes to know Christ can believe in evolution – even an evolution that supposedly is a work of God. The Bible gives us no basis to accept evolution. Moreover, to the contrary, it clearly teaches a sudden creation.

1 **In the beginning God created the heavens and the earth.** (Genesis 1:1).

6 By the word of the LORD were the heavens made, their starry host by the breath of his mouth. 9 For he spoke, and it came to be; he commanded, and it stood firm. (Psalm 33:6,9).

5 Let them praise the name of the LORD, for he commanded and they were created. (Psalm 148:5).

We see that it was not necessary for God to resort to some long drawn-out process of evolution over a period of millions or billions of years. He just spoke what He wanted, and it was done.

5 ...long ago by God's word the heavens existed ... (2 Peter 3:5).

3 By faith we understand that the universe was formed at God's command, so that what is seen was not made out of what was visible. (Hebrews 11:3).

3 And God said, "Let there be light," and there was light. (Genesis 1:3).

As we look further at the account of creation, we find that one type of fish, bird, or animal did not come from some other kind of animal, but that God created them according to their own kind.

20 And God said, "Let the water teem with living creatures, and let birds fly above the earth across the expanse of the sky." 21 So God created the great creatures of the sea and every living and moving thing with which the water teems, according to their kinds, and every winged bird according to its kind. And God saw that it was good. 24 And God said, "Let the land produce living creatures according to their kinds: livestock, creatures that move along the ground, and wild animals, each according to its kind." And it was so. (Genesis 1:20-21,24). (Emphasis mine)

We see in Genesis 1:21 that God created the great creatures of the sea. When the whale was created, it did not have to evolve from a tiny one-cell organism.

After God created the fish, birds, and animals, He then created man. However, man was created in God's image and was given dominion over the animals.

> **26 Then God said, "Let us make man in our image, in our likeness, and let them rule over the fish of the sea and the birds of the air, over the livestock, over all the earth, and over all the creatures that move along the ground."**
> **27 So God created man in his own image,**
> **in the image of God he created him;**
> **male and female he created them.** (Genesis 1:26-27).

God is spirit. Being created in the image of God does not have anything to do with physical appearance. Commentators have various opinions as to exactly what is included in "God's image", but most agree that it includes moral likeness – the moral dispositions of man's spirit. Man before "The Fall" was without sin and was morally righteous. Some refer to this as original righteousness.

> **29 This only have I found:**
> **God made mankind upright...** (Ecclesiastes 7:29).

The fall of man has greatly affected his ability to exemplify being made in God's image. Nonetheless, though corrupted and distorted, the image is still valid. It has meaning to God and therefore should have meaning to us.

> **5 ... And from each man, too, I will demand an accounting for the life of his fellow man. 6 "Whoever sheds the blood of man, by man shall his blood be shed; for in the image of God has God made man.** (Genesis 9:5-6).

The more one looks at the account of creation, the more preposterous evolution appears. It is so obvious that man is not just a higher animal, one who is different only in degree. No, man is different in kind. Man has a place of real importance in God's creation. He was created to be God's representative on earth – to rule over the earth. It is true that man is not what he was before Adam sinned; however, God is working in his people to renew them in knowledge and in righteousness thus making their image of Him much clearer.

> **10 ...and have put on the new self, which is being renewed in knowledge in the image of its Creator.** (Colossians 3:10).

> **24 ...and to put on the new self, created to be like God in true righteousness and holiness.** (Ephesians 4:24).

5. Scripture indicates that before the fall both man and beast ate plants and fruit.

> **29 Then God said, "I give you every seed-bearing plant on the face of the whole earth and every tree that has fruit with seed in it. They will be yours for food. 30 And to all the beasts of the earth and all the birds of the air and all the creatures that move on the ground—everything that has the breath of life in it—I give every green plant for food." And it was so.** (Genesis 1:29-30).

After the fall all the creatures were given to man as food. There are different opinions as to how long it was after the fall before this took place. Some commentators think man began eating meat without permission before the flood. Others say that animals were sacrificed and their skins used before the flood, but that they were not eaten until after the flood. The first time eating animals is mentioned in the Bible is after the flood. Regardless, God's covenant with Noah makes it clear that eating meat was then permissible.

> **1 Then God blessed Noah and his sons, saying to them, "Be fruitful and increase in number and fill the earth. 2 The fear and dread of you will fall upon all the beasts of the earth and all the birds of the air, upon every creature that moves along the ground, and upon all the fish of the sea; they are given into**

your hands. *3* Everything that lives and moves will
be food for you. Just as I gave you the green plants,
I now give you everything. (Genesis 9:1-3).

The Biblical account of creation in Genesis 1:29-30 shows us that neither man nor beast ate meat before the fall. Before the fall there was no death. Neither man nor animal died. Man did not eat meat, and animals did not eat each other. Death came to man and animal when Adam sinned.

12 **Therefore, just as sin entered the world through**
one man, and death through sin, and in this way
death came to all men, because all sinned...
(Romans 5:12).

Evolution would have millions of animals dying before man finally evolved. A man who evolved through the process of animals living and dying would certainly be expected to die, as they did. Therefore, death would not be as a result of sin (which is what the Bible teaches) but just the natural process of evolution.

6. If the Bible is true, evolution is false. If evolution is true, the Bible is false. It can't be both ways. Evolution has never been proven – it is only a theory (really, a religion). Moreover, there are and have been different theories of evolution over the years. The account of creation, though also unproven, has remained the same over the centuries. The evolutionists have even attempted to build a case for evolution by publishing drawings of their idea of what they imagine prehistoric man looked like. In some cases their idea of what the man looked like was based on nothing more than fragments of a jawbone or a few teeth. There have been cases where an animal's tooth or bone was mistakenly used in doing this, and in a few cases purposefully used. Some of these mistakes and hoaxes have never been removed from school textbooks and are being used today to teach evolution.

The evolutionist would have us believe the first man was nothing more than a grunting, hairless ape. There are no fossil remains showing a transition from ape to man, nor do we see any living examples existing in the world today. One has to ask, if evolution once took place, where is the evidence and why is it not still happening? Why did all the species stop changing into other species?

Let's assume for a moment that evolution happened. Before man evolved, picture an ape. Now this is the ape from which man is going to come. This ape is going to be the ancestor of the first man. Let's say it is going to take fifty generations to come down the line from this ape to the first man. Can you imagine how difficult it would be, if you were there and could see it happening, to determine if the first man was really number fifty or could he be number forty-seven? Supposedly, going down the line from ape number one, ape number five would still be a lot like ape number one. But we would expect ape number forty to be more like the first man than like ape number one. Surely number forty-nine would be so much like the first man that it would be difficult to tell which was the ape and which the man. It appears to me, it would be almost impossible. Assuming that after fifty generations a 100% human is born. This human, whether male or female, is a human baby. We would then have to wonder, did it grow up and mate with a 100% ape or did it mate with a creature that was 50% ape and 50% man or 25% ape and 75% man. It would seem that to have an offspring that was 100% human, it would have to mate with another human or at least an ape that was the next thing to human. However, it also seems it would be too much to expect that two human or almost human babies (one male and one female) would be born about the same time, in the same jungle neighborhood, survive to grow up, and end up mating with each other instead of the numerous part ape, part man creatures.

7. The evolutionist would have us believe that the first man was one grunt away from being an ape. The Bible indicates that the first man was created as a grown man (not a baby), and that he was very intelligent. Before the fall

his intelligence and understanding were not corrupted by sin. God created him intelligent enough to name all the animals. That would be a feat too great for a man one grunt, three grunts, or even thirty grunts past being an ape.

> **19 Now the LORD God had formed out of the ground all the beasts of the field and all the birds of the air. He brought them to the man to see what he would name them; and whatever the man called each living creature, that was its name. 20 So the man gave names to all the livestock, the birds of the air and all the beasts of the field.** (Genesis 2:19-20).

8. The origin of the races has always been a subject of interest to most people. The scientists who believe in evolution have nothing clearer to say on this subject than they do about the rest of evolution. The scientists who believe in creation have a plausible explanation for the races as we know them. I use the expression "races as we know them", because the Bible, and creation scientist speak of only one race, the human race. The Bible tells us all people descended from Adam and Eve. And remember, Eve was made from one of Adam's ribs, so all people come from one bloodline – that of Adam.

> **26 From one man he made every nation of men, that they should inhabit the whole earth; and he determined the times set for them and the exact places where they should live.** (Acts 17:26).

Even among evolutionists the theory that all mankind evolved from one man is becoming popular. Creation scientist point to the account of "The Tower of Babel" in the Bible as the reason for different languages. They also think this is probably the cause of the so-called different races.

> *1* **Now the whole world had one language and a common speech.** *2* **As men moved eastward, they found a plain in Shinar and settled there.**
> **3 They said to each other, "Come, let's make bricks and bake them thoroughly." They used brick instead**

of stone, and tar for mortar. 4 Then they said, "Come, let us build ourselves a city, with a tower that reaches to the heavens, so that we may make a name for ourselves and not be scattered over the face of the whole earth."
5 But the LORD came down to see the city and the tower that the men were building. 6 The LORD said, "If as one people speaking the same language they have begun to do this, then nothing they plan to do will be impossible for them. 7 Come, let us go down and confuse their language so they will not understand each other."
8 So the LORD scattered them from there over all the earth, and they stopped building the city. 9 That is why it was called Babel—because there the LORD confused the language of the whole world. From there the LORD scattered them over the face of the whole earth. (Genesis 11:1-9).

Once man was scattered over the earth, the inbreeding among the smaller groups perpetuated the genetic characteristics found within that group. This accounts for the difference seen in features and skin color of the human species.

9. If one believes in evolution, why not believe in reincarnation too? Evolution is a matter of evolving physically, while reincarnation is a matter of evolving spiritually. However, both are equally far fetched. One theory of evolution would have us to believe that a lump of matter just happened to be in space. It then exploded and expanded to make all the planets. At some point in time, somehow, from somewhere, life appeared. This may have been a one-cell organism, but it appeared out of nowhere and came from nothing. One moment there was no life, and the next moment there was life. This life then grew, divided and changed, continually improving itself until it produced all the species of life we know now exist and those that no longer exist.

One theory of reincarnation would have us believe that man is a soul or spirit-being that is at present inhabiting a human body. It may have inhabited an animal body in its last life, and if it doesn't do good this time around, it may find itself in another animal body the next time. The next body, whether animal or human, would be its mother's womb. How the soul or spirit being is supposed to get from the present body when it dies to the next body is a mystery. How physical evolution produces just the right number of bodies to accommodate the spirit-beings who need these bodies is another mystery.

God's Word will oppose the idea of reincarnation in many ways, one of the most obvious being that man lives only once.

> **27 Just as man is destined to die once, and after that to face judgment...** (Hebrews 9:27).

Of course, reincarnation is not as widely accepted in this country as is evolution. However, it is tragic that whether or not it is evolution, reincarnation, or something else, man will go out of his way to suppress the truth of God and believe a lie.

> *18* **The wrath of God is being revealed from heaven against all the godlessness and wickedness of men who suppress the truth by their wickedness...** (Romans 1:18).

> **25 They exchanged the truth of God for a lie...** (Romans 1:25).

10. In the final analysis, when it comes to the question of which to believe, creation or evolution, we are actually facing the question of whom to believe, God or man. Men of science and academia originate, teach, and promote theories of evolution. But to keep things in the right perspective it should be noted that some in the world of science and academia, both Christians and non-Christians, do believe in creation. Each of us must ask ourselves, do I believe God's Word or man's word? Have we any evidence of God being mistaken in what He says? What about man?

Did not the best minds at one time think the earth was flat? Do not the best minds today on occasion find that what they once thought was correct is really wrong? This is not to put science down or to put down the people who have contributed so much to our welfare. Those in the scientific world have done great things that benefit us all, but they are still men with finite minds. God is God, the sovereign ruler of the universe, the source of all truth and wisdom. He has given us His account of creation in the Bible. In view of what we have in the Bible concerning creation, does one professing Christ dare say he is a Christian but believes in evolution? Dare we tell God that we had rather believe that things are the way we think they are than the way He says they are? Knowledge and experiences that coincide with Scripture are true. Those that neither coincide with nor contradict Scripture may or may not be true. Those that contradict Scripture are definitely false.

If you give thought to evolution and creation, you will see that these are in conflict. They are on a collision course. Ultimately, one must either bow to the thinking of man or the Word of God. To which do you bow?

Self-Image

As the Bible is truth, I believe that all Christians could agree that our true self-image is to be based on what the Bible says about us. Contrary to anything we think, the way the Bible describes us is the way God our Creator sees us and knows us to be. Therefore, it is the way we actually are. Consequently, without knowledge of what God says, we are not in a position to have a correct self-image. Sadly, most people do not know what God says. They have done little reading of the Bible and even less study of it. The result is that most people, both Christians and non-Christians, base their self-image on the world's system, and the world's system is one of pride. It is the pride one has in what they have achieved or what they have become: the pride one takes in having pulled themselves up by their own boot straps and the greater the adversity they faced in doing this the more pride they take in the accomplishment. The world's system holds in high esteem those who have achieved fame, fortune, and powerful positions.

The world encourages pride that leads to boasting and arrogance. We see these arrogant attitudes and proud boasting in all walks of life and in all fields of endeavor. Having pride in yourself and your achievements is not only the accepted thing, but is the desired thing. In fact, some people say that self-esteem is so important that a lack of it is one of the reasons we have kids killing kids today. Be something or do something that makes you proud. That is the world's system. But what does God think of pride? His Word makes it clear that He not only does not like man's pride but He hates it.

> **13 ...I hate pride and arrogance,**
> **evil behavior and perverse speech.** (Proverbs 8:13).

God also tells us that pride is a destructive thing, and it causes man to fall.

> **16 But after Uzziah became powerful, his pride led to**
> **his downfall...** (2 Chronicles 26:16).

> **18 Pride goes before destruction,**
> **a haughty spirit before a fall.** (Proverbs 16:18).

God opposes the proud.

> **5 Young men, in the same way be submissive to**
> **those who are older. All of you, clothe yourselves**
> **with humility toward one another, because, "God**
> **opposes the proud but gives grace to the humble." 6**
> **Humble yourselves, therefore, under God's mighty**
> **hand, that he may lift you up in due time.**
> (1 Peter 5:5-6).

We find that love is not proud.

> **4 Love is patient, love is kind. It does not envy, it**
> **does not boast, it is not proud.** (1 Corinthians 13:4).

God commands us not to be proud.

16 Live in harmony with one another. Do not be proud, but be willing to associate with people of low position. Do not be conceited. (Romans 12:16).

We find that the world's system of having pride in order to have a good self-image is in direct and strong opposition to God's Word. The world's system also recognizes and rewards those who devote their lives to humanitarian concerns. Many humanitarians, whether they become well known or not, take pride in being the good person they have become. They see their self-sacrifice and good they do as a real achievement. It becomes their driving force in life, constantly feeding their pride. Humanitarian work done at the leading of the Holy Spirit and for God's glory should be the desire of Christians. Then we see right work being done for the right reason. Humanitarian work done to win the approval of the world may be right work, but it is for the wrong reason. It is sin.

23 ...and everything that does not come from faith is sin. (Romans 14:23).

Others seeking self-esteem take pride and base their self-image on being a good parent and molding their children into good citizens. Some derive their self-image from the one they marry. They take pride in marrying someone who is either very attractive, rich, famous, or powerful.

The world stresses our need to have self-esteem, a good self-image. We are told that we need to have such a good self-image that we actually love ourselves. In fact, we are told that unless we love ourselves we cannot love others. Many who are truly born again have bought into that idea, but they are in error. The Bible does not teach that we need to love ourselves; it teaches that we need to love God. The Bible assumes we love ourselves when it tells us to love our neighbor as our self (Mark 12:31). The idea in this command is that we should do by our neighbor as we would have our neighbor do by us. We seek our own welfare, and we should have concern for our neighbor's welfare.

> *4* **Each of you should look not only to your own interests, but also to the interests of others.** (Philippians 2:4).

Furthermore, as we would not intentionally harm ourselves we should not seek to harm our neighbor.

> *10* **Love does no harm to its neighbor. Therefore love is the fulfillment of the law.** (Romans 13:10).

Rather than loving ourselves as the world tells us to do, we need to deny ourselves as Christ tells us to do.

> **24 Then Jesus said to his disciples, "If anyone would come after me, he must deny himself and take up his cross and follow me. "** (Matthew 16:24)

We can only deny ourselves in the power of the Holy Spirit for our sinful human nature is selfish and seeks to have its own way.

> *3* **All of us also lived among them at one time, gratifying the cravings of our sinful nature and following its desires and thoughts.** (Ephesians 2:3).

Controlled by his human nature man's love for himself is condemned by the Bible.

> *1* **But mark this: There will be terrible times in the last days.** *2* <u>**People will be lovers of themselves**</u>**, lovers of money, boastful, proud, abusive, disobedient to their parents, ungrateful, unholy,** *3* **without love, unforgiving, slanderous, without self-control, brutal, not lovers of the good,** *4* **treacherous, rash, conceited, lovers of pleasure rather than lovers of God—** *5* **having a form of godliness but denying its power. Have nothing to do with them.**
> (2 Timothy 3:1-5). (emphasis mine)

Christ tells a parable about a Pharisee and a tax collector in Luke 18:9-14. The world encourages us to have the ego of the Pharisee, but the Bible makes it clear that we should seek to be humble like the tax collector.

9 To some who were confident of their own righteousness and looked down on everybody else, Jesus told this parable: 10 "Two men went up to the temple to pray, one a Pharisee and the other a tax collector. 11 The Pharisee stood up and prayed about himself: 'God, I thank you that I am not like other men—robbers, evildoers, adulterers—or even like this tax collector. 12 I fast twice a week and give a tenth of all I get.'
13 "But the tax collector stood at a distance. He would not even look up to heaven, but beat his breast and said, 'God, have mercy on me, a sinner.'
14 "I tell you that this man, rather than the other, went home justified before God. For everyone who exalts himself will be humbled, and he who humbles himself will be exalted." (Luke 18:9-14).

The self-image seekers are like the Pharisee; they are looking for something of which to be proud. They want to be able to boast and brag. The Bible condemns these types of behavior.

16 As it is, you boast and brag. All such boasting is evil. (James 4:16).

7 For who makes you different from anyone else? What do you have that you did not receive? And if you did receive it, why do you boast as though you did not? (1 Corinthians 4:7).

We should be like the tax collector and rather than seek self-esteem, seek salvation. Where we spend eternity is far more important than even the essentials of food, clothing, and shelter, much less a so-called good self-image.

31 So do not worry, saying, 'What shall we eat?' or 'What shall we drink?' or 'What shall we wear?' 32 For the pagans run after all these things, and your heavenly Father knows that you need them. 33 But seek first his kingdom and his righteousness, and all these things will be given to you as well.
(Matthew 6:31-33).

People who base their hopes and happiness on what they achieve and gain in this world just don't understand: to attain heaven is to win; anything else is to lose. No one in hell will have reason to have a good self-image. We should not be concerned at all with seeking a self-image, but we should be very concerned with seeking the image – the image of Christ. Moreover, when God says we are sinners, objects of wrath deserving hell, how can we claim to have a good self-image? Does that not contradict God? Is it not sinful to tell God He is wrong?

> **1 As for you, you were dead in your transgressions and sins, 2 in which you used to live when you followed the ways of this world and of the ruler of the kingdom of the air, the spirit who is now at work in those who are disobedient. 3 All of us also lived among them at one time, gratifying the cravings of our sinful nature and following its desires and thoughts. Like the rest, we were by nature objects of wrath.** (Ephesians 2:1-3).

A number of people base their self-esteem on how they look to others rather than how they actually are. To them looking the part is as good as living the part. Some pursue face-lifts, suctioning of fat, etc. to look good. They are concerned with looking physically fit rather than being fit. In a similar manner there are Christians who say things and do things in order to appear spiritual, rather than seeking to be spiritual. One wants to present an image of being physically fit, the other an image of being spiritually fit. In both cases it is all a façade.

Self-esteem has always been an important issue with man, but I don't believe it has ever been more important than it is today. One reason for this is that it is being taught to our children and sold to us adults as a cure-all for many problems. If we just have a good self-image, we can overcome most anything. The negative side to this is that, if we cannot find reasons to have a good self-image then we cannot solve our problems or overcome life's obstacles. Consequently people in general, and teen-agers in particular react to the pressure from the world and especially the pressure from their peers by grasping at most anything as a way to find a good self-image. The sad thing about it is that often they base their self-image on very frivolous and ridiculous things. And when these things don't "pan out" as they expect, they are prone to develop a bad self-image and feel that life has dealt unfairly with them. Too often they seek to offset their disappointment and to be comforted by turning to drugs, excessive drinking, illicit sex, overeating, constant pursuit of fun, cult religions, etc. It is bad enough when those who don't know Christ do these things, but when those who profess to be Christians do them, we have to ask the question: why do you do it, are these things of more help to you than God and His Word? Is there more power in these things than in God's indwelling Holy Spirit? The Christian is not to be ruled by any desire but one, and that is the desire to be obedient to God and thereby glorify Him.

> **31 So whether you eat or drink or whatever you do, do it all for the glory of God.** (1 Corinthians 10:31).

> **17 And whatever you do, whether in word or deed, do it all in the name of the Lord Jesus, giving thanks to God the Father through him.** (Colossians 3:17).

> **11 If anyone speaks, he should do it as one speaking the very words of God. If anyone serves, he should do it with the strength God provides, so that in all things God may be praised through Jesus Christ. To him be the glory and the power for ever and ever. Amen.** (1 Peter 4:11).

We see from the above verses that Christians are not to seek gain for themselves but are to seek glory for God. On the other hand, the non-Christian does what he does not for God's glory but his own. He is only concerned with his perceived needs. As Christians we must guard against being more concerned with having our needs met than we are with meeting our responsibilities. God will meet our needs.

19 And my God will meet all your needs according to his glorious riches in Christ Jesus. (Philippians 4:19).

One way we glorify God is by living in total dependency on Him. If the dependency of our feeling good in a given situation is more on the "support group" than God, it is wrong. If we are facing surgery and we are depending more on the surgeon than God, it is wrong. However, knowing that we are totally dependent on God does not relieve us of the responsibility to do and to achieve. In our dependency on God, we are to look to Him to lead us as to what to do and to give us the where-with-all to do it. In God's plan He may enable us to do it, or He may allow us to fail. However, unlike the unbeliever, our failure or success doesn't affect our self-image. We recognize that the outcome is in the hands of our sovereign Lord and that however it turns out, He will make it work for our good.

With God's glory rather than self-image our priority, we should be careful of our concerns. We do not want to be more concerned with the state of our house than the state of our souls. We don't want to have more concern for the work we do on the job than the work we do for God. As Christians, we are concerned about all the evil we see in the world, and rightly so. However, we are not to be more concerned about what we see in the world than what the world sees in us. Christ's cause would be advanced if we Christians would be less concerned about attracting others physically and more concerned about attracting them spiritually. It is easy to see the reigning power of Satan in the kingdom of the world, but should we not be good examples of Christ's reigning power in His Kingdom?

Those who have gone for the idea that you need a good self-image fail to realize how many people have a high opinion of themselves based on morally wrong and sinful achievements. The successful bank robber, the head of a gang, a crooked politician, the madam of a whorehouse, an abortionist, and an adulterous philanderer, etc. may take pride in, and feel good about, what they do and how well they do it.

On the other end of the spectrum are those who base their high opinion of themselves on the fact that they are morally good and are upstanding and successful people. But if it is done without Christ, what good is it?

> **6 And without faith it is impossible to please God...**
> (Hebrews 11:6).

> **23 ...and everything that does not come from faith is sin.** (Romans 14:23).

If it is done through Christ, then how can they take credit for it? They are enabled by God to do it.

> **19 The Sovereign LORD is my strength...**
> (Habakkuk 3:19).

> *13* **I can do everything through him who gives me strength.** (Philippians 4:13).

There are those whose self-image is based on what certain people, to whom they are close, think of them. These may be parents, siblings, spouse, boss, fellow workers, friends, etc. The question we ought to consider is how should we respond to what others think of us? Some might expect us to be or to do something that God condemns. From man there are so many ideas as to what we should be like that it becomes confusing. God has only one idea of what we should be like, His Son – there is no confusion. Our understanding of who we are and what we are is not to be based on the opinion of man but on what God says about us. Other people's opinions are important to us, and we can respect their opinion. However, if to the best of our discernment we are being obedient to God, we should not let man's opinion affect us. The Bible makes it clear that we are not here to please man but to glorify God in our obedience to Him.

Some Christians find it easy enough to ignore or overlook unfavorable opinions of themselves that others hold but find it hard to escape a condemning opinion they hold about themselves. They spend a great amount of time looking back at their "old man" instead of concentrating on the "new man". They dwell on past sins and failures in such a manner, and to such a degree, that it becomes a hindrance to their spiritual health and growth. Christians need to see themselves not as what they once were but as what they are now. They should do as Paul did and not look at what lies behind but at what lies ahead. They need not only to keep the reality of heaven in mind but also to keep the surety of going to heaven in mind.

> *12* **Not that I have already obtained all this, or have already been made perfect, but I press on to take hold of that for which Christ Jesus took hold of me. *13* Brothers, I do not consider myself yet to have taken hold of it. But one thing I do: Forgetting what is behind and straining toward what is ahead, *14* I press on toward the goal to win the prize for which God has called me heavenward in Christ Jesus.**
> (Philippians 3:12-14).

Christians should learn from past sins and Christians should feel sorrow for past sins, but they are exactly that – they are past. We have repented of them and God, through Christ, has forgiven us for them. Therefore, it is un-Scriptural to dwell on them, worry about them, and continually feel guilty about them. Instead we need to put our energy and effort on trying to not sin from this point on.

> **10 Jesus straightened up and asked her, "Woman, where are they? Has no one condemned you?"**
> **11 "No one, sir," she said.**
> **"Then neither do I condemn you," Jesus declared.**
> **"Go now and leave your life of sin."** (John 8:10-11).

As Christians we are members of the body of Christ, and we have a command from Christ to carry out the Great Commission.

> *18* **Then Jesus came to them and said, "All authority in heaven and on earth has been given to me. *19* Therefore go and make disciples of all nations,**

> baptizing them in the name of the Father and of the
> Son and of the Holy Spirit, *20* and teaching them to
> obey everything I have commanded you. And surely
> I am with you always, to the very end of the age."
> (Matthew 28:18-20).

We have work to do, and we can't spend time feeling guilty about the past. We need to get busy, and in obedience to God and by the grace of God, do the work He has ordained us to do. However, we do not want to forget the pit from which we were pulled. Remembering our sinful and lost condition before we were saved reminds us that it is by God's grace that we are saved. Being aware of what we were and what we did makes us mindful that, except for God's grace, we could again be like we were and again do what we did. Although Paul did not dwell on his past, he was aware of it, and by comparing it with the present he could see what a change God's grace had made in him.

> 9 For I am the least of the apostles and do not even
> deserve to be called an apostle, because I
> persecuted the church of God. 10 But by the grace
> of God I am what I am, and his grace to me was not
> without effect. No, I worked harder than all of them—
> yet not I, but the grace of God that was with me.
> (1 Corinthians 15:9-10).

Paul's life is certainly evidence of God's work and God's power. We also see God's hand at work as the shepherd David faces the giant Goliath. Abraham worshiped idols before God called him. When we look at the achievements of God's people, whether they lived in the past or live in the present, their achievements are due to the work of God in them and through them. That should encourage us to seek the potential we have in Christ – to be whatever He chooses for us to be. What an adventure lies before Christians if they just pursue God's will for their life. We are never to pursue our will. Self-will is a spiritual cancer that must be cured before it kills. Self-will leads to a false self-image, whether or not that image is good or bad. We have mentioned those who base their good self-image on wealth, appearance, position, etc. There is also a false self-image that is a bad image. It has to do with the opposite of those things that bring the good image. If we don't like the way we look, the clothes we have, the house in which we live, etc. we may develop a bad self-image. Too often we also judge others by the clothes they wear, car they drive, house they have, color of their skin, or ethnic background. We do the same with people who are disabled or disfigured. Often when a person is in an accident and is disabled or disfigured, we treat him as though he was a different person because of it. He is the same person as before. The body may be changed but the person inside is the same. The real you is in the body, and that body can be black, white, red, yellow, or brown. It can be tall, short, fat or skinny, healthy or crippled. We are not to judge a person by his body but by the actual person living in that body. If a nice person lived in a run-down house, we would not say the person was no good, just that he lives in a run-down house. If someone lives in a crippled or run-down body, it doesn't mean he is no good. Men are inclined to form their opinions of others based on their outward appearance, but God looks at the heart.

> 7 But the LORD said to Samuel, "Do not consider his appearance or his height, for I have rejected him. The LORD does not look at the things man looks at. Man looks at the outward appearance, but the LORD looks at the heart." (1 Samuel 16:7).

We cannot read other's hearts as God can, but we should make every effort to form our opinions of others based on the inner man rather than the outward appearance.

When we consider ourselves, we should never be resentful toward God or condemning of ourselves for a lack of talent and ability or for an unattractive appearance with which we were born. We should do our best with what God has given us, knowing that He made us the way He did to fit His plan. Our sovereign Lord has decreed our mental ability, physical ability, appearance, length of life, whether or not we can have children, good or bad circumstances of our life, etc.

11 The LORD said to him, "Who gave man his mouth? Who makes him deaf or mute? Who gives him sight or makes him blind? Is it not I, the LORD? (Exodus 4:11).

If we belong to God, do we believe these things are working to our good? Do you know Christ as Savior and Lord? Do you have assurance that you will go to spend eternity with Him? Then what if you aren't popular, successful, married, healthy, etc. down here. This is but a very brief time. If you are being obedient, you have His peace and joy regardless of these other things. Would you rather be who you are, headed to heaven, or the best looking, most talented, highly successful person of all the people who are headed to hell? God's objective is not to make us feel good about ourselves; it is to get us to be good and to do good for His glory. Humanly speaking, we may not like the way we look or our circumstances, but we are to be good and do good in whatever situation we find ourselves. God has determined our gifts, talents, and abilities, and they may be few or plentiful. He has also decreed our successes and failures. He had decreed great success for some and less or no success for others. However, He commands obedience from all. Therefore, Christians knowing that God controls the results should do what they do at the direction and in the power of the Holy Spirit. For the Christian then, success is not in what you accomplish but in how hard you try, how obedient you are. This really takes the pressure off the Christian who understands and believes this truth of Scripture. It is not a "cop out", but it removes the pressure to succeed and achieve according to the world's standard. It also enables those Christians, who God gives much in the way of success, not to look down on others as they realize their successes are from God's hand.

17 You may say to yourself, "My power and the strength of my hands have produced this wealth for me." 18 But remember the LORD your God, for it is he who gives you the ability to produce wealth, and so confirms his covenant, which he swore to your forefathers, as it is today. (Deuteronomy 8:17-18).

7 For who makes you different from anyone else? What do you have that you did not receive? And if you did receive it, why do you boast as though you did not? (1 Corinthians 4:7).

We see God's hand in David defeating Goliath and Abraham becoming wealthy.

45 David said to the Philistine, "You come against me with sword and spear and javelin, but I come against you in the name of the LORD Almighty, the God of the armies of Israel, whom you have defied. 46 This day the LORD will hand you over to me, and I'll strike you down and cut off your head. Today I will give the carcasses of the Philistine army to the birds of the air and the beasts of the earth, and the whole world will know that there is a God in Israel. 47 All those gathered here will know that it is not by sword or spear that the LORD saves; for the battle is the LORD's, and he will give all of you into our hands." (1 Samuel 17:45-47).

34 So he said, "I am Abraham's servant. 35 The LORD has blessed my master abundantly, and he has become wealthy. He has given him sheep and cattle, silver and gold, menservants and maidservants, and camels and donkeys.
(Genesis 24:34-35).

For the Christian who understands and puts into practice what we have discussed, self-image is not a problem. Failure cannot give him a bad self-image nor can success give him a good one. If he is walking in obedience to God, he has nothing to be ashamed of and nothing to brag about for it is the result God has purposed and decreed. We should not be concerned with comparing ourselves with others and feeling either superior or inferior. For we, as well as they, can only do what God has decreed. We are free from the pressure of being the best. However, let us not be complacent and forget that we should always be our best. Being your best is different from being the best. Being your best is, in obedience to and in dependence upon the Holy Spirit, being all that God enables you to be. You can do no more — you should desire to do no less.

As we conclude our discussion on self-image, let us not forget that pride is a great sin, and humility is a virtue. True humility acknowledges that one is a sinner, and in and of one's self can do nothing to please God. However, by the grace of God, one can do good things (sometimes great things) and achieve much to God's glory. As a Christian, it is important to know yourself as God says you are, for that is the true picture. Know that you are a sinner, but you are one whom God has saved, one whom God is keeping saved, one who is to be salt and light in this corrupt and dark world, - one who is to be <u>different</u> and to <u>act differently</u> from those of the world. But never forget that all that is good about you and all the good that you do is God's work and to His glory. Christ makes it clear that without Him we can do nothing that is pleasing to God, but in Him we can bear much fruit for God.

> *4* Remain in me, and I will remain in you. No branch can bear fruit by itself; it must remain in the vine. Neither can you bear fruit unless you remain in me.
> 5 "I am the vine; you are the branches. If a man remains in me and I in him, he will bear much fruit; apart from me you can do nothing. (John 15:4-5).

It is not the truth of knowing that we are nothing and can do nothing without Christ that makes us feel content about who we are. It is the truth of knowing that in Christ we are who He created us to be and we can do whatever He has ordained for us to do in and through His strength.

> *10* For we are God's workmanship, created in Christ Jesus to do good works, which God prepared in advance for us to do. (Ephesians 2:10).

What is your self-image? What is your main goal in life? What are you trying to accomplish? Is it to be obedient to God and to glorify Him? If not, why not? If so, are you striving to achieve your goal? Are you making progress? Being obedient and glorifying God is what Christ did when He walked on earth. Therefore, we should seek to do the same if we would be conformed to His image. As we focus on this and strive by God's grace to achieve it, we will see progress. We will find that we have a good self-image, which is truly not a self-image but our image in Him.

Poverty

For a number of Christians, poverty is a lifelong problem. It is something they must contend with daily. The Health, Wealth, and Prosperity folks would tell you God doesn't want any of His people to be poor. However, Christ says we will always have the poor.

> **11 The poor you will always have with you, but you will not always have me.** (Matthew 26:11).

Christians should always be ready, as God leads and provides, to help those in need and in particular to help fellow Christians.

> *15* **Suppose a brother or sister is without clothes and daily food.** *16* **If one of you says to him, "Go, I wish you well; keep warm and well fed," but does nothing about his physical needs, what good is it?** (James 2:15-16).

> **17 He who is kind to the poor lends to the LORD, and he will reward him for what he has done.** (Proverbs 19:17).

> **9 A generous man will himself be blessed, For he shares his food with the poor.** (Proverbs 22:9).

The Apostle Paul took up a collection for the poor Christians at Jerusalem. He didn't suggest that they needed to plant a seed by making a contribution to his ministry in order to get out of their poverty. Nor did he suggest that all they needed was more faith.

> *25* **Now, however, I am on my way to Jerusalem in the service of the saints there.** *26* **For Macedonia and**

> **Achaia were pleased to make a contribution for the poor among the saints in Jerusalem.**
> (Romans 15:25-26).

The Bible warns us about turning our backs on the poor. However, it also teaches us not to be "easy marks", not to be taken in by the lazy person, the idle person, and those that will not work.

> **13 If a man shuts his ears to the cry of the poor, he too will cry out and not be answered.**
> (Proverbs 21:13).

> **15 Laziness brings on deep sleep, and the shiftless man goes hungry.** (Proverbs 19:15).

> **6 In the name of the Lord Jesus Christ, we command you, brothers, to keep away from every brother who is idle and does not live according to the teaching you received from us. 10 For even when we were with you, we gave you this rule: "If a man will not work, he shall not eat."**
> **11 We hear that some among you are idle. They are not busy; they are busybodies. 12 Such people we command and urge in the Lord Jesus Christ to settle down and earn the bread they eat.**
> (2 Thessalonians 3:6,10-12).

Christians who are in poverty today may not be tomorrow. And some who are not in poverty today may be tomorrow. Others never experience poverty while some live in it all their lives. However, whether our poverty is temporary or continual, God says He will meet all our needs. It is not necessarily our wants, but our needs that He will meet. He alone knows our needs. He alone can meet our needs.

> **19 And my God will meet all your needs according to his glorious riches in Christ Jesus.** (Philippians 4:19).

A Christian who is poor in the material things of this world should take heart and be glad that he is saved. He is a child of the King and has spiritual treasure that greatly exceeds all earthly treasures. He has an inheritance being kept in heaven for him.

**6 Better a poor man whose walk is blameless
than a rich man whose ways are perverse.**
(Proverbs 28:6).

**9 The brother in humble circumstances ought to
take pride in his high position.** (James 1:9).

**5 Listen, my dear brothers: Has not God chosen
those who are poor in the eyes of the world to be
rich in faith and to inherit the kingdom he promised
those who love him?** (James 2:5).

**4 ...and into an inheritance that can never perish,
spoil or fade—kept in heaven for you...** (1 Peter 1:4).

A Christian who is rich in the material things of this world can delight in his blessing, but he must remember that he is called to be a good steward of what God has given him. Furthermore, he is not to feel superior to someone who has less, for God has made both of them and has determined what each will have.

**2 Rich and poor have this in common:
The LORD is the Maker of them all.** (Proverbs 22:2).

**7 For who makes you different from anyone else?
What do you have that you did not receive? And if
you did receive it, why do you boast as though you
did not?** (1 Corinthians 4:7).

God warns us not to love money but to be content with whatever we have because He is always with us.

**5 Keep your lives free from the love of money and be
content with what you have, because God has said,
"Never will I leave you; never will I forsake you."**
(Hebrews 13:5).

The Apostle Paul was one who had learned to be content in any situation. As Christians, we know that God loves us, that He is in control, that He works all things for our good. Whether it is poverty or some other problem we face, should we not strive to learn to be content, as Paul had learned to be?

12 I know what it is to be in need, and I know what it is to have plenty. I have learned the secret of being content in any and every situation, whether well fed or hungry, whether living in plenty or in want. (Philippians 4:12).

Disease and Pain

A very common trial that Christians face is that of disease and pain. A temporary short-term illness is one thing, but a prolonged illness with much pain is another. A long-term illness can be not only physically debilitating but it can drain one spiritually. Therefore, it must be fought tooth and nail by prayer and meditation on God's Word. In fighting that battle, a firm belief in the truth of Romans 8:28 is essential to our spiritual well being. Often, we may take personal suffering easier than we take the suffering of a loved one. Do we acknowledge God's love and sovereignty in our suffering but rebel against God when our loved one suffers? How about when one is born deaf, mute, or blind or becomes that way through an illness or injury? Perhaps one becomes a paraplegic or disfigured. Does this not put a strain on our faith?

With many Christians the tendency is not to rebel against God but to acknowledge that He is a God of love and to think that He has nothing to do with this. It is as though He has no control or power over the problem or situation. Therefore, it has to all be caused by Satan.

Now we readily agree that Satan is involved in much of our suffering and pain as he was in that of Job. However, he could only do to Job that which God allowed, and he can only do to us that which God permits. We must remember that at no time in history has Satan or anyone else ever been able to do something that God did not have complete control over.

8 Then the LORD said to Satan, "Have you considered my servant Job? There is no one on earth like him; he is blameless and upright, a man who fears God and shuns evil."

9 "Does Job fear God for nothing?" Satan replied. 10 "Have you not put a hedge around him and his household and everything he has? You have blessed the work of his hands, so that his flocks and herds are spread throughout the land. 11 But stretch out your hand and strike everything he has, and he will surely curse you to your face."
12 The LORD said to Satan, "Very well, then, everything he has is in your hands, but on the man himself do not lay a finger."
Then Satan went out from the presence of the LORD. (Job 1:8-12).

3 Then the LORD said to Satan, "Have you considered my servant Job? There is no one on earth like him; he is blameless and upright, a man who fears God and shuns evil. And he still maintains his integrity, though you incited me against him to ruin him without any reason."
4 "Skin for skin!" Satan replied. "A man will give all he has for his own life. 5 But stretch out your hand and strike his flesh and bones, and he will surely curse you to your face."
6 The LORD said to Satan, "Very well, then, he is in your hands; but you must spare his life." (Job 2:3-6).

God either causes something to happen or allows it to happen when He could prevent it. In either case, it happened because God decreed it would.

11 The LORD said to him, "Who gave man his mouth? Who makes him deaf or mute? Who gives him sight or makes him blind? Is it not I, the LORD? (Exodus 4:11).

1 As he went along, he saw a man blind from birth. 2 His disciples asked him, "Rabbi, who sinned, this man or his parents, that he was born blind?"
3 "Neither this man nor his parents sinned," said Jesus, "but this happened so that the work of God might be displayed in his life." (John 9:1-3).

When we are confronted with disease and pain, we need to look to God for strength, and believe His guarantee of Romans 8:28. Then we should be able to do as Job did.

7 So Satan went out from the presence of the LORD
and afflicted Job with painful sores from the soles of
his feet to the top of his head. 8 Then Job took a
piece of broken pottery and scraped himself with it
as he sat among the ashes.
9 His wife said to him, "Are you still holding on to
your integrity? Curse God and die!"
10 He replied, "You are talking like a foolish woman.
Shall we accept good from God, and not trouble?"
In all this, Job did not sin in what he said.
(Job 2:7-10).

Death

Death is an issue that all mankind must face sooner or
later. Some people make light of death because of their fear
of it. However, it is not just the act of dying itself that causes
man concern, but there is the uncertainty of when and how.
Of course, for the unbeliever there is also the disturbing
question of what, if anything, happens after death. For the
Christian the afterlife is a settled issue.

People think of death more often than most of us realize.
When we are young we have thoughts of death, but with age
the prospect of death gets even more attention. However,
death is not something that just happens. It too is part of
God's plan.

6 "The LORD brings death and makes alive;
he brings down to the grave and raises up.
(1 Samuel 2:6).

We see that in the early Old Testament days man lived a
long time in spite of the fact that he did not have the
medicine and medical skills that are available to us today.
However, in that day as in our day, each man lived the
length of time that God has decreed – no more and no less.

5 Man's days are determined;
you have decreed the number of his months
and have set limits he cannot exceed. (Job 14:5).

The writer of Psalm 39 knew that God ordained his time on earth, and he asked God to tell him how much time he had. It may be that he was inquiring about how long it would be before he was released from his troubles through death. He was aware of the brevity of life.

> 4 "Show me, O LORD, my life's end
> and the number of my days;
> let me know how fleeting is my life. (Psalm 39:4).

Under the heavy burden of severe trials and suffering, Christians sometimes ask God to take them in death. The question of whether or not this is right or wrong could be raised. Arguments both pro and con could be made depending on individual circumstances. However, it seems that any correct answer would have to be based on the Christian's attitude of, "Yet not as I will, but as you will" (Matthew 26:39). A correct understanding of, and belief in Romans 8:28 is a tremendous help toward having that attitude in times of trial. Whether right or wrong, we find in the Bible where some godly men asked God to take them in death. Moses did under the burden of leading the Israelites.

> 14 I cannot carry all these people by myself; the burden is too heavy for me. 15 If this is how you are going to treat me, put me to death right now—if I have found favor in your eyes—and do not let me face my own ruin." (Numbers 11:14-15).

Elijah did as he fled from Jezebel.

> 3 Elijah was afraid and ran for his life. When he came to Beersheba in Judah, he left his servant there, 4 while he himself went a day's journey into the desert. He came to a broom tree, sat down under it and prayed that he might die. "I have had enough, LORD," he said. "Take my life; I am no better than my ancestors." (1 Kings 19:3-4).

Job did under the weight of his suffering.

> 8 "Oh, that I might have my request,
> that God would grant what I hope for,
> 9 that God would be willing to crush me,
> to let loose his hand and cut me off!" (Job 6:8-9).

This shows not only the frailty of human nature but also the lack of fear of death that the sure hope of heaven gives the believer. The unbeliever lacks this sure hope and therefore fears death, and with good reason. It is at death that the unbeliever's troubles really begin. It is at death the believer's troubles come to an end. The curse of sin in the believer's life is brought to an end as he is released totally from sin. Death has been swallowed up in victory.

> **54 When the perishable has been clothed with the imperishable, and the mortal with immortality, then the saying that is written will come true: "Death has been swallowed up in victory."** (1 Corinthians 15:54).

For the Christian death is the door between earth and heaven. Go through it and you are in heaven. When an unbeliever steps through the door of death, he takes with him all the sins he has accumulated in his lifetime. On the other side he will have to pay for those sins, and it would seem that he will continue to commit sins as he reacts to God's judgment and punishment. Revelation 22:11 indicates that if one continues in this life without repentance and faith in Christ, his character is set, and he will grow more wicked with time in hell. He will have no opportunity in hell to repent, but even if he did, there is no reason to believe that controlled by his sinful nature he would want to repent. Certainly we know nothing of the devil and the other fallen angels wanting to repent. They continue to sin.

Even though Christians go to an infinitely better place at death, we are often reluctant to leave our loved ones when our time comes. The fact that we will no longer be here to help them or to enjoy them can be troubling to us. Also there is sadness and sorrow when one of our loved ones dies. If they belong to the Lord, we know they are better off, but we still experience the trial of grieving. Our grief is greater if they don't know Christ. Nonetheless, from what we have seen, for those of us who know Christ, death works for our good. It has no hold on us, and it holds no terror for us. Christ has destroyed death, conquered death, and in Him we have conquered death. We can say with Paul that to die is gain. However, does the life we now live qualify us to say with Paul that to live is Christ? If we go on living in our bodies, can we say with Paul that it will mean fruitful labor? If not, why not?

> **21 For to me, to live is Christ and to die is gain. 22 If I am to go on living in the body, this will mean fruitful labor for me.**
> (Philippians 1:21-22).

Abortion

The issue of legalized abortion is something that Christians have been faced with for so long that many of today's young adults do not remember when abortion was not legal. To them it is simply "the way of life in America". They view it much like they view "sleeping around". In fact abortion lessens one potential problem of "sleeping around" because people can abort an unwanted child. Sometimes the process of "sleeping around", becoming pregnant, and having an abortion is repeated several times by the same couple.

Why is it that some people condone abortion, some oppose it, and some are neutral toward it? In my opinion most of those who condone abortion are not believers. They do not know God, do not understand His Word, and are concerned only with pleasing themselves. Most of those that are neutral are also not believers. They are very proud of their tolerance and their "hands off" approach toward the issue of abortion. Most true believers will oppose abortion, but there are also many who oppose abortion who are not true believers. However, they do oppose it on moral grounds that spring from the Bible. On the other hand there are some true Christians that condone abortion and some that even have had one. Although it is no excuse, I believe most of them are ignorant of what God's Word says. I assume others are in a back-slidden condition at the time and have not really considered the high cost of disobedience to God. King David paid a price for his sin, and they may find that they will too (2 Samuel Chapters 11 and 12).

Let us look at abortion from a Christian perspective to see what our position should be. We should not oppose abortion only on moral grounds, but rather because God opposes it. It is sin in God's eyes, and it should be sin in our eyes. God sees it as murder, and we should see it as murder.

People who believe in legalized abortion somehow seem to think that if it is legal then it is all right. They do not seem to realize that much of what is legal finds opposition from various groups. However, in the end we are not concerned with what man declares to be legal, but rather what God declares to be right.

To get a better understanding of this whole issue, let us see if we can find some ground on which most pro-choice and pro-life people agree. I believe that would be this: When one has an abortion something is killed. The question remaining is, what is killed? Some people say it is a fetus, some a glob, some a baby, some a person (a baby is a person); however, no one would say that abortion does not kill something or someone. They all recognize that the "something or someone" continues to grow if it does not die, therefore giving evidence that it is alive. Abortion kills it and it stops growing. Let us see if Scripture sheds any light on what that something or someone is

In the first place, God is the giver of life.

> **5 This is what God the LORD says—**
> **he who created the heavens and stretched them out,**
> **who spread out the earth and all that comes out of it,**
> **who gives breath to its people,**
> **and life to those who walk on it...** (Isaiah 42:5).

God gives the spirit or soul of man.

> **7 and the dust returns to the ground it came from,**
> **and the spirit returns to God who gave it.**
> (Ecclesiastes 12:7).

> This is the word of the LORD concerning Israel. The LORD, who stretches out the heavens, who lays the foundation of the earth, and who forms the spirit of man within him, declares... (Zechariah 12:1).

It would seem that the spirit or soul of man is given from conception because God speaks of those in the womb as children, babies, or persons.

> *18* This is how the birth of Jesus Christ came about: His mother Mary was pledged to be married to Joseph, but before they came together, she was found to be with child through the Holy Spirit. (Matthew 1:18).

> *4* The word of the LORD came to me, saying,
> 5 "Before I formed you in the womb I knew you,
> before you were born I set you apart;
> I appointed you as a prophet to the nations."
> (Jeremiah 1:4-5).

> 13 For you created my inmost being;
> you knit me together in my mother's womb.
> 16 your eyes saw my unformed body.
> All the days ordained for me
> were written in your book
> before one of them came to be. (Psalm 139:13,16).

> 5 As you do not know the path of the wind,
> or how the body is formed in a mother's womb,
> so you cannot understand the work of God,
> the Maker of all things. (Ecclesiastes 11:5).

> *39* At that time Mary got ready and hurried to a town in the hill country of Judea, *40* where she entered Zechariah's home and greeted Elizabeth. *41* When Elizabeth heard Mary's greeting, the baby leaped in her womb, and Elizabeth was filled with the Holy Spirit. *42* In a loud voice she exclaimed: "Blessed are you among women, and blessed is the child you will bear! *43* But why am I so favored, that the mother of my Lord should come to me? *44* As soon as the sound of your greeting reached my ears, the baby in my womb leaped for joy. (Luke 1:39-44).

> **3 The angel of the LORD appeared to her and said, "You are sterile and childless, but you are going to conceive and have a son. 5 because you will conceive and give birth to a son. No razor may be used on his head, because the boy is to be a Nazirite, set apart to God from birth, and he will begin the deliverance of Israel from the hands of the Philistines."** (Judges 13:3,5).

That living thing in a woman's womb is a living human being regardless of whether you call it a fetus, baby, or person. When you abort it, you have killed a human being.

> **22 "If men who are fighting hit a pregnant woman and she gives birth prematurely but there is no serious injury, the offender must be fined whatever the woman's husband demands and the court allows. 23 But if there is serious injury, you are to take life for life, 24 eye for eye, tooth for tooth, hand for hand, foot for foot, 25 burn for burn, wound for wound, bruise for bruise.** (Exodus 21:22-25).

The unjustified killing of a human being is murder and is condemned by God.

> **13 "You shall not murder.** (Exodus 20:13).

God creates us. The unborn are God's creatures, and we have no right to kill them. Children are a gift from God and aborting them is refusing to receive God's gift.

> **5 Then Esau looked up and saw the women and children. "Who are these with you?" he asked. Jacob answered, "They are the children God has graciously given your servant."** (Genesis 33:5).

> **3 Sons are a heritage from the LORD, children a reward from him.** (Psalm 127:3).

Those who are pro-choice should realize that they make their choice when they decide to have sex – not after they have gotten pregnant. Once pregnant, right-minded people do not have a choice. To them legalized abortion is still legalized murder. It is a "cop out" on the part of our "feel good" society. People talk pro-choice, but we really do not have the right to choose to do anything that God does not want us to do. Furthermore, we are held responsible to do everything that God tells us to do. In other words, we are not to choose what we want to do, but rather to seek what God would have us do. So often you hear those who favor abortion say that "abortion should be a choice of the woman, her doctor and her god." One has to wonder who is her god? Certainly the God of the Bible is not helping anyone choose to have an abortion. Chances are good that the devil is playing a role in the decision in the same way he did when Cain killed Abel.

> **12 Do not be like Cain, who belonged to the evil one and murdered his brother.** (1 John 3:12).

Also, the odds are great that the abortionist is a child of the devil and probably the woman too. According to the Bible, all who are not children of God have the devil for a father.

> **42 Jesus said to them, "If God were your Father, you would love me, for I came from God and now am here. I have not come on my own; but he sent me. 43 Why is my language not clear to you? Because you are unable to hear what I say. 44 You belong to your father, the devil, and you want to carry out your father's desire. He was a murderer from the beginning, not holding to the truth, for there is no truth in him. When he lies, he speaks his native language, for he is a liar and the father of lies. 45 Yet because I tell the truth, you do not believe me! 46 Can any of you prove me guilty of sin? If I am telling the truth, why don't you believe me? 47 He who belongs to God hears what God says. The reason you do not hear is that you do not belong to God."** (John 8:42-47).

At this point in our discussion let me ask a question. If you are coming from a pro-choice position do you still hold to it? In considering what you have read up to this point, why do you think that is the case? Please look again at the above passage of Scripture. Do you ever say the "Lord's Prayer" calling God your father? Jesus said, "If God were your Father, you would love me." Do you love Jesus? How do you show your love for Jesus? Jesus tells us that we show our love for Him by obeying Him. Being obedient does not save us, but if we are saved we will strive to obey.

> *15* **"If you love me, you will obey what I command."**
> (John 14:15).

Are you obeying the commands Christ has given us? Do you know what the commands are? Or are you even concerned with finding out? Jesus says, "If anyone loves me, he will obey my teaching." Do you know what Jesus taught? Do you obey it? If you do not, Jesus tells us you do not love Him. Moreover, if you do not love Him, then you do not belong to Him, you are not a child of God.

> **23 Jesus replied, "If anyone loves me, he will obey my teaching. My Father will love him, and we will come to him and make our home with him. 24 He who does not love me will not obey my teaching. These words you hear are not my own; they belong to the Father who sent me.** (John 14:23-24).

If you would like to be a child of God and have God save you, you can. If your heart longs for God and in all sincerity you want to repent (turn) from your sinful way to God's way, then you can right now ask Christ to forgive your sins and to come into your heart and make you the person He wants you to be. In doing so you are asking Christ to save you, and you are trusting Him to do it. You can do nothing to help save yourself; it is all of Christ. You trust Christ and Christ alone for salvation.

Getting back to the issue of abortion, we need to consider another thing that the abortionists do not talk about. That is that an abortion, at any stage of pregnancy, is not just killing a human being, but it is doing it in a violent and painful manner. Sometimes the baby is burned in a saline solution, or dissected by a sharp instrument, or sucked apart by a strong suction machine, or its brains are sucked out just before it is born. It is truly amazing that some women, who otherwise are seemingly genteel and nice, could do this to an unborn child – their own child.

One has to wonder how the doctors and nurses can continue to do these procedures day after day. I have heard that in one procedure they have to reassemble the body parts after the abortion to be sure they have removed them all.

The reasons given for why people should be able to have an abortion can vary. Rape and incest are two that are talked about the most, but actually very few of the number of abortions done each year are for either reason. Sometimes it is because the baby is known to have a deformity, and the mother or parents will say they do not want to bring a deformed child into the world. When they do that, they are "playing God". God says He has a purpose for all of His creation, and in His sovereignty He has determined that some would be deformed.

> **11 The LORD said to him, "Who gave man his mouth? Who makes him deaf or mute? Who gives him sight or makes him blind? Is it not I, the LORD?** (Exodus 4:11).

God also corrects some deformities by miracles or through medicine.

> **1 As he went along, he saw a man blind from birth. 2 His disciples asked him, "Rabbi, who sinned, this man or his parents, that he was born blind?"**
> **3 "Neither this man nor his parents sinned," said Jesus, "but this happened so that the work of God might be displayed in his life. 4 As long as it is day, we must do the work of him who sent me. Night is coming, when no one can work. 5 While I am in the world, I am the light of the world."**
> **6 Having said this, he spit on the ground, made some mud with the saliva, and put it on the man's eyes. 7 "Go," he told him, "wash in the Pool of Siloam" (this word means Sent). So the man went and washed, and came home seeing.** (John 9:1-7).

How do you tell the God who made a deformed child that you thought it best to kill it?

> **9 "Woe to him who quarrels with his Maker,**
> **to him who is but a potsherd among the potsherds**
> **on the ground.**
> **Does the clay say to the potter,**
> **'What are you making?'**
> **Does your work say,**
> **'He has no hands'?**
> **10 Woe to him who says to his father,**
> **'What have you begotten?'**
> **or to his mother,**
> **'What have you brought to birth?'**
> **11 "This is what the LORD says—**
> **the Holy One of Israel, and its Maker:**
> **Concerning things to come,**
> **do you question me about my children,**
> **or give me orders about the work of my hands?**
> (Isaiah 45:9-11).

Regardless of the reasons given for having an abortion, the people who keep up with statistics tell us that most abortions are done as a matter of convenience. In some of these cases it is not necessarily the choice of the woman to have an abortion, but she consents at the urging or insistence of the baby's father or her parents.

Often the pro-choice people like to tell everyone that it is the mother's body and she has a right to do with her body as she pleases. But, that is not the case. The baby is not part of the mother's body – it is another body within the mother's body. It was not a missing part of the mother's body before conception and it is not a lost part once it is born, grows up, and goes off to college. It was just another body, so completely separate from the mother's body, that it sometimes has a different blood type from the mother.

A baffling thing about some people is that they will travel and go to great lengths to demonstrate against the death penalty. They will work hard to keep a condemned murderer from being executed and then turn around and support the killing of millions of unborn children. People will talk and fight against child abuse and then go murder their own baby. Politicians talk about government doing something for the children in this country and then go promote and support the murder of children through legalized abortion. Our society sends troops to foreign lands to prevent people, especially children, from being slaughtered and then condones laws that encourage and help people to slaughter our own unborn children.

I read where there were approximately 4,000 abortions a day in America in the mid 1980s. I would assume it is still around that number today. I also read that from 1973 through 1999 we have killed by abortion at least 20 times more babies than we lost soldiers in all the wars in which we have fought, starting with the Revolutionary War.

Where do we go from here as a country and as a society: I believe we are moving toward infanticide and euthanasia. Anyone that does not have his head in the sand can see that this is happening. I would not be surprised, if things continue on the present path, to see it become legal for a mother or a couple to "try out a baby." In other words, have a baby and see for a period of one year if they like being parents. If they do, then continue. If they do not, then infanticide would be legal up to one year old, and the baby could then be killed. Sounds far fetched, even crazy, but so did legalized abortion fifty years ago. This nation has turned its back on God and in doing so; society is becoming more pagan each passing year. God will hold us accountable, and there will be a price to pay for our disobedience.

> **7 Do not be deceived: God cannot be mocked. A man reaps what he sows.** (Galatians 6:7).

> **8 He who sows wickedness reaps trouble...** (Proverbs 22:8).

How should true Christians behave in facing this issue of abortion? First, we need to remember that, as horrible a thing as abortion is, God has promised to make it work together with all other things to our good. What is that good?

It is to make us more like His Son Christ. Knowing that, let each of us then seek what God would have us to do, if anything, about the abortion issue. Abortion is not the only evil that is taking place, and God may have something else for us to do. However, there are two passages of Scripture to which I believe we should definitely give thought as we consider abortion.

> 8 "Speak up for those who cannot speak for themselves,
> for the rights of all who are destitute.
> 9 Speak up and judge fairly;
> defend the rights of the poor and needy."
> (Proverbs 31:8-9).

> 11 Rescue those being led away to death;
> hold back those staggering toward slaughter.
> 12 If you say, "But we knew nothing about this,"
> does not he who weighs the heart perceive it?
> Does not he who guards your life know it?
> Will he not repay each person according to what he has done? (Proverbs 24:11-12).

Let Christians abide by the law and do what they can in a non-violent and legal manner. Let no one say that I have encouraged or provoked him or her to commit a crime. True Christians do not advocate violence and killing to stop abortion. That is a form of terrorism and killing an abortionist is just as much murder in God's eyes as is the killing of babies. Let those who choose to demonstrate do so in a peaceful and godly manner. Regardless of how much or how little we feel led of God to fight actively against abortion, we all can speak out and speak up when the subject arises. We can write letters or articles putting abortion in a true light. Above all, we can do that which is probably the hardest and most neglected, pray. If we want to see a change in people's attitude toward abortion, then let us pray to our God who can change them.

> 1 The king's heart is in the hand of the LORD;
> he directs it like a watercourse wherever he pleases.
> (Proverbs 21:1).

In closing our discussion on abortion, let us read a proclamation by one of our past presidents.

Proclamation 5761 of January 14, 1988

A PROCLAMATION

America has given a great gift to the world, a gift that drew upon the accumulated wisdom derived from centuries of experiments in self-government, a gift that has irrevocably changed humanity's future. Our gift is twofold: the declaration, as a cardinal principle of all just law, of the God-given, unalienable rights possessed by every human being; and the example of our determination to secure those rights and to defend them against every challenge through the generations. Our declaration and defense of our rights have made us and kept us free and have sent a tide of hope and inspiration around the globe.

One of those unalienable rights, as the Declaration of Independence affirms so eloquently, is the right to life. In the 15 years since the Supreme Court's decision in Roe v. Wade, however, America's unborn have been denied their right to life. Among the tragic and unspeakable results in the past decade and a half have been the loss of life of 22 million infants before birth; the pressure and anguish of countless women and girls who are driven to abortion; and a cheapening of our respect for the human person and the sanctity of human life.

We are told that we may not interfere with abortion. We are told that we may not "impose our morality" on those who wish to allow or participate in the taking of the life of infants before birth; yet no one calls it "imposing morality" to prohibit the taking of life after people are born. We are told as well that there exists a "right" to end the lives of unborn children; yet no one can explain how such a right can exist in stark contradiction of each person's fundamental right to life.

That right to life belongs equally to babies in the womb, babies born handicapped, and the elderly or infirm. That we have killed the unborn for 15 years does not nullify this right, nor could any number of killings ever do so. The unalienable right to life is found not only in the Declaration of Independence but also in the Constitution that every President is sworn to preserve, protect, and defend. Both the Fifth and Fourteenth Amendments guarantee that no person shall be deprived of life without due process of law.

All medical and scientific evidence increasingly affirms that children before birth share all the basic attributes of human personality – that they in fact are persons. Modern medicine treats unborn children as patients. Yet, as the Supreme Court itself has noted, the decision in Roe v. Wade rested upon an earlier state of medical technology. The law of the land in 1988 should recognize all of the medical evidence.

Our Nation cannot continue down the path of abortion, so radically at odds with our history, our heritage, and our concepts of justice. This sacred legacy, and the well-being and the future of our country, demand that protection of the innocents must be guaranteed and that the personhood of the unborn be declared and defended throughout our land. In legislation introduced at my request in the First Session of the 100th Congress, I have asked the Legislative branch to declare the "humanity of the unborn child and the compelling interest of the several states to protect the life of each person before birth." This duty to declare on so fundamental a matter falls to the Executive as well. By this Proclamation I hereby do so.

NOW, THEREFORE, I, RONALD REAGAN, President of the United States of America, by virtue of the authority vested in me by the Constitution and laws of the United States, do hereby proclaim and declare the unalienable personhood of every American, from the moment of conception until natural death, and I do proclaim, ordain, and declare that I will take care that the Constitution and laws of the United States are faithfully executed for the protection of America's unborn children. Upon this act, sincerely believed to be an act of justice, warranted by the Constitution, I invoke the considerate judgment of mankind and the gracious favor of Almighty God. I also proclaim Sunday, January 17, 1988, as National Sanctity of Human Life Day. I call upon the citizens of this blessed land to gather on that day in their homes and places of worship to give thanks for the gift of life they enjoy and to reaffirm their commitment to the dignity of every human being and the sanctity of every human life.

IN WITNESS WHEREOF, I have hereunto set my hand this 14th day of January, in the year of our Lord nineteen hundred and eighty-eight, and of the Independence of the United States of America the two hundred and twelfth.

Signed,
Ronald Reagan

Crime and Corruption

Crime and corruption are issues that are growing in proportion around the world. They have always been bad in some foreign countries, but they are now bad in America. The biggest deterrent to crime and all immoral behavior is God. Yet society goes to great lengths to teach our youth that God either does not exist or that He is not an important factor. The more society succeeds in doing this, the greater our problems become.

There are those who think you can educate people to do right. They think everyone would live right and do right if they were told how to and were given the opportunity to do so. They remove God from people's lives and the moral dam breaks. They fail to understand that man is a creation of the Sovereign God; therefore, as a creature created by God, he is subject to the law of God. This was the case before the "Fall" and it is the case after the Fall. (Genesis 2:15-17, Deuteronomy 5:6-21).

God's law forbids much that man's law allows. Man's law prevents crime because of fear of the law. God's law prevents it because of fear of God.

20 Moses said to the people, "Do not be afraid. God has come to test you, so that the fear of God will be with you to keep you from sinning." (Exodus 20:20).

Man can consider God – animals cannot. A pet dog will react to its master's training. It will fear punishment when it knows it did wrong and will act guilty. People aware of God's laws and fearing His punishment feel guilty when they do wrong. For many people the fear of God is a greater deterrent to doing wrong than the fear of the government. Unfortunately, we continue to do away with this deterrent in society. The result is increased crime and corruption.

One thing that is common to both crime and corruption is lying. Lying, directly or indirectly, is involved in most crime and corruption. Many people do not realize the degree to which lying is a hindrance to law enforcement bringing people to justice. There are legal penalties for lying under certain conditions but regardless; lying appears to be a growing problem for law enforcement.

Being hindered in bringing a criminal to justice can actually lead to an increase in crime. For example, a man robs a bank and gets away. The police suspect a person and go to his home where he lives with his mother and brothers and sisters. The police question his family, a couple of the man's good friends, and the next-door neighbors. All of these have information that would allow the police to arrest this suspect but they all lie and claim not to know anything. As a result, an investigation that might have taken one or two weeks to conduct now takes sixteen months. In the meantime the bank robber has committed three more robberies, shooting someone during one of them.

As the moral fiber of our society continues its downhill run, lying seems to be increasingly accepted by society in the same manner as is obscene language. Just as God's Word speaks against obscene language (Colossians 3:8), it also speaks against lying. It appears to indicate that lying originated with Satan, calling him "the father of lies".

44 ...for he is a liar and the father of lies. (John 8:44).

Liars are one group of people among several groups that the Bible says will go to hell.

> 8 But the cowardly, the unbelieving, the vile, the murderers, the sexually immoral, those who practice magic arts, the idolaters and all liars—their place will be in the fiery lake of burning sulfur. This is the second death." (Revelation 21:8).

Crime and corruption are not a matter of poor self-image or what happened to us as children or our economic status. All of these things may contribute to criminal attitudes – but the root cause is man's sinful nature. A number of Kings and other high officials from the pages of Scripture are examples of this, (1 Kings and 2 Kings). For more recent examples all one has to do is read the daily newspaper.

Communist countries remove God from their society and put in brutal enforcement of law. We remove God from our society and put in liberal laws. How can we expect anything less than we are getting?

> 11 When the sentence for a crime is not quickly carried out, the hearts of the people are filled with schemes to do wrong. (Ecclesiastes 8:11).

The loss of material things due to crime and corruption is a fear that many people have. Sixty years ago many people seldom locked their doors, even at night. Now we see signs all over that tell us a house is protected by a security system or a neighborhood watch program. People today not only fear the loss of material things, they also fear physical harm. With God being removed from the picture, man's sinful nature asserts itself even more.

> The fool says in his heart,
> "There is no God."
> They are corrupt, their deeds are vile;
> there is no one who does good.
> 2 The LORD looks down from heaven
> on the sons of men
> to see if there are any who understand,

any who seek God.
3 All have turned aside,
they have together become corrupt;
there is no one who does good,
not even one. (Psalm 14:1-3).

The need for laws and those who enforce them points to the sinful nature of man. Our pagan society and those in authority are ignoring the great benefit that the church has been in the past and could be again. The cost of controlling crime in a godly influenced society is much less than that of a pagan society. No society ever will be perfect, but a strong and vibrant church would do much to encourage goodness and to restrain wickedness. If those in power would stop tearing down the church and begin building it up, and if they would stop restricting God from the schools and public places, then they might be surprised at the flavor of the salt and the brightness of the light that would permeate society.

Satan

One of the most important issues Christians face is what to believe about Satan and how to resist his influence and temptations. The name Satan means "adversary" One definition of "adversary" is "enemy". Satan is certainly our enemy, as we will see in this discussion. Peter calls him our adversary, the devil.

> **8 Be of sober *spirit,* be on the alert. Your adversary,**
> **the devil, prowls about like a roaring lion, seeking**
> **someone to devour.** (1 Peter 5:8).

Sadly, many who profess Christ do not believe there is a devil, much less the devil (Satan) as he is portrayed in the Bible. Then there are those who say they believe there is a devil but live as though there is not. They go for days and weeks on end without even giving Satan a thought. What a dangerous thing to do!

Satan is one of the three commonly referred to enemies of the Christian – "the world, the flesh, and the devil".

Moreover, it would appear that Satan is the most powerful of the three. He was instrumental in the fall of man and the corruption of the earth.

We speak of the "world" as our enemy, and it is. But, behind the world is Satan. He is controlling the systems of the world. In fact Christ calls him "the ruler of this world".

> **30 "I will not speak much more with you, for the ruler of the world is coming...** (John 14:30).

When we refer to "the flesh" as our enemy, we are not talking about our physical body but our sinful human nature. The flesh causes us to sin without any help from Satan, but when tempted by him it is even more likely to do so. Satan influenced King David to sin by counting his soldiers.

> *1* THEN **Satan stood up against Israel and moved David to number Israel.***2* **So David said to Joab and to the princes of the people, "Go, number Israel from Beersheba even to Dan, and bring me** *word* **that I may know their number."***3* **And Joab said, "May the** LORD **add to His people a hundred times as many as they are! But, my lord the king, are they not all my lord's servants? Why does my lord seek this thing? Why should he be a cause of guilt to Israel?"***4* **Nevertheless, the king's word prevailed against Joab. Therefore, Joab departed and went throughout all Israel, and came to Jerusalem.***5* **And Joab gave the number of the census of** *all* **the people to David. And all Israel were 1,100,000 men who drew the sword; and Judah** *was* **470,000 men who drew the sword.***6* **But he did not number Levi and Benjamin among them, for the king's command was abhorrent to Joab.***7* **And God was displeased with this thing, so He struck Israel.***8* **And David said to God, "I have sinned greatly, in that I have done this thing. But now, please take away the iniquity of Thy servant, for I have done very foolishly."** (1 Chronicles 21:1-8).

Satan influenced Peter to sin when Peter told Jesus that He did not have to go to the cross and die. Jesus knew it was Satan's influence that caused Peter to do it.

21 From that time Jesus Christ began to show His disciples that He must go to Jerusalem, and suffer many things from the elders and chief priests and scribes, and be killed, and be raised up on the third day.22 And Peter took Him aside and began to rebuke Him, saying, "God forbid *it*, Lord! This shall never happen to You."23 But He turned and said to Peter,"Get behind Me, Satan! You are a stumbling block to Me; for you are not setting your mind on God's interests, but man's." (Matthew 16:21-23).

Another example of the influence Satan can have is found in that of Ananias and Sapphira.

32 And the congregation of those who believed were of one heart and soul; and not one *of them* claimed that anything belonging to him was his own; but all things were common property to them.33 And with great power the apostles were giving witness to the resurrection of the Lord Jesus, and abundant grace was upon them all.34 For there was not a needy person among them, for all who were owners of land or houses would sell them and bring the proceeds of the sales, 35 and lay them at the apostles' feet; and they would be distributed to each, as any had need.
36 And Joseph, a Levite of Cyprian birth, who was also called Barnabas by the apostles (which translated means, Son of Encouragement),37 and who owned a tract of land, sold it and brought the money and laid it at the apostles' feet. (Acts 4:32-37).

1 BUT a certain man named Ananias, with his wife Sapphira, sold a piece of property,*2* and kept back *some* of the price for himself, with his wife's full knowledge, and bringing a portion of it, he laid it at the apostles' feet.*3* But Peter said, "Ananias, why has Satan filled your heart to lie to the Holy Spirit, and to keep back *some* of the price of the land?*4* "While it remained *unsold,* did it not remain your own? And after it was sold, was it not under your control? Why is it that you have conceived this deed in your heart? You have not lied to men, but to God."*5* And as he heard these words, Ananias fell down and breathed his last; and great fear came upon all who heard of it.*6* And the young men arose

and covered him up, and after carrying him out, they buried him.
7 Now there elapsed an interval of about three hours, and his wife came in, not knowing what had happened.8 And Peter responded to her, "Tell me whether you sold the land for such and such a price?" And she said, "Yes, that was the price."9 Then Peter *said* to her, "Why is it that you have agreed together to put the Spirit of the Lord to the test? Behold, the feet of those who have buried your husband are at the door, and they shall carry you out *as well*."10 And she fell immediately at his feet, and breathed her last; and the young men came in and found her dead, and they carried her out and buried her beside her husband.11 And great fear came upon the whole church, and upon all who heard of these things. (Acts 5:1-11).

The above examples of Satan's ability to influence the thinking and ultimately the actions of those who profess to be Christians should cause us to be on our guard. He is still influencing people today. If we only knew how he has injected himself into the world's affairs as well as the countless individual and family lives, we would be astonished. Of course, when we refer to Satan, we are not speaking of just the one spirit being but all the other demons that follow him as well. They are not only numerous, but they are intelligent and powerful. Together, they accomplish much for their side. To speak of "their side" is correct as the Bible makes it clear that there are two sides and only two sides in this world: God's side which is good and Satan's side which is evil. Whether they recognize it or not, everyone in the world is on one of these two sides. All unbelievers are on the side of Satan, although the vast majority are unaware that they are. The few who have knowingly chosen to side with Satan must not believe in hell, or else they don't realize how awful it will be. It's truly a sad situation.

All believers are on the side of God. There is a great conflict that is constantly taking place between these two sides. However, many Christians seem to be either unaware that there is a conflict, or they do not recognize how serious the conflict its. God's Word makes it very clear, this is a major conflict – it is war!

10 Finally, be strong in the Lord, and in the strength of His might.11 Put on the full armor of God, that you may be able to stand firm against the schemes of the devil.12 For our struggle is not against flesh and blood, but against the rulers, against the powers, against the world forces of this darkness, against the spiritual *forces* of wickedness in the heavenly *places*.13 Therefore, take up the full armor of God, that you may be able to resist in the evil day, and having done everything, to stand firm.14 Stand firm therefore, HAVING GIRDED YOUR LOINS WITH TRUTH, and HAVING PUT ON THE BREASTPLATE OF RIGHTEOUSNESS,15 and having shod YOUR FEET WITH THE PREPARATION OF THE GOSPEL OF PEACE; 16 in addition to all, taking up the shield of faith with which you will be able to extinguish all the flaming missiles of the evil *one*.17 And take THE HELMET OF SALVATION, and the sword of the Spirit, which is the word of God.18 With all prayer and petition pray at all times in the Spirit, and with this in view, be on the alert with all perseverance and petition for all the saints... (Ephesians 6:10-18).

This war is really between God and Satan, and as Ephesians 6:12 tells us, it is a spiritual war. Satan is trying to prevent or hinder God from carrying out His plan and achieving His purpose. Because Christians belong to God, Satan attacks them. We must learn by God's grace to defend ourselves. Furthermore, because God has been so loving and merciful in saving us, we should want to defend His name and seek every opportunity to faithfully serve Him in this war. This means we are to fight to increase His kingdom and to bring honor and glory to His name.

The apostle Paul knew the Christian life was a struggle and a fight, as he made clear to Timothy.

8 This command I entrust to you, Timothy, my son, in accordance with the prophecies previously made concerning you, that by them you may fight the good fight... (1 Timothy 1:18).

3 Suffer hardship with *me,* as a good soldier of Christ Jesus. (2 Timothy 2:3).

According to tradition Paul was beheaded at Rome. He had reached a degree of spiritual maturity for which each of us would do well to strive. He could look back over his walk with God and say, "I have fought the good fight". He had fought sin; he had fought the devil; and by the grace of God he had kept the faith.

> **7 I have fought the good fight, I have finished the course, I have kept the faith...** (2 Timothy 4:7).

Paul found living the Christian life to be such a struggle that he referred to it as running the race and fighting the fight, should we not expect to do the same? Should we not be willing to fight? If we are not fighting the world, the flesh, and the devil, if we are not struggling with the sin in our lives and trying to rid ourselves of it, then we should examine ourselves. If we are content with our lack of obedience to God, we may not even be Christians.

Whether we are fighting the war or not, you can be sure Satan and his demons are.

> **4 ... in whose case the god of this world has blinded the minds of the unbelieving, that they might not see the light of the gospel of the glory of Christ, who is the image of God.** (2 Corinthians 4:4).

> **24 And the Lord's bond-servant must not be quarrelsome, but be kind to all, able to teach, patient when wronged,25 with gentleness correcting those who are in opposition, if perhaps God may grant them repentance leading to the knowledge of the truth,26 and they may come to their senses *and* escape from the snare of the devil, having been held captive by him to do his will.** (2 Timothy 2:24-26).

> **8 Be of sober *spirit,* be on the alert. Your adversary, the devil, prowls about like a roaring lion, seeking someone to devour.** (1 Peter 5:8).

Christ points out how Satan tries to hinder God's plan in the Parable of the Sower and the Parables of the Weeds.

1 AND He began to teach again by the sea. And such a very great multitude gathered to Him that He got into a boat in the sea and sat down; and the whole multitude was by the sea on the land.*2* And He was teaching them many things in parables, and was saying to them in His teaching,*3* "Listen *to this*! Behold, the sower went out to sow;*4* and it came about that as he was sowing, some *seed* fell beside the road, and the birds came and ate it up.*5* "And other *seed* fell on the rocky *ground* where it did not have much soil; and immediately it sprang up because it had no depth of soil.*6* "And after the sun had risen, it was scorched; and because it had no root, it withered away.*7* "And other *seed* fell among the thorns, and the thorns came up and choked it, and it yielded no crop.*8* "And other *seeds* fell into the good soil and as they grew up and increased, they yielded a crop and produced thirty, sixty, and a hundredfold."*9* And He was saying, "He who has ears to hear, let him hear."

10 And as soon as He was alone, His followers, along with the twelve, *began* asking Him *about* the parables.11 And He was saying to them, "To you has been given the mystery of the kingdom of God; but those who are outside get everything in parables,12 in order that WHILE SEEING, THEY MAY SEE AND NOT PERCEIVE; AND WHILE HEARING, THEY MAY HEAR AND NOT UNDERSTAND LEST THEY RETURN AND BE FORGIVEN."

13 And He *said to them, "Do you not understand this parable? And how will you understand all the parables?*14* "The sower sows the word.*15* "And these are the ones who are beside the road where the word is sown; and when they hear, immediately Satan comes and takes away the word which has been sown in them.*16* "And in a similar way these are the ones on whom seed was sown on the rocky *places,* who, when they hear the word, immediately receive it with joy;*17* and they have no *firm* root in themselves, but are *only* temporary; then, when affliction or persecution arises because of the word, immediately they fall away.*18* "And others are the ones on whom seed was sown among the thorns; these are the ones who have heard the word,*19* and the worries of the world, and the deceitfulness of riches, and the desires for other things enter in and

choke the word, and it becomes unfruitful.20 "And those are the ones on whom seed was sown on the good soil; and they hear the word and accept it, and bear fruit, thirty, sixty, and a hundredfold."
(Mark 4:1-20).

24 He presented another parable to them, saying, "The kingdom of heaven may be compared to a man who sowed good seed in his field.25 "But while men were sleeping, his enemy came and sowed tares also among the wheat, and went away.26 "But when the wheat sprang up and bore grain, then the tares became evident also.27 "And the slaves of the landowner came and said to him, 'Sir, did you not sow good seed in your field? How then does it have tares?'28 "And he said to them, 'An enemy has done this!' And the slaves *said to him, 'Do you want us, then, to go and gather them up?'29 "But he *said, 'No; lest while you are gathering up the tares, you may root up the wheat with them.30 'Allow both to grow together until the harvest; and in the time of the harvest I will say to the reapers, "First gather up the tares and bind them in bundles to burn them up; but gather the wheat into my barn.""'
36 Then He left the multitudes, and went into the house. And His disciples came to Him, saying, "Explain to us the parable of the tares of the field."37 And He answered and said, "The one who sows the good seed is the Son of Man,38 and the field is the world; and as for the good seed, these are the sons of the kingdom; and the tares are the sons of the evil one; 39 and the enemy who sowed them is the devil, and the harvest is the end of the age; and the reapers are angels.40 "Therefore just as the tares are gathered up and burned with fire, so shall it be at the end of the age.41 "The Son of Man will send forth His angels, and they will gather out of His kingdom all stumbling blocks, and those who commit lawlessness,42 and will cast them into the furnace of fire; in that place there shall be weeping and gnashing of teeth.43 "Then THE RIGHTEOUS WILL SHINE FORTH AS THE SUN in the kingdom of their Father. He who has ears, let him hear.
(Matthew 13:24-30,36-43).

Satan is evil. Think of the most evil person of whom you have ever heard or read about throughout history and Satan is more evil. He is the ultimate evil. In fact, "the evil one" is a common way of referring to Satan in Scripture. Some examples are as follows:

> *15* "I do not ask Thee to take them out of the world, but to keep them from the evil *one.* (John 17:15).

> *3* But the Lord is faithful, and He will strengthen and protect you from the evil *one.* (2 Thessalonians 3:3).

> 14 I have written to you, fathers, because you know Him who has been from the beginning. I have written to you, young men, because you are strong, and the word of God abides in you, and you have overcome the evil one. (1 John 2:14).

> *12...*not as Cain, *who* was of the evil one...
> *(*1 John 3:12).

> 18 We know that no one who is born of God sins; but He who was born of God keeps him and the evil one does not touch him. (1 John 5:18).

> 19 We know that we are of God, and the whole world lies in *the power of* the evil one. (1 John 5:19).

As evil as he is, Satan is able to masquerade as an angel of light.

> *13* For such men are false apostles, deceitful workers, disguising themselves as apostles of Christ.*14* And no wonder, for even Satan disguises himself as an angel of light.*15* Therefore it is not surprising if his servants also disguise themselves as servants of righteousness; whose end shall be according to their deeds. (2 Corinthians 11:13-15).

Notice in the above passage that the same men that Paul calls "false apostles" he also calls servants of Satan. This bears out the fact that, according to Scripture, all unbelievers are serving Satan in his war with God.

> *8* ...the one who practices sin is of the devil; for the devil has sinned from the beginning. (1 John 3:8).

1 AND you were dead in your trespasses and sins, *2* in which you formerly walked according to the course of this world, according to the prince of the power of the air, of the spirit that is now working in the sons of disobedience. (Ephesians 2:1-2).

44 "You are of *your* father the devil, and you want to do the desires of your father. (John 8:44).

Another name for Satan is "Tempter". It is an appropriate name because he is continually tempting people to sin in one-way or another.

5 For this reason, when I could endure *it* no longer, I also sent to find out about your faith, for fear that the tempter might have tempted you, and our labor should be in vain. (1 Thessalonians 3:5).

Satan even tempted Christ.

1 AND Jesus, full of the Holy Spirit, returned from the Jordan and was led about by the Spirit in the wilderness*2* for forty days, being tempted by the devil. And He ate nothing during those days; and when they had ended, He became hungry.*3* And the devil said to Him, "If You are the Son of God, tell this stone to become bread."*4* And Jesus answered him, "It is written, 'MAN SHALL NOT LIVE ON BREAD ALONE.'"*5* And he led Him up and showed Him all the kingdoms of the world in a moment of time.*6* And the devil said to Him, "I will give You all this domain and its glory; for it has been handed over to me, and I give it to whomever I wish.*7* "Therefore if You worship before me, it shall all be Yours."*8* And Jesus answered and said to him, "It is written, 'YOU SHALL WORSHIP THE LORD YOUR GOD AND SERVE HIM ONLY.'"*9* And he led Him to Jerusalem and had Him stand on the pinnacle of the temple, and said to Him, "If You are the Son of God, throw Yourself down from here; *10* for it is written,
'HE WILL GIVE HIS ANGELS CHARGE CONCERNING YOU TO GUARD YOU,'**11** and, 'ON *their* HANDS THEY WILL BEAR YOU UP, LEST YOU STRIKE YOUR FOOT AGAINST A STONE.'"
12 And Jesus answered and said to him, "It is said,

'YOU SHALL NOT PUT THE LORD YOUR GOD TO THE TEST.'"
13 And when the devil had finished every
temptation, he departed from Him until an opportune
time. (Luke 4:1-13).

As Christians we should remember that being tempted is
not a sin, but yielding to the temptation is. However, God
tells us that whenever we are tempted we do not have to
yield to it. We do not have to sin for He has given us a way
out of the temptation.

> *13* No temptation has overtaken you but such as is
> common to man; and God is faithful, who will not
> allow you to be tempted beyond what you are able,
> but with the temptation will provide the way of
> escape also, that you may be able to endure it.
> (1 Corinthians 10:13).

We must keep in mind that God is absolutely sovereign;
therefore, Satan can only do what God allows him to do. The
classic example of this is found in the Book of Job.

> *1* THERE was a man in the land of Uz, whose name
> was Job, and that man was blameless, upright,
> fearing God, and turning away from evil. *2* And seven
> sons and three daughters were born to him. *3* His
> possessions also were 7,000 sheep, 3,000 camels,
> 500 yoke of oxen, 500 female donkeys, and very
> many servants; and that man was the greatest of all
> the men of the east. *4* And his sons used to go and
> hold a feast in the house of each one on his day, and
> they would send and invite their three sisters to eat
> and drink with them. *5* And it came about, when the
> days of feasting had completed their cycle, that Job
> would send and consecrate them, rising up early in
> the morning and offering burnt offerings *according
> to* the number of them all; for Job said, "Perhaps my
> sons have sinned and cursed God in their hearts."
> Thus Job did continually. *6* Now there was a day
> when the sons of God came to present themselves
> before the LORD, and Satan also came among them. *7*
> And the LORD said to Satan, "From where do you
> come?" Then Satan answered the LORD and said,

"From roaming about on the earth and walking around on it."8 And the LORD said to Satan, "Have you considered My servant Job? For there is no one like him on the earth, a blameless and upright man, fearing God and turning away from evil."9 Then Satan answered the LORD, "Does Job fear God for nothing?10 "Hast Thou not made a hedge about him and his house and all that he has, on every side? Thou hast blessed the work of his hands, and his possessions have increased in the land.11 "But put forth Thy hand now and touch all that he has; he will surely curse Thee to Thy face."12 Then the LORD said to Satan, "Behold, all that he has is in your power, only do not put forth your hand on him." So Satan departed from the presence of the LORD.

13 Now it happened on the day when his sons and his daughters were eating and drinking wine in their oldest brother's house,14 that a messenger came to Job and said, "The oxen were plowing and the donkeys feeding beside them,15 and the Sabeans attacked and took them. They also slew the servants with the edge of the sword, and I alone have escaped to tell you."16 While he was still speaking, another also came and said, "The fire of God fell from heaven and burned up the sheep and the servants and consumed them, and I alone have escaped to tell you."17 While he was still speaking, another also came and said, "The Chaldeans formed three bands and made a raid on the camels and took them and slew the servants with the edge of the sword; and I alone have escaped to tell you."18 While he was still speaking, another also came and said, "Your sons and your daughters were eating and drinking wine in their oldest brother's house, 19 and behold, a great wind came from across the wilderness and struck the four corners of the house, and it fell on the young people and they died; and I alone have escaped to tell you."

20 Then Job arose and tore his robe and shaved his head, and he fell to the ground and worshiped.21 And he said,"Naked I came from my mother's womb, And naked I shall return there.

The LORD gave and the LORD has taken away.

Blessed be the name of the LORD."

22 Through all this Job did not sin nor did he blame God. (Job 1:1-22).

> 1 AGAIN there was a day when the sons of God came to present themselves before the LORD, and Satan also came among them to present himself before the LORD.2 And the LORD said to Satan, "Where have you come from?" Then Satan answered the LORD and said, "From roaming about on the earth, and walking around on it."3 And the LORD said to Satan, "Have you considered My servant Job? For there is no one like him on the earth, a blameless and upright man fearing God and turning away from evil. And he still holds fast his integrity, although you incited Me against him, to ruin him without cause."4 And Satan answered the LORD and said, "Skin for skin! Yes, all that a man has he will give for his life.5 "However, put forth Thy hand, now, and touch his bone and his flesh; he will curse Thee to Thy face."6 So the LORD said to Satan, "Behold, he is in your power, only spare his life."
> 7 Then Satan went out from the presence of the LORD, and smote Job with sore boils from the sole of his foot to the crown of his head.8 And he took a potsherd to scrape himself while he was sitting among the ashes.9 Then his wife said to him, "Do you still hold fast your integrity? Curse God and die!"10 But he said to her, "You speak as one of the foolish women speaks. Shall we indeed accept good from God and not accept adversity?" In all this Job did not sin with his lips. (Job 2:1-10).

God in His sovereignty tested Job; Satan, allowed by God, tempted Job. Satan had suggested God inflict Job (Chapter 1:11), but God left this to Satan to do. God does not tempt anyone to sin.

> 13 Let no one say when he is tempted, "I am being tempted by God"; for God cannot be tempted by evil, and He Himself does not tempt anyone.
> (James 1:13).

Many Christians wonder if Satan is powerful enough to possess them. The answer is no! If you are truly a Christian, you can be influenced by Satan but not possessed by him. This is not the case with unbelievers. The Bible makes it clear that evil spirits can, and on occasion do, possess unbelievers.

13 And they were casting out many demons and were anointing with oil many sick people and healing them. (Mark 6:13).

7 For *in the case of* many who had unclean spirits, they were coming out *of them* shouting with a loud voice; and many who had been paralyzed and lame were healed. (Acts 8:7).

11 And God was performing extraordinary miracles by the hands of Paul, *12* so that handkerchiefs or aprons were even carried from his body to the sick, and the diseases left them and the evil spirits went out. (Acts 19:11-12).

In America demon possession has never been the problem that is has been in some other parts of the world. However, it does happen here and it may be on the increase. We should keep in mind that often what some call demon possession is actually something else. It could be a physical disease or condition, a mental or emotional problem, or drugs. The work of Satan and his demons is troubling enough without our attributing other things to it. In not making more of it than we should though, let us not make less of it than we should. When we consider Satan's possession of Judas, we see what an important role he and his demons play. They play a role in contributing to the evil events in this world and actually have an effect on the course of history.

1 Now the Feast of Unleavened Bread, which is called the Passover, was approaching. *2* And the chief priests and the scribes were seeking how they might put Him to death; for they were afraid of the people. 3 And Satan entered into Judas who was called Iscariot, belonging to the number of the twelve. *4* And he went away and discussed with the chief priests and officers how he might betray Him to them. *5* And they were glad, and agreed to give him money. *6* And he consented, and *began* seeking a good opportunity to betray Him to them apart from the multitude. (Luke 22:1-6).

In this spiritual war with Satan, we do not want to misjudge the capability of the enemy. We are no match for any of the evil spirits. Paul had planned on going to Thessalonica, but Satan was able to stop him.

> **17 But we, brethren, having been bereft of you for a short while—in person, not in spirit—were all the more eager with great desire to see your face.18 For we wanted to come to you—I, Paul, more than once—and *yet* Satan thwarted us.**
> (1 Thessalonians 2:17-18).

Even the archangel Michael looked to God for help with Satan.

> **9 But Michael the archangel, when he disputed with the devil and argued about the body of Moses, did not dare pronounce against him a railing judgment, but said, "The Lord rebuke you."** (Jude 9).

As we face temptation or other problems placed before us by Satan, let us remember that we need to do so in God's strength, not our own. Let us come in faith and submission to God, and by His grace we can resist the devil.

> **16 ...in addition to all, taking up the shield of faith with which you will be able to extinguish all the flaming missiles of the evil *one*.** (Ephesians 6:16).

> **7 Submit therefore to God. Resist the devil and he will flee from you.** (James 4:7).

Also, let us not forget that one of the reasons Christ came was to destroy the work of Satan.

> **8 The Son of God appeared for this purpose, that He might destroy the works of the devil.** (1 John 3:8).

> **14 Since then the children share in flesh and blood, He Himself likewise also partook of the same, that through death He might render powerless him who had the power of death, that is, the devil...**
> (Hebrews 2:14).

One great comfort that Christians have is the knowledge that Christ has defeated Satan. He has destroyed his work and broken it into pieces. However, all the pieces have not been put away yet. Regardless, Satan's days are numbered, and he knows it. The Bible spells out what happens when the last piece is put away.

> 31 "Now judgment is upon this world; now the ruler of this world shall be cast out. (John 12:31).

> 11 and concerning judgment, because the ruler of this world has been judged. (John 16:11).

> 1 AND I saw an angel coming down from heaven, having the key of the abyss and a great chain in his hand.2 And he laid hold of the dragon, the serpent of old, who is the devil and Satan, and bound him for a thousand years,3 and threw him into the abyss, and shut it and sealed it over him, so that he should not deceive the nations any longer, until the thousand years were completed; after these things he must be released for a short time. (Revelation 20:1-3).

> 7 And when the thousand years are completed, Satan will be released from his prison,8 and will come out to deceive the nations which are in the four corners of the earth, Gog and Magog, to gather them together for the war; the number of them is like the sand of the seashore.9 And they came up on the broad plain of the earth and surrounded the camp of the saints and the beloved city, and fire came down from heaven and devoured them.10 And the devil who deceived them was thrown into the lake of fire and brimstone, where the beast and the false prophet are also; and they will be tormented day and night forever and ever. (Revelation 20:7-10).

In the Apostle John's day, Pergamum was a very evil city. Much of this was apparently due to Satan, as Christ said it was where Satan had his throne.

> 12 "And to the angel of the church in Pergamum write:The One who has the sharp two-edged sword says this:13 'I know where you dwell, where Satan's

> **throne is; and you hold fast My name, and did not
> deny My faith, even in the days of Antipas, My
> witness, My faithful one, who was killed among you,
> where Satan dwells.** (Revelation 2:12-13).

Does it not appear that Satan is becoming more and
more active in America? Do we not see how he is influencing
our society? Moreover, in a more subtle way and sometimes
as an "angel of light" he is having an influence on many of
our churches. More preachers are failing to preach and
teach the truth of God's Word. More people who profess to
be Christians are living in sin and with "itching ears" they are
looking for someone to tell them it is all right. More people
are looking for a religion that does not make them
uncomfortable, one where they are entertained by man
rather than enlightened by God. As a result, we find that
Christians are less and less the salt of society or a light to
those in darkness. As the Christian influence in America
declines, we can be sure that Satan will attempt to take over
even more than he has in the last thirty years. However,
Christ said the church at Pergamum remained true to His
name in spite of the strong influence of Satan. We too must
remain true to Christ regardless of whatever increased effort
Satan throws against us. In the power of the Holy Spirit, let
us do as the Apostle Peter tells us to do and resist Satan.

> **9 But resist him, firm in *your* faith, knowing that the
> same experiences of suffering are being
> accomplished by your brethren who are in the world.**
> (1 Peter 5:9).

Lastly, let us never forget that the indwelling Holy Spirit is
God, and God is greater than Satan.

> **4 You are from God, little children, and have
> overcome them; because greater is He who is in you
> than he who is in the world.** (1 John 4:4).

The Family

A great change has taken place in the American family since 1960, and it continues to change today. The family, as ordained by God, is a man and woman who are married to each other. They usually have children. This is a picture of the normal family according to Scripture. I understand that in the last forty years the normal family has declined in percentage of the total number of households. Unless marriage makes a comeback the family as the Bible describes it and as past history has recorded it, will eventually cease to exist. Today, there are groups who would like to see this happen and are doing what they can to bring it about. Some businesses as well as some people in state and federal government are also contributing to the downfall of the American family. There are other factors such as a general weakening of the moral fiber of society. Many things that are detrimental to families spring from this lowering of our morals. Divorce laws become so lax that for all practical purposes we have "no fault divorce". There was a time when divorce was a bad word. It was something of which to be ashamed. People took their marriage oath seriously, and most of them tried hard to stay together until "death do us part". Christians and non-Christians grew up believing that God did not like it when people got divorced. They were correct in their belief.

> 4 "Haven't you read," he replied, "that at the beginning the Creator 'made them male and female,' 5 and said, 'For this reason a man will leave his father and mother and be united to his wife, and the two will become one flesh'? 6 So they are no longer two, but one. Therefore what God has joined together, let man not separate." (Matthew 19:4-6).

No marriage is perfect, and all marriages require work to be successful. Some, of course, require more work than others. However, when succeeding in building a marriage is more important than succeeding in having your own way, a marriage is on the right track.

Think of the advantage Christians have over the unbeliever in building a marriage. They have God with them, for them, and in them. They have His blueprint in Scripture concerning forgiveness, love, sacrifice, submission, purpose, etc. They know that their marriage exists for one reason, to glorify God. There are many facets to a Christian marriage, and there should be much pleasure in it for the married couple. However, it still remains that the ultimate purpose for the marriage is to glorify God. After all, the command to each Christian is to glorify God in everything, and that would include their marriage.

31 So whether you eat or drink or whatever you do, do it all for the glory of God. (1 Corinthians 10:31).

How can two Christians build, not just a good marriage, but also a godly marriage? There is only one way. It takes depending totally on God. The couple must actively and continually seek to have God's Holy Spirit control them and order their steps so that the marriage is built according to His will. God wants His people to live godly lives. He wants their marriages to be godly. Therefore, keep God in your marriage by depending on and submitting to His Holy Spirit. Then your marriage cannot fail. Leave God out of your marriage, and it can fall apart.

5 "I am the vine; you are the branches. If a man remains in me and I in him, he will bear much fruit; apart from me you can do nothing." (John 15:5).

Living under the control of the Holy Spirit is not something Christians can do all the time because their old nature, which is sinful, is always at odds with the Spirit.

5 Those who live according to the sinful nature have their minds set on what that nature desires; but those who live in accordance with the Spirit have their minds set on what the Spirit desires. 6 The mind of sinful man is death, but the mind controlled by the Spirit is life and peace; 7 the sinful mind is

> **hostile to God. It does not submit to God's law, nor can it do so. 8 Those controlled by the sinful nature cannot please God.** (Romans 8:5-8).

> **16 So I say, live by the Spirit, and you will not gratify the desires of the sinful nature. 17 For the sinful nature desires what is contrary to the Spirit, and the Spirit what is contrary to the sinful nature. They are in conflict with each other, so that you do not do what you want.** (Galatians 5:16-17).

Imagine two Christians trying to build a marriage without the Holy Spirit's control. You can see how their sinful natures would clash with each other and cause all kinds of problems. We can visualize two people with each one wanting to have his own way, expecting the other one to meet all his needs, and holding the other one responsible to make him happy. Sheer determination may hold the marriage together, but what a miserable and un-Christian like marriage it would be.

Divorce, by definition, is a tearing down of the family. It is the act of dissolving or terminating a marriage. Marriage, according to one definition in Webster's Dictionary is, "being joined for the purpose of founding and maintaining a family." God instituted marriage. Contrary to popular thinking, God did not institute divorce – man did.

> **7 "Why then," they asked, "did Moses command that a man give his wife a certificate of divorce and send her away?" 8 Jesus replied, "Moses permitted you to divorce your wives because your hearts were hard. But it was not this way from the beginning.**
> (Matthew 19:7-8).

Once man insisted on divorce, God stepped in to regulate it. There is much that can be said about divorce as it relates to what the Bible teaches. There is the question of Biblical grounds for divorce and also the question of Biblical grounds for remarriages. It is not my intent to inject these aspects of divorce into our discussion. There are already a number of good books on those subjects. For this discussion, the emphasis is on the effect divorce is having on the family – regardless of whether or not the divorce is Biblical.

There appear to be three popular views about grounds for divorce. Some hold that Scripture does not allow for divorce under any circumstances. Others say that the offended party can get a divorce when a spouse commits adultery. Still others would say both adultery and desertion are Biblical grounds. The view that there are no grounds for divorce is totally wrong. Christ Himself tells us differently. The view that desertion is a Biblical ground comes from Paul's writings. However, it appears that Paul is referring to a marriage between a believer and an unbeliever who deserts the marriage. If this is clear-cut, there should not be a problem. However, this could be confusing if it came down to people who professed to be Christians but were not, or people who were Christians but at the time were not living as though they were. The deserted party could be tempted to make a wrong decision. The only clear and sure answer for Biblical grounds for a divorce between two believers is adultery. Christ makes this clear.

> **9 I tell you that anyone who divorces his wife, except for marital unfaithfulness, and marries another woman commits adultery."** (Matthew 19:9).

If someone gets a divorce on Scriptural grounds, it is not a sin. However, in most cases the divorce is probably not based on Scriptural grounds and therefore is a sinful act. Furthermore, if the persons remarry they have sinned again. However, even in these situations let us remember that these sins, like all others sins, are forgiven the Christian.

> **9 If we confess our sins, he is faithful and just and will forgive us our sins and purify us from all unrighteousness.** (1 John 1:9).

If you have been divorced and remarried one or more times, before or after becoming a Christian, you will not have to pay for these sins in eternity, but you may pay a temporal price for them. As with all sin, there are consequences to suffer – particularly if there are children involved.

If you find yourself in this situation, you need to turn to God, seek to be obedient to Him, and ask Him to lead and guide you in dealing with the consequences of your divorce. Also, if you are remarried, determine to do all you can to make your marriage a godly one. Study God's Word to find out what He expects of you in your marriage and then ask His Holy Spirit to enable and empower you to fulfill those requirements.

As Christians, we should never be seeking grounds for divorce, but rather we should always be seeking ways to strengthen our marriages. Actually, we should hate divorce. God hates divorce and we should hate what God hates.

> **16 "I hate divorce," says the LORD God of Israel...**
> (Malachi 2:16).

It is not the process of going through a divorce that God hates; it is the results and the repercussions of it. Look at what is happening today because people take the position that divorce is the easy way out of a situation they do not like. It does not even seem to matter when there are children involved. In most divorces involving children, the children suffer. They miss out on the love and help of a mother or father as the case may be. Children living with the mother are deprived of the father's discipline. Often this can make the difference in a child staying in school, staying off drugs, or keeping out of jail. Children, as they see their parents and the parents of their friends getting divorces, can become apprehensive about marriage. They can actually develop a fear of getting married, because they fear their marriage will fail and end up in a divorce. If they do get married, the chances are good that they will enter into the marriage with an erroneous idea of what marriage is all about. The fear they had about a failed marriage could become a reality.

The children are not the only ones hurt. The parents of the couple getting divorced are hurt and may wonder if somehow they failed their children. In a number of cases it leads to grandparents seldom being able to see their grandchildren. Occasionally, in a bitter divorce, grandparents may be completely deprived of seeing their grandchildren. Often when a divorce takes place, one or both of the divorced partners are left with a low opinion of themselves and a real feeling of inadequacy and failure. This can make it difficult for them to develop and build a sound relationship with one of the opposite sex. They, too, can develop a fear of getting married again. They fear another failure. Two Christians who get divorced leave themselves open to the temptation of fornication. This temptation can be more intense for some than others. In these cases, if they are serious about obeying God, it becomes a burden. In general, this would be a bigger problem for men than women. The problem of financial and physical security would be important for most women.

Man's quest to satisfy his sexual appetite and woman's desire to be financially and physically secure, have played a strong role in causing people to want to get married. That is the way it has been for years; however, it has changed in recent times due to the moral decay of society and the feminist movement. In the past society strongly condemned sex outside of marriage. As a result, many men and most women refrained from sex until marriage. At the same time a large number of households existed where the man earned the living, and the woman kept the house and raised the children. The young people grew up with this, and it was a way of life to follow. I am not saying that a permanent source of sex for the male and security for the woman were what caused two people to marry each other. They were strong basic drives that caused people to want to get married. However, a person's looks, personality, character, etc. were the factors that determined with whom they fell in love. With these basic drives pushing toward marriage, once two people fell in love, they were inclined to get married.

Look how different things are today. Sex is free and easy to come by for men. So-called liberated women are ready and willing to give it away to show how equal they are to men. To further show how liberated they are, many of these feminists pursue a career at the expense of getting married or having children. When women take on the man's roll, it leads to problems, not the least of which is a moral decline in society. God made women equal to men, but He gave them a different role in life. When a woman seeks to live life in her God-given role, she is not only a blessing to her husband but to society in general. She contributes to making the moral standard of society higher. As a whole, the American male has always been more immoral than the female. Therefore, when women begin to act like men morally, the standard for society is lowered. Whether it is male "machismo" or something else, the male's morals then sink even lower, and a downward spiral is begun. On the other hand, women can lead morals in an upward spiral. Imagine if:

Most of the unmarried women in American were virgins.
Most of the women were strong and outspoken in their opposition to adultery.
Most women did not drink to excess.
Most women did not use drugs of any kind.
Most women did not use profanity.
Most women would not watch the filth on TV and the Internet.
Most women would not watch a filthy movie or video.
Most women made it a point to dress modestly.
Most women considered themselves fortunate if they did not have to work, could be married, have children and stay at home.

Does anyone think that most males would not upgrade their moral standard in a hurry? Without a doubt they would.

We are speaking of women as a whole and men as a whole. There are always those exceptions in society where the man is the moral leader in a relationship or a household. Also, in a believer's household the man is to be the head and the spiritual leader. Even though we know that this is the way it is suppose to be, we also know that very often it is the woman that sets the moral standard in the Christian family. I believe it is also safe to say that the hand that rocks the cradle is the glue that holds society together. Moreover, when women go bad, society begins to come apart at the seams.

We know that in God's sovereign plan, Adam and Eve were going to eat the forbidden fruit. However, we have to wonder what Adam would have done if Eve had not lowered her moral standard and disobeyed God. Adam was responsible for his disobedience. However, regardless of that fact, it does appear that Eve had some influence in his eating the fruit. After all, God's Word tells us that Eve not only was the first to eat, but that she actually handed some of the fruit to Adam to eat. We are also told that Eve said she was deceived, but Adam just said he ate because Eve gave him some to eat.

> **11 And he said, "Who told you that you were naked? Have you eaten from the tree that I commanded you not to eat from?"**
> **12 The man said, "The woman you put here with me—she gave me some fruit from the tree, and I ate it."**
> **13 Then the LORD God said to the woman, "What is this you have done?"**
> **The woman said, "The serpent deceived me, and I ate."** (Genesis 3:11-13).

Another thing that contributes to the decline of the family, as the Bible defines family, is the increasing number of single parents. We have said that a number of single parents are single because of divorce. However, divorce is not the only cause. There are the teenage mothers whose boyfriends move on when they become pregnant. Of course there are the unmarried mothers of various ages who have babies that are mostly unplanned. A few follow Hollywood's lead and plan to have a baby out of wedlock. This is not to put down single moms. It is to bring out the fact that a single mom generally has more of a problem trying to keep teenage boys and girls off alcohol and drugs and in school and out of trouble, than a mom with the benefit of a husband to help.

Think of the number of children growing up today who do not know who their father is. Their mother slept around with a number of different men of which any one might be the father. If you do not know who your father is, you do not know who your grandparents are on your father's side. This carries over to aunts, uncles, cousins, etc. In addition, if your mother was living in an area removed from her family and did not maintain contact with them, then you would grow up with only one relative – your mother. In essence you would be a person with no family and no real knowledge of your roots.

Government and some businesses encourage redefining the term family when they advocate that the same rights be given to homosexuals and lesbians living together as are given to married couples. In fact some businesses have actually done this. Certain states are considering doing it.

Materialism is another thing that is harmful to building healthy families. Making money, having things, going places and doing things is replacing building the family and enjoying ones family. Even among many Christians, the state of the bank account is more important than the state of the soul. Building an empire is more important than building God's Kingdom. The idea that both the husband and wife have to work to get by is true in fewer cases than most realize. Many married women are working for luxuries not for needs. Bigger houses, finer cars, expensive clothes, costly jewelry, etc. are not things everyone has to have but things they want. To the world material things can be very important, but the Christian should be concerned with God's Kingdom.

> **29 And do not set your heart on what you will eat or drink; do not worry about it. 30 For the pagan world runs after all such things, and your Father knows that you need them. 31 But seek his kingdom, and these things will be given to you as well.**
> (Luke 12:29-31).

There is nothing wrong in having wealth, but we sin when we let money become too important to us – so important that we seek money instead of seeking God. Scripture warns against the love of money.

> 24 "No one can serve two masters. Either he will hate the one and love the other, or he will be devoted to the one and despise the other. You cannot serve both God and Money. (Matthew 6:24).

> 6 But godliness with contentment is great gain. 7 For we brought nothing into the world, and we can take nothing out of it. 8 But if we have food and clothing, we will be content with that. 9 People who want to get rich fall into temptation and a trap and into many foolish and harmful desires that plunge men into ruin and destruction. 10 For the love of money is a root of all kinds of evil. Some people, eager for money, have wandered from the faith and pierced themselves with many griefs. (1 Timothy 6:6-10).

There are other things that have a detrimental effect on the family. Let us never forget the important role that Satan plays in trying to destroy the family. He started with the first family, that of Adam and Eve, and he has been attacking the family structure ever since. The family is such an important target for Satan because one of the main ways that God keeps His Kingdom here on earth replenished is through the family.

> 15 Has not the LORD made them one? In flesh and spirit they are his. And why one? Because he was seeking godly offspring. So guard yourself in your spirit, and do not break faith with the wife of your youth. (Malachi 2:15).

Of course there have always been and still are converts like Rehab and Zacchaeus, but it is more often through being a member of a Christian family that children of the Covenant find salvation in Jesus Christ.

> 38 Peter replied, "Repent and be baptized, every one of you, in the name of Jesus Christ for the forgiveness of your sins. And you will receive the

gift of the Holy Spirit. 39 The promise is for you and your children and for all who are far off—for all whom the Lord our God will call." (Acts 2:38-39).

25 And you are heirs of the prophets and of the covenant God made with your fathers. He said to Abraham, 'Through your offspring all peoples on earth will be blessed.' (Acts 3:25).

8 He remembers his covenant forever, the word he commanded, for a thousand generations...
(Psalm 105:8).

We see that the family is not just another issue that we face, but rather it is a very important issue. God uses the family to help propagate the Christian community. These children who become new believers, grow up, get married, and have children – many of which find salvation. In this manner, true Christianity is passed down from one generation to the next. Many families can point to four or more generations of believers before them.

What do we do to defend and strengthen the family against the attacks of Satan and his pawns? I believe the most important thing we can do, after shoring up our own walk with God, is to do a much better job of teaching our children at home, as well as at church. At church and at home, we need to keep the world out and the Word in. Our children need to know more than how to be saved – they need to know how to live. They need to know God's Word, so it can continue to be passed down through the generations.

9 Teach them to your children and to their children after them. (Deuteronomy 4:9).

6 These commandments that I give you today are to be upon your hearts. 7 Impress them on your children. Talk about them when you sit at home and when you walk along the road, when you lie down and when you get up. (Deuteronomy 6:6-7).

**5 He decreed statutes for Jacob
and established the law in Israel,
which he commanded our forefathers
to teach their children,
6 so the next generation would know them,
even the children yet to be born,
and they in turn would tell their children.
7 Then they would put their trust in God
and would not forget his deeds
but would keep his commands.** (Psalm 78:5-7).

Racism

Racism is an issue that has been around since God scattered man at the Tower of Babel. There is a tendency in man to feel superior and harbor suspicion toward others who live in a foreign land, speak a different language, and have a different culture. If this attitude exists between people of the same skin color, it is considered an ethnic problem. If it exists between people of different skin color, it is considered a problem of race. However, both ethnocentrism and racism boil down to the belief that one ethnic group or one race is superior to others. This superior attitude may lead to snobbery, discrimination, prejudice, and even hatred. A belief in evolution opens the door to these possibilities.

Today, there are many people who think that there are five different races in the world. These would be white, black, brown, red, and yellow. Most of those who think this way are convinced that some races evolved earlier than others and therefore have had more time to develop as humans. It then follows that those races that have had the longest period of time to develop are the most advanced humans and have moved the farthest from their animal ancestors. As a result, they are superior to the other races; therefore, they have a right to think of themselves as being superior. There are even some who profess Christ that have bought the theory of evolution. They attempt to reconcile the Bible with evolution by believing that God created man through evolution; however, the Bible does not, in any way, support this idea.

Let us look at what God's Word says about how man came to be and how the different nations of people came about. God says He created man in His own image.

> **27 So God created man in his own image,**
> **in the image of God he created him;**
> **male and female he created them.** (Genesis 1:27).

God tells us He formed man from the dust of the ground.

> **7 ...the LORD God formed the man from the dust of**
> **the ground and breathed into his nostrils the breath**
> **of life, and the man became a living being.**
> (Genesis 2:7).

God further tells us He formed woman from one of the man's ribs.

> **21 So the LORD God caused the man to fall into a**
> **deep sleep; and while he was sleeping, he took one**
> **of the man's ribs and closed up the place with flesh.**
> **22 Then the LORD God made a woman from the rib**
> **he had taken out of the man, and he brought her to**
> **the man.** (Genesis 2:21-22).

From looking at God's Word, we see that all mankind is descended from Adam and Eve. As Eve was made from Adam's rib, we all have the same blood and descend from Adam.

> **26 From one man he made every nation of men, that**
> **they should inhabit the whole earth; and he**
> **determined the times set for them and the exact**
> **places where they should live.** (Acts 17:26).

We see from the above verse that there is only one race, the human race. There are not different races of people, but there are different groups of people within the one human race. These are often referred to as nations or tribes. Let us see what God's Word says about how these different groups of people came to be.

Most everyone is familiar with the fact that man became so wicked that God sent a flood to destroy mankind. Only eight people survived: Noah, his wife, his three sons, and their wives. Noah and his family carried the genetic information (genes) for a wide range of physical characteristics including the color of skin, hair, eyes, etc. As the population increased, there would emerge a large group of people in the middle that would be considered average. They would be average in height, skin color, and all psychical characteristics. The average skin color would very likely have been mid-brown. Of course the extremes of white and dark black would be found in the group, but the interbreeding would maintain the average of mid-brown.

Skin color is determined by the amount of melanin we produce. Melanin is a dark brownish pigment in special cells in the skin. If we produce little melanin, we will have white skin, and if we produce a lot of it, we will have dark black skin. Sunlight has an effect on melanin causing it to increase. If you take a group of people who have basically the same shade of white skin and expose them to an equal amount of sunlight daily for a period of six weeks, you would find varying degrees of tan. This would be due to the genetic potential of each person to produce melanin.

For a period of time after the flood, all the people spoke the same language and shared the same culture. They married, had children, and thus the average physical characteristics of the group remained much the same. However, the people disobeyed God by not scattering across the earth. So God determined to scatter them by confusing their language.

1 Now the whole world had one language and a common speech. 2 As men moved eastward, they found a plain in Shinar and settled there.
3 They said to each other, "Come, let's make bricks and bake them thoroughly." They used brick instead of stone, and tar for mortar. 4 Then they said, "Come, let us build ourselves a city, with a tower

> that reaches to the heavens, so that we may make a
> name for ourselves and not be scattered over the
> face of the whole earth."
> 5 But the LORD came down to see the city and the
> tower that the men were building. 6 The LORD said,
> "If as one people speaking the same language they
> have begun to do this, then nothing they plan to do
> will be impossible for them. 7 Come, let us go down
> and confuse their language so they will not
> understand each other."
> 8 So the LORD scattered them from there over all the
> earth, and they stopped building the city. 9 That is
> why it was called Babel—because there the LORD
> confused the language of the whole world. From
> there the LORD scattered them over the face of the
> whole earth. (Genesis 11:1-9).

Once the people were scattered into many groups, they would tend to stay within their group, marry and have children. As a result they would perpetuate the most dominant and the most common genes within their group. Over time the physical characteristics of each group would become different from the others. In addition when God dispersed the groups, there would have been unequal dispersion of knowledge, skill, and talent. The different groups would also end up in different environments. All of these things would combine to insure that the cultures were also different. Therefore, it is understandable that people who have been taught that evolution is fact would look around and think they saw evidence for it. However, once you know what God's Word says you can readily understand how these different groups of people came about.

Someone may ask from where the Jews came. The Jews are descendents of Adam and Eve like everyone else. They became a group of people when God established them. The first Jew was Abraham, and again God's Word tells us how this came about. Sometime after the people were scattered at the Tower of Babel, Abram (God later changed his name to Abraham) was living in Ur of the Chaldeans. Ur was in ancient Babylonia, and it appears that Abram and his family were idol worshipers. Abram went to Haran with his father, Terah.

> 31 Terah took his son Abram, his grandson Lot son of Haran, and his daughter-in-law Sarai, the wife of his son Abram, and together they set out from Ur of the Chaldeans to go to Canaan. But when they came to Haran, they settled there. (Genesis 11:31).

God called Abram to leave Haran.

> 1 The LORD had said to Abram, "Leave your country, your people and your father's household and go to the land I will show you.
> 2 "I will make you into a great nation
> and I will bless you;
> I will make your name great,
> and you will be a blessing.
> 3 I will bless those who bless you,
> and whoever curses you I will curse;
> and all peoples on earth
> will be blessed through you."
> 4 So Abram left, as the LORD had told him; and Lot went with him. Abram was seventy-five years old when he set out from Haran. 5 He took his wife Sarai, his nephew Lot, all the possessions they had accumulated and the people they had acquired in Haran, and they set out for the land of Canaan, and they arrived there. (Genesis 12:1-5).

God changed Abram's name to Abraham, and Abraham became the first Jew when he was circumcised at age ninety-nine.

> 1 When Abram was ninety-nine years old, the LORD appeared to him and said, "I am God Almighty; walk before me and be blameless. 2 I will confirm my covenant between me and you and will greatly increase your numbers."
> 3 Abram fell facedown, and God said to him, 4 "As for me, this is my covenant with you: You will be the father of many nations. 5 No longer will you be called Abram; your name will be Abraham, for I have made you a father of many nations. 6 I will make you very fruitful; I will make nations of you, and kings will come from you. 7 I will establish my covenant as an everlasting covenant between me and you and

your descendants after you for the generations to come, to be your God and the God of your descendants after you. 8 The whole land of Canaan, where you are now an alien, I will give as an everlasting possession to you and your descendants after you; and I will be their God
9 Then God said to Abraham, "As for you, you must keep my covenant, you and your descendants after you for the generations to come. 10 This is my covenant with you and your descendants after you, the covenant you are to keep: Every male among you shall be circumcised. 11 You are to undergo circumcision, and it will be the sign of the covenant between me and you. (Genesis 17:1-11).

If we are all descendents of Adam and Eve, does God distinguish between us in any manner? The answer from the Bible is yes; God does make distinctions. He speaks of two basic groups of people, but it has nothing to do with physical differences. It is a spiritual difference. God sees people as either those who have trusted Christ for their salvation or those who have not. In other words, those who are truly believers and those who are not. This is made clear in the Parable of the Weeds.

24 Jesus told them another parable: "The kingdom of heaven is like a man who sowed good seed in his field. 25 But while everyone was sleeping, his enemy came and sowed weeds among the wheat, and went away. 26 When the wheat sprouted and formed heads, then the weeds also appeared.
27 "The owner's servants came to him and said, 'Sir, didn't you sow good seed in your field? Where then did the weeds come from?'
28 "'An enemy did this,' he replied.
"The servants asked him, 'Do you want us to go and pull them up?'
29 "'No,' he answered, 'because while you are pulling the weeds, you may root up the wheat with them. 30 Let both grow together until the harvest. At that time I will tell the harvesters: First collect the weeds and tie them in bundles to be burned; then gather the wheat and bring it into my barn.'"

36 Then he left the crowd and went into the house. His disciples came to him and said, "Explain to us the parable of the weeds in the field."
37 He answered, "The one who sowed the good seed is the Son of Man. 38 The field is the world, and the good seed stands for the sons of the kingdom. The weeds are the sons of the evil one, 39 and the enemy who sows them is the devil. The harvest is the end of the age, and the harvesters are angels.
40 "As the weeds are pulled up and burned in the fire, so it will be at the end of the age. 41 The Son of Man will send out his angels, and they will weed out of his kingdom everything that causes sin and all who do evil. 42 They will throw them into the fiery furnace, where there will be weeping and gnashing of teeth. 43 Then the righteous will shine like the sun in the kingdom of their Father. He who has ears, let him hear. (Matthew 13:24-30,36-43).

Christ also makes this clear in the Gospel of John.

42 Jesus said to them, "If God were your Father, you would love me, for I came from God and now am here. I have not come on my own; but he sent me. 43 Why is my language not clear to you? Because you are unable to hear what I say. 44 You belong to your father, the devil, and you want to carry out your father's desire. He was a murderer from the beginning, not holding to the truth, for there is no truth in him. When he lies, he speaks his native language, for he is a liar and the father of lies. 45 Yet because I tell the truth, you do not believe me! 46 Can any of you prove me guilty of sin? If I am telling the truth, why don't you believe me? 47 He who belongs to God hears what God says. The reason you do not hear is that you do not belong to God." (John 8:42-47).

In view of all that we have discussed above, what action (if any) should we take? If you do not know Christ as your Savior and Lord, let me urge you to repent and trust Him for your salvation now! If you are already a Christian but have been harboring wrong thoughts about other people, let me suggest that you repent of those thoughts now! Remember, we are told to love our neighbor (Matthew 22:39). Let us not be among those people who claim the name of Christ while doing the deeds of the devil. We should show love to all men, but particularly to a fellow believer. We should show love regardless of their skin color, the language they speak, or the culture in which they live. All believers are joined together in Christ. They are part of the spiritual body of Christ. They are spiritual brothers and sisters in Christ.

> **27 Now you are the body of Christ, and each one of you is a part of it.** (1 Corinthians 12:27).

All believers are children of God. God loves His children and commands His children to love each other.

> **19 We love because he first loved us. 20 If anyone says, "I love God," yet hates his brother, he is a liar. For anyone who does not love his brother, whom he has seen, cannot love God, whom he has not seen. 21 And he has given us this command: Whoever loves God must also love his brother.**
> (1 John 4:19-21).

> **2 This is how we know that we love the children of God: by loving God and carrying out his commands.**
> (1 John 5:2).

In the Gospel of John, Christ gives the command for us to love one another.

> **34 "A new command I give you: Love one another. As I have loved you, so you must love one another. 35 By this all men will know that you are my disciples, if you love one another."**
> (John 13:34-35).

As we close this discussion, let us remember that regardless of what man says, God's Word is where we find the truth. Christ tells us it is the truth.

> **17 Sanctify them by the truth; your word is truth.**
> (John 17:17).

Sanctification

The issue of sanctification is somewhat different than the other issues we have discussed. The others are issues that proceed from the world, the flesh, or the devil. Sanctification proceeds from God. The others are issues that would tear us down and weaken our faith. Sanctification will build us up and strengthen our faith. We must fight against the other issues if we are to win. We must yield to sanctification if we are to win.

Sanctification is a process by which God makes us more like Christ by working spiritual maturity in us. Although it is God's working in us that sanctifies us, we are to be actively working to be sanctified. We should be seeking and striving to grow in the grace and knowledge of Jesus Christ.

18 But grow in the grace and knowledge of our Lord and Savior Jesus Christ. (2 Peter 3:18).

Willfully <u>resisting</u> sanctification <u>may</u> indicate a lack of justification. Willfully <u>refusing</u> sanctification <u>does</u> indicate a lack of it. If one refuses to grow in Christ, one has no reason to think they are in Christ. Many who profess to be Christians show much concern about being justified but little concern about being sanctified. That is a grievous error. Through the process of sanctification we grow closer to God. As we grow closer to God, we move further from sin. Sanctification actually begins the moment we experience spiritual birth and continues until we draw our last breath. Just as God must work a change in us to make us suitable for heaven, He must work a change in us to make us suitable for His kingdom here on earth. On earth He allows (but restrains) the sin in us. In heaven He forbids and removes the sin from us. Christians need to know not only what sanctification is but also how important it is. Sanctification works holiness in us and without holiness no one will see heaven.

14 ...without holiness no one will see the Lord. (Hebrews 12:14).

We will not achieve holiness by passive dependence on God, nor will we achieve it by working independently of God. It is true that it is God who works to make us holy. But it is also true that we are to work to be made holy. Our sanctification involves both.

The more mature we grow in Christ, the more we come to depend on Him. We reach a greater realization that without Christ we can do nothing of value, but through Him we can do all that He wills. The more we learn about the work of Christ the more we will understand the love of Christ.

> **4 Remain in me, and I will remain in you. No branch can bear fruit by itself; it must remain in the vine. Neither can you bear fruit unless you remain in me.**
> **5 "I am the vine; you are the branches. If a man remains in me and I in him, he will bear much fruit; apart from me you can do nothing. 6 If anyone does not remain in me, he is like a branch that is thrown away and withers; such branches are picked up, thrown into the fire and burned. 7 If you remain in me and my words remain in you, ask whatever you wish, and it will be given you. 8 This is to my Father's glory, that you bear much fruit, showing yourselves to be my disciples.** (John 15:4-8).

> **13 I can do everything through him who gives me strength.** (Philippians 4:13).

A word of caution concerning sanctification: We must guard against overconfidence. The slightest confidence in ourselves is overconfidence. When God has been doing a sanctifying work in us, we must be careful to not think that somehow we have a strength built up that is now our own. It was God's work in the beginning; it is God's work at present; it will be God's work in the future. We can never rest in our own strength or think that we have developed spiritual muscles that are sufficient for the task at hand. We must always look to God and be aware of our total dependence on Him.

> **13 ...for it is God who works in you to will and to act according to his good purpose.** (Philippians 2:13).

23 May God himself, the God of peace, sanctify you through and through. May your whole spirit, soul and body be kept blameless at the coming of our Lord Jesus Christ. 24 The one who calls you is faithful and he will do it. (1 Thessalonians 5:23-24).

God works sanctification in us by His Holy Spirit applying His Word to our lives. Knowledge of the Bible unattended by the Holy Spirit is next to useless. On the other hand, the Holy Spirit unaccompanied by knowledge of the Bible is certainly hindered. The Holy Spirit applies the Word to our hearts. If we do not read the Word, we do not give Him anything to apply. God has done something wonderful in giving us His Word to teach us. We certainly should make an effort to learn. It would seem hypocritical to thank God for the Bible and then not read or study it. Our thanks would seem insincere.

Even when we are sincere in wanting to grow spiritually the task is not easy. In the believer's life there is a continual conflict between doing God's will and doing our own will – between our love for God and our affection for other things. Wanting to grow spiritually is one thing – actually growing is another. There should always be concern if we find ourselves not growing spiritually. We know we will not be made perfect in this life, but if we are not moving toward holiness we could be in great danger. If we do not see growth, we have to ask the question, is there life? Are we really saved?

However, if we are truly Christians we can take heart. We will face tough issues in the future, but our God controls the future. And, until God takes the Christian out of the world, He is working to take the world out of the Christian. Therefore, let all of us who profess the name of Christ seek to be obedient to Him. It is in obedience to Christ that we prove we belong to Christ.

21 "Whoever has my commands and obeys them, he is the one who loves me. He who loves me will be loved by my Father, and I too will love him and show myself to him." (John 14:21).

My Grandchildren and Romans 8:28

While writing my first book, <u>Let God Speak</u>, I became aware of the great comfort we enjoy when we truly believe and rely upon Romans 8:28. It is amazing to realize that once you become a Christian, everything that happens after that will be made to work to your good. God will work all tragic events, sickness, and failures, as well as pleasant events, good health, and success for the good of His children.

I began to have a strong desire that my grandchildren understand and believe the truth of Romans 8:28. I wanted them to face life knowing the depth of its meaning. I knew that this would enable them to glorify God, while benefiting from the comfort and joy that comes from living by it.

All four of my grandchildren trusted Christ for their salvation at an early age and were still quite young in 1989 when I began to have these thoughts and desires. I decided to put something on paper that they could keep and memorize over time. Meanwhile, I planned to spend some time teaching them the doctrine contained in Romans 8:28. This worked very well. They memorized what I had written about the verse and recited it for me each year when we took our family vacation together. They also grasped the doctrine and as a whole have done a good job of facing life in light of it. As they have become older (one is a college junior, one a college sophomore, two are high school juniors), I have not had them recite the verse and information for the past several years. I plan to ask them to do it one more time when we go on vacation. By the end of the year 2001 or in early 2002, I hope to have this book in print. They will then have their own copy as a reminder.

They are four wonderful grandchildren. Their names are: Taylor Joseph, Edmund Joseph, Lyndsay McDavid, and Michael McDavid. It is my hope that they will always remember to take whatever comes their way, whether it is good, bad, or otherwise with Romans 8:28 in mind. What I wrote for them and had them memorize is printed here. Perhaps they will pass it down to their children and grandchildren.

August 1, 1989

God is in control of everything so everything happens as God has planned.

Romans 8:28 says:

> **28 And we know that in all things God works for the good of those who love him, who have been called according to his purpose.**

All things means good things and bad things – big things and little things.

Those who love Him are those who are trusting Jesus Christ to forgive their sins and save them.

Those who have been called are those God has chosen to be His children.

His purpose for them is to grow more like Jesus and in doing this to glorify God.

I love God – I am one of those He has chosen – my purpose in life is to grow more like Jesus and glorify God.

Random Thoughts and Questions

The Bible declares itself to be God's Word and therefore to be absolute truth.

> **44 He said to them, "This is what I told you while I was still with you: Everything must be fulfilled that is written about me in the Law of Moses, the Prophets and the Psalms."**
> **45 Then he opened their minds so they could understand the Scriptures. 46 He told them, "This is what is written: The Christ will suffer and rise from the dead on the third day, 47 and repentance and forgiveness of sins will be preached in his name to all nations, beginning at Jerusalem.** (Luke 24:44-47).

> **4 Jesus answered, "It is written: 'Man does not live on bread alone, but on every word that comes from the mouth of God.'"** (Matthew 4:4).

> **3 Then Moses went up to God, and the LORD called to him from the mountain and said, "This is what you are to say to the house of Jacob and what you are to tell the people of Israel...** (Exodus 19:3).

Do you believe the Bible is absolute truth? If not, why not? After thirty-five years of studying the Bible, I am more convinced than ever that it is absolute truth. Make a study of the fulfilled prophecies of the Bible and see if you don't find them to be a compelling reason to believe the Bible is true. There are also the letters of the Apostles who had seen the resurrected Christ. One had to have seen the resurrected Christ to be an Apostle.

> **21 Therefore it is necessary to choose one of the men who have been with us the whole time the Lord Jesus went in and out among us, 22 beginning from John's baptism to the time when Jesus was taken up from us. For one of these must become a witness with us of his resurrection."** (Acts 1:21-22).

There are eyewitness accounts from men of integrity. Do you have reason not to believe them?

> **32 God has raised this Jesus to life, and we are all witnesses of the fact.** (Acts 2:32).

> **3 For what I received I passed on to you as of first importance: that Christ died for our sins according to the Scriptures, 4 that he was buried, that he was raised on the third day according to the Scriptures, 5 and that he appeared to Peter, and then to the Twelve. 6 After that, he appeared to more than five hundred of the brothers at the same time, most of whom are still living, though some have fallen asleep. 7 Then he appeared to James, then to all the apostles...** (1 Corinthians 15:3-7).

> **1 That which was from the beginning, which we have heard, which we have seen with our eyes, which we have looked at and our hands have touched—this we proclaim concerning the Word of life. 2 The life appeared; we have seen it and testify to it, and we proclaim to you the eternal life, which was with the Father and has appeared to us. 3 We proclaim to you what we have seen and heard, so that you also may have fellowship with us. And our fellowship is with the Father and with his Son, Jesus Christ.**
> (1 John 1:1-3).

We also have the conformation of Christ Himself as He quotes the Old Testament – there was no New Testament in His day.

> **10 Jesus said to him, "Away from me, Satan! For it is written: 'Worship the Lord your God, and serve him only.'"** (Matthew 4:10).

> **17 "Do not think that I have come to abolish the Law or the Prophets; I have not come to abolish them but to fulfill them.** (Matthew 5:17).

> **39 You diligently study the Scriptures because you think that by them you possess eternal life. These are the Scriptures that testify about me...**
> (John 5:39).

44 He said to them, "This is what I told you while I was still with you: Everything must be fulfilled that is written about me in the Law of Moses, the Prophets and the Psalms." (Luke 24:44).

If you believe the Bible is God's Word, do you study it? If you don't study the Bible, what does that indicate? Could it indicate that you do not really believe it is God's Word? Could it be that you believe the Bible is God's Word but you just don't think God's Word is important enough for you to spend your time studying it?

Have you ever read about what is often referred to as Noah's Flood? Some people think it is a myth. Do you think it is? Jesus Christ believed it really happened.

37 As it was in the days of Noah, so it will be at the coming of the Son of Man. 38 For in the days before the flood, people were eating and drinking, marrying and giving in marriage, up to the day Noah entered the ark; 39 and they knew nothing about what would happen until the flood came and took them all away. That is how it will be at the coming of the Son of Man. (Matthew 24:37-39).

Do you claim to be a Christian? A Christian is one who is "saved", one who is going to heaven when their physical body dies. Does that describe you? Why do you think so?

A Christian loves Jesus Christ. Do you love Him? Christ says we show our love for Him by our obedience to His commands.

15 "If you love me, you will obey what I command. (John 14:15).

Christ also says that if we do not love Him we will not obey His teaching.

24 He who does not love me will not obey my teaching. (John 14:24).

Are you obeying Christ's commands? Have you even given thought to His commands in the last two weeks? How about in the last few days? What about today? Do you know what Christ teaches? Are you studying God's Word in order to find out?

Christ says we are to teach others to obey everything He has commanded us. Are you doing that?

> **20 ...and teaching them to obey everything I have commanded you. And surely I am with you always, to the very end of the age."** (Matthew 28:20).

Do you believe in prayer? Do you pray? The Bible tells us to pray without ceasing, to pray continually.

> **17 pray continually...** (1 Thessalonians 5:17).

Praying is talking with God. We should be talking with Him all through the day. Biblical prayer is not confined to folding your hands and saying prayers at bedtime. It is an on-going conversation with God that can take place while driving a car (with your eyes open), walking down the street, attending a business meeting, or watching your child's ball game. After all, if you know Christ as your Saviour and Lord, isn't He always with you wherever you are and in whatever you are doing? Talk with Him. Ask Him what He would have you do. Then ask Him to enable you to do it. Get to know God well – He is a wonderful God and a loving Saviour.

How often do you speak to people about God? Do you ever tell anyone that Christ is your Saviour and Lord? Do you ever tell them how they can know Christ? If not, why not? Don't you believe you are to be a witness? The Bible says you are.

> *19* **Therefore go and make disciples of all nations, baptizing them in the name of the Father and of the Son and of the Holy Spirit,** *20* **and teaching them to obey everything I have commanded you.**
> (Matthew 28:19-20).

Perhaps you don't tell people how they can know Christ because you don't know Him yourself. There are many people who don't know Christ as their personal Saviour and Lord, but they think they are going to heaven when they die. They mistakenly think that where the Bible says you must believe in Jesus Christ that it means you are to believe about Him.

> **16 "For God so loved the world that he gave his one and only Son, that whoever believes in him shall not perish but have eternal life.** (John 3:16).

However, believing about Christ is only an intellectual acknowledgement of who He is. People make this type of acknowledgement all the time when they acknowledge someone is the head of a country, the coach of a sports team, or the principal of a school. Many people who do not have a personal relationship with Christ will acknowledge that there is a God and that Christ is the Son of God. Before I became a Christian I certainly did that. However, that does not save you. Even the demons do that.

> **19 You believe that there is one God. Good! Even the demons believe that—and shudder.** (James 2:19).

The demons' destination is not heaven but rather the lake of fire. They are not saved. What does it mean then to believe in Jesus Christ? It means much more than believing about Christ. It means believing that in His death on the cross your sins were paid for. It means to trust in Christ – to rely on Him to save you. It is an individual thing, a personal thing. True belief in Christ is not just believing that He can save you, but it is acting on that belief and trusting Him to save you. You must first acknowledge that you are a sinner who needs saving and then repent (turn from your sin) and ask Christ to forgive your sins and save you. By faith you trust Christ and Christ alone to save you.

> **19 Repent, then, and turn to God, so that your sins may be wiped out, that times of refreshing may come from the Lord...** (Acts 3:19).

> **21 I have declared to both Jews and Greeks that they must turn to God in repentance and have faith in our Lord Jesus.** (Acts 20:21).

> **22 "Turn to me and be saved,**
> **all you ends of the earth;**
> **for I am God, and there is no other.** (Isaiah 45:22).

Because we are all sinners no one can earn their way into heaven. We should try to live as God would have us to and do the good works that He would have us do. However, we are not, and cannot be saved by our good work. Our good work is the result of our being saved.

> **16 ...know that a man is not justified by observing the law, but by faith in Jesus Christ. So we, too, have put our faith in Christ Jesus that we may be justified by faith in Christ and not by observing the law, because by observing the law no one will be justified.** (Galatians 2:16).

> **20 Therefore no one will be declared righteous in his sight by observing the law; rather, through the law we become conscious of sin.** (Romans 3:20).

Our salvation is a free gift from God. It is something we do not deserve and cannot earn by our works. It is by grace, which means unmerited favor.

> **8 For it is by grace you have been saved, through faith—and this not from yourselves, it is the gift of God— 9 not by works, so that no one can boast.** (Ephesians 2:8-9).

Many people hear what has just been said in the several paragraphs above, but they do nothing about it. In so many words you have been reading about the Gospel of Salvation, but if you have never turned to Christ and do not turn now it will be of no value to you.

> **1 Therefore, since the promise of entering his rest still stands, let us be careful that none of you be found to have fallen short of it. 2 For we also have**

had the gospel preached to us, just as they did; but the message they heard was of no value to them, because those who heard did not combine it with faith. (Hebrews 4:1-2).

Be aware that everyone that has ever lived will end up one day in either heaven or hell.

36 "Whoever believes in the Son has eternal life, but whoever rejects the Son will not see life, for God's wrath remains on him." (John 3:36).

15 If anyone's name was not found written in the book of life, he was thrown into the lake of fire. (Revelation 20:15).

28 Do not be afraid of those who kill the body but cannot kill the soul. Rather, be afraid of the One who can destroy both soul and body in hell. (Matthew 10:28).

Some people think that there are many different ways to heaven, but they are mistaken. There is only one way and that is through Jesus Christ.

6 Jesus answered, "I am the way and the truth and the life. No one comes to the Father except through me. (John 14:6).

21 She will give birth to a son, and you are to give him the name Jesus, because he will save his people from their sins." (Matthew 1:21).

12 Salvation is found in no one else, for there is no other name under heaven given to men by which we must be saved." (Acts 4:12).

God showed His approval and acceptance of Christ's work on the cross by raising Him from the dead.

32 God has raised this Jesus to life, and we are all witnesses of the fact. (Acts 2:32).

> **25 He was delivered over to death for our sins and was raised to life for our justification.**
> (Romans 4:25).

Some who refuse to follow the teaching of the Bible think they will get to heaven anyway. However, the Bible tells us differently.

> **21 "Not everyone who says to me, 'Lord, Lord,' will enter the kingdom of heaven, but only he who does the will of my Father who is in heaven. 22 Many will say to me on that day, 'Lord, Lord, did we not prophesy in your name, and in your name drive out demons and perform many miracles?' 23 Then I will tell them plainly, 'I never knew you. Away from me, you evildoers!'** (Matthew 7:21-23).

If you have never repented and turned to Christ for the forgiveness of your sins asking Him to be your Lord and Saviour, let me urge you to do so now – at this moment. In sincerity and faith pray the following prayer:

Dear God, I confess I am a sinner. I am lost in my sins. Please have mercy on me. I thank you that your Son Jesus Christ died for my sins. I ask Him to come into my life, to be my Lord and Saviour, to forgive my sins, and to do with my life as He pleases. I thank you that as I pray this is done. In Jesus' name I pray. Amen.

Many Christians fail to recognize the importance of the first eleven chapters of the Book of Genesis. How about you? Those eleven chapters are the foundation for much of the doctrine that is taught in the New Testament. Throw out these eleven chapters and you throw out the Fall of Man, God's curse on the earth, the entrance of sin and death into the world, etc. The New Testament writers would have no reference to which they could point and say this is when it happened or this is why it happened.

What about creation and evolution? Where do you stand on this issue? God's Word teaches creation in six literal days. Make a study of it and your eyes may be opened to some wonderful things. Read some of the books on the subject put out by the Institute for Creation Research in California and Answers in Genesis located in Kentucky.

Before the fall of man there was no death among men or animals. Man did not eat animals nor did animals eat other animals. Both man and animals ate plants.

> **29 Then God said, "I give you every seed-bearing plant on the face of the whole earth and every tree that has fruit with seed in it. They will be yours for food. 30 And to all the beasts of the earth and all the birds of the air and all the creatures that move on the ground—everything that has the breath of life in it—I give every green plant for food." And it was so.** (Genesis 1:29-30).

After the fall man ate animals and animals ate animals.

> **1 Then God blessed Noah and his sons, saying to them, "Be fruitful and increase in number and fill the earth. 2 The fear and dread of you will fall upon all the beasts of the earth and all the birds of the air, upon every creature that moves along the ground, and upon all the fish of the sea; they are given into your hands. 3 Everything that lives and moves will be food for you. Just as I gave you the green plants, I now give you everything.** (Genesis 9:1-3).

It was at the fall that sin and death came into the world. It was through Adam that sin entered the world and through sin that death entered it.

> **16 And the LORD God commanded the man, "You are free to eat from any tree in the garden; 17 but you must not eat from the tree of the knowledge of good and evil, for when you eat of it you will surely die."** (Genesis 2:16-17).

> **12 Therefore, just as sin entered the world through one man, and death through sin, and in this way death came to all men, because all sinned—** (Romans 5:12).

If animals were living and dying, killing and eating each other for millions of years before Adam then Romans 5:12 is untrue. But Romans 5:12 is true, it is God's Word and God not only does not lie, He cannot lie.

2 ...which God, who does not lie... (Titus 1:2).

18 ...it is impossible for God to lie... (Hebrews 6:18).

Are you aware that if you are a Christian that you are indwelt by God's Holy Spirit? If you are not a Christian the Spirit does not indwell you.

9 You, however, are controlled not by the sinful nature but by the Spirit, if the Spirit of God lives in you. And if anyone does not have the Spirit of Christ, he does not belong to Christ. (Romans 8:9).

19 Do you not know that your body is a temple of the Holy Spirit, who is in you, whom you have received from God? You are not your own... (1 Corinthians 6:19).

13 We know that we live in him and he in us, because he has given us of his Spirit. (1 John 4:13).

Apart from the Holy Spirit the Christian can do nothing that pleases God.

4 Remain in me, and I will remain in you. No branch can bear fruit by itself; it must remain in the vine. Neither can you bear fruit unless you remain in me. 5 "I am the vine; you are the branches. If a man remains in me and I in him, he will bear much fruit; apart from me you can do nothing. (John 15:4-5).

It is God working in you that causes you to do things that please Him.

13 ...for it is God who works in you to will and to act according to his good purpose. (Philippians 2:13).

The Holy Spirit is your source of power for living the Christian life.

8 "But you will receive power when the Holy Spirit comes on you; and you will be my witnesses in Jerusalem, and in all Judea and Samaria, and to the ends of the earth." (Acts 1:8).

3 His divine power has given us everything we need for life and godliness through our knowledge of him who called us by his own glory and goodness. (2 Peter 1:3).

13 I can do everything through him who gives me strength. (Philippians 4:13).

Your sinful human nature rebelled against God before you became a Christian, and it rebels against God now that you are a Christian. There is a conflict within you between your sinful nature and God's Spirit. It is only as you follow the leading of the Spirit that you do anything good in God's eyes.

5 Those who live according to the sinful nature have their minds set on what that nature desires; but those who live in accordance with the Spirit have their minds set on what the Spirit desires. 6 The mind of sinful man is death, but the mind controlled by the Spirit is life and peace; 7 the sinful mind is hostile to God. It does not submit to God's law, nor can it do so. 8 Those controlled by the sinful nature cannot please God. (Romans 8:5-8).

16 So I say, live by the Spirit, and you will not gratify the desires of the sinful nature. 17 For the sinful nature desires what is contrary to the Spirit, and the Spirit what is contrary to the sinful nature. They are in conflict with each other, so that you do not do what you want. (Galatians 5:16-17).

8 The one who sows to please his sinful nature, from that nature will reap destruction; the one who sows to please the Spirit, from the Spirit will reap eternal life. (Galatians 6:8).

Therefore, God's command to the Christian is to be filled with the Holy Spirit.

18 Do not get drunk on wine, which leads to debauchery. Instead, be filled with the Spirit. (Ephesians 5:18).

To be filled with the Spirit means to be controlled by the Spirit. It is not a one-time thing or a momentary thing, but rather it is to be a continuous way of life. Christians are to seek to be controlled by the Spirit moment by moment each and every day.

If you will learn to submit to the control of the Holy Spirit and begin to practice this every day you will find a dramatic change in your Christian life. You will be shown ways to be used of God in order to glorify Him. When Christ walked this earth He did so as fully God but also as fully man. It was Christ as man that God worked through in order to bring glory to Himself.

> **10 Don't you believe that I am in the Father, and that the Father is in me? The words I say to you are not just my own. Rather, it is the Father, living in me, who is doing his work.** (John 14:10).

> **22 "Men of Israel, listen to this: Jesus of Nazareth was a man accredited by God to you by miracles, wonders and signs, which God did among you through him, as you yourselves know.** (Acts 2:22).

Seek the control and power of the Holy Spirit for your life and you will be pleasantly surprised at what God does through you. You may find that you can say with the Apostle Paul that you no longer live, but Christ lives in you. You may find that your body is under His control doing the work that God planned for you to do.

> **10 For we are God's workmanship, created in Christ Jesus to do good works, which God prepared in advance for us to do.** (Ephesians 2:10).

> **20 I have been crucified with Christ and I no longer live, but Christ lives in me. The life I live in the body, I live by faith in the Son of God, who loved me and gave himself for me.** (Galatians 2:20).

The Author's Testimony

Before I became a Christian, I thought I was one. I had always believed there was a God and that Jesus was the Son of God. I lived in a Christian country, was a member of a church, and I accepted the fact that Jesus died for the sins of the world. I felt this made me a Christian. I believed I would go to heaven when I died, although I had no real basis for believing it. I believed that some people would go to hell, but like most everyone, I thought it would always happen to the other fellow. I knew I was a sinner who did some wrong things. However, I knew that I tried to be a good citizen, husband, and father. I felt the good I did outweighed the bad. I thought that in comparing my good and bad deeds, I was keeping the scales tipped in my favor. I envisioned that when this world is brought to an end, if all the people who had ever lived stood in a long line before the gates of heaven and God made a cut-off, the people on one side going to heaven and those on the other side going to hell, I would be on the side that got into heaven. I did not expect to be at the front of the line, but I did expect to make the cut-off.

There came a time in my life when I realized how fortunate I was. I had a nice home, a good marriage, two fine children (too young to get into real trouble), and good health. My wife Peg and I both felt blessed. Sometimes we would sit in our kitchen drinking coffee and wonder what life was all about. We wondered if enjoying life, as we were, and then one day dying with the uncertain hope of going to heaven, was all there was to life. We became restless as we continued to wonder about the purpose of life.

While traveling in my work, I would often listen to preachers on the car radio. Looking back, I feel sure some were good and some were not, but I did not know the difference. However, I heard and understood enough to make me question if I was truly a Christian. I found myself praying as I drove, asking God to please make my family and me Christians.

Peg started taking our children to Sunday school. She felt it would be good for them, and I certainly agreed. She would attend an adult class while the children were in their classes. She suggested that I might want to join them, and I did. With time Peg and I became very religious – attending Sunday school and church on a regular basis. Peg became active in the women's work, and I became an officer of the church. We even helped to start a mission church. We were religious but not saved. We still carried the guilt of sin and were still under the penalty of sin. We were religiously active but spiritually dead. If we had died while in that condition, we would have gone straight to hell.

My younger sister Mitzi told us about a lady, Elizabeth Newbold, who was a Bible teacher. It seemed that Elizabeth said the Bible taught that to be a Christian a person had to have a personal relationship with Jesus Christ. Mitzi said that she now had this relationship. Peg and I did not understand what was meant by a personal relationship with Christ but decided to find out.

One night I called Elizabeth. I told her that I was Mitzi's brother, and that Peg and I would like to talk with her. She said that she had to go to Huntsville the next day to teach a Bible class but would come to our house that night when she got back. Wanting to be a gentleman and do the right thing, I told her we would come to her house. However, she insisted on coming to ours. The next night we got a phone call about 9:30. Elizabeth had just gotten back from Huntsville, and it would be 10:30 before she could get to our house. She wanted to know if that was too late for us. The time was fine with us, but I felt it was too late for her. However, again she insisted. The fact that she was so eager and willing to do this for strangers made us even more desirous of hearing what she had to say.

We had made a list of questions to ask Elizabeth, and she obligingly answered them. However, she kept returning the conversation to the Gospel. She made us aware that we were counting on living lives good enough to deserve heaven. In other words, we were attempting to earn the right to go there when we died. She showed us where the Bible says that no one is saved by good deeds. We found that we could not tip the scales in our favor by doing good – our good deeds could not erase the sin on our record.

Elizabeth explained that God would not allow sin into heaven. She then pointed out that if we have committed just one sin, it is the same as breaking all of God's Law. We realized that no matter how hard we tried, we could not live the life God required – life without any sin. And even if that were now possible, we were already condemned by our past sins. It became clear that we were lost sinners, without hope and headed to hell.

Elizabeth had given us the bad news. Next, she gave us the good news. She told us that Christ had died for us. He had already paid for every sin we had ever committed in the past, and every one we would ever commit in the future. Christ had lived a sinless life, suffered and died for our sins, was resurrected, and had ascended to heaven. He offered us the free gift of salvation. We could go to heaven because of what Christ did for us, not because of anything we do. He did it all. We could contribute nothing. Our sin debt was paid in full; all we needed to do was accept the gift.

Elizabeth pointed out that it seems so simple, many people have trouble believing it. She explained that we should acknowledge that we were sinners, repent, ask Jesus Christ to forgive us and to come into our hearts and lives as our Saviour and Lord. She explained that this involved more than an intellectual assent of fact about Jesus. It is a personal thing. A person must not only believe about Jesus, but must personally commit his life to Him, trusting and relying on Him to save him.

She then asked us if we would like to receive Christ as Saviour and Lord. We were both only too glad to be able to do so, and about one o'clock in the morning, we knelt in our living room and asked Christ to save us. He did, and our lives were changed.

This was in the early part of 1966. We no longer had reason to wonder what life was all about. We soon learned we were to live and serve God in whatever way pleased Him. We were now Christians, and the purpose of the Christian life was to glorify God.

Before I became a Christian, there were things that I knew were wrong to do, but I did them anyway. After Christ saved me, I began to try to stop doing those things. One of the first things I stopped was cursing. In time I found there were things that were sinful that I had never thought of before as being sinful. Like all Christians, I sinned even though I did not want to nor intended to. And like all Christians, I still sin today. We will not reach perfection and be without sin until we get to heaven. However, as time passes, I sin less and less as I learn, by God's grace, to walk more consistently in the control and power of His Holy Spirit.

When I do sin, I know I can turn to God and, in the name of His precious Son Jesus Christ, ask Him to forgive me – and He does. Having been forgiven so much by God, I want to be forgiving of others. I would hope that any one I have wronged, intentionally or unintentionally, would forgive me too. However, all wrongdoing is actually sin against God, and it is His forgiveness that we must have. I am fully confident that I have that forgiveness based on the fact that Christ paid the penalty for my sins. I received the benefit of His payment when I accepted Him as my Saviour and Lord. I have confidence that I will go to heaven when I die, not because I deserve to but because God has promised salvation to all who put their trust in His Son. Knowing that I do not deserve heaven makes me very grateful to God for His love and mercy in saving me.

I think it is normal for Christians, having experienced the joy of salvation, to want to tell others how they might come to know Christ personally. We want our families, friends, and strangers to hear the Good News about salvation. That is one reason this book and my first book Let God Speak were written. It is my hope that, through these books, many who do not know Christ will come to a saving knowledge of Him.

Ed McDavid III